W9-ADS-004

FAIR PLAY

FAIR PLAY

The Ethics of Sport

THIRD EDITION

Robert L. Simon

HAMILTON COLLEGE

**WESTVIEW
PRESS**

A Member of the Perseus Books Group

Find us on the World Wide Web at www.westviewpress.com.

Westview Press books are available at special discounts for bulk purchases in the United States by corporations, institutions, and other organizations. For more information, please contact the Special Markets Department at the Perseus Books Group, 2300 Chestnut Street, Suite 200, Philadelphia, PA 19103, or call (800) 810-4145, ext. 5000, or e-mail special.markets@perseusbooks.com.

Designed by Trish Wilkinson
Set in 10 point Minion

Library of Congress Cataloging-in-Publication Data
    Simon, Robert L., 1941–
Fair play : the ethics of sport / Robert L. Simon.—3rd ed.
        p.   cm.
Includes bibliographical references and index.
ISBN 978-0-8133-4368-6 (alk. paper)
    1. Sports—Moral and ethical aspects. 2. Sports—Social aspects. I. Title.
GV706.3.S56 2010
796.01—dc22   2010007325

10 9 8 7 6 5 4 3 2 1

To my grandchildren:
Chika, Maya, Kayla, Jake, Zakary, and Travis
I hope they will enjoy sports as much as I have

CONTENTS

PREFACE

S ports play a significant role in the lives of millions of people throughout the world. Many men and women participate actively in sports and still more are spectators, fans, and critics of sports. Even those who are uninvolved in sports, bored by them, or critical of athletic competition often will be significantly affected by them, either because of their relationships with enthusiasts or, more important, because of the impact of sports on our language, thought, and culture.

Because sports are a significant form of social activity that affects the educational system, the economy, and perhaps the values of citizens, they raise a wide range of issues, some of which are factual or empirical in character. Social scientists, historians, physicians, and writers have raised many such issues that concern sports. For example, sociologists may be concerned with whether participation in sports affects the values of the participants, and psychologists might try to determine what personality features contribute to success or failure in competitive athletics.

In addition to factual and explanatory questions, sports also raise philosophical issues that are conceptual and ethical. Conceptual questions concern how we are to understand the concepts and ideas that apply in the world of sports. What are sports, anyway? How are sports related to rules? Do those who intentionally break the rules of a game even play it or are they doing something else? Are there different forms of competition in sports? Is it possible to compete against oneself?

Ethical questions raise the moral concerns many of us have about sports. Should sports be accorded the importance they are given in our society? Is there too much emphasis on winning and competition? Are college sports getting out of hand? Why shouldn't we cheat in a game if it will bring us a championship? What, if anything, makes the use of steroids to enhance performance in sports unethical? How should men and women be treated in sports if they are to be treated equitably and fairly? Should we be aiming more for excellence in competition among highly skilled athletes, or should we place greater value on more participation? Does the commercialization of sports actually corrupt the game? *Fair Play* examines such questions and evaluates the principles to which thoughtful people might appeal in trying to formulate answers.

Not only are questions in the philosophy of sport important in their own right, they can also serve as a useful introduction to broader philosophical issues. Most students come to philosophy courses with knowledge of sports, and many have a deep interest in ethical issues raised by sports. This initial interest can serve as a launching pad to introduce students to the nature and value of philosophical inquiry. For example, questions about whether the use of steroids to enhance athletic performance is fair can lead to broad inquiry into the nature of fairness and the just society.

Perhaps most important, issues in the philosophy of sport are of great intrinsic interest and are well worth our attention. Philosophical questions force us to stretch our analytical powers to the fullest and to question basic presuppositions. Those that arise in the philosophical examination of sports, like any others, require us to test and evaluate fundamental justificatory principles and engage in rigorous critical inquiry.

Readers of earlier editions of this book will find significant changes in the current edition. Among the most significant is the addition of a section on genetic enhancement of athletic abilities, including a discussion of Michael Sandel's recent work on the topic, in Chapter 4, and an expanded discussion of the issues in intercollegiate sports, including an examination of recent contributions by Peter French and Myles Brand, in Chapter 6. Myles focused on strengthening the relationship between academics and athletics during his tenure as president of the NCAA, and his untimely death in September 2009 saddened all of us who knew him. It also must have saddened all those who did not know him personally but who applauded his efforts at strengthening the academic requirements that applied to athletes participating at NCAA member institutions.

Other changes in the new edition range from the concrete to the theoretical and include a discussion of the recent steroid scandals in Major League Baseball, an expanded account of Bernard Suits's analysis of games and its influence on the philosophy of sport, and a fuller discussion of the alleged link between participation in sports and moral development. The latter focuses on the complications of assessing the effects of participation in competitive athletics on character development. The discussion of the ethics of strategic or "professional" fouling, as it sometimes has been called, also has been expanded and includes a discussion of Warren Fraleigh's most recent criticism of the argument of earlier editions of this book. Many other sections also have been revised, and new, more contemporary examples have been incorporated whenever possible. Accordingly, I hope this book provides a deeper insight into major issues in the philosophy of sport while remaining accessible to students and others new to the philosophical investigation of sport.

Fair Play never would have been written had it not been for the challenges to my own views of sports put forth by friends, colleagues in the philosophy department at Hamilton College, and especially my students, who have been critical of many of my views but always helpful and insightful. I have also benefited from the tough questions posed by Scott Kretchmar's students at Penn State, who have always presented me with challenging questions whenever I have been able to visit their classes.

Although I cannot acknowledge and sort out all my intellectual debts here, I would like to thank the original editors of the first edition of this book, Ray O'Connell and Doris Michaels of Prentice-Hall, for their initial encouragement, and Spencer Carr and Sarah Warner, my original editors at Westview Press, for their insights as to how the earlier editions could be expanded and improved upon. Indeed, all the staff members at Westview have been wonderful in helping to prepare this edition as well as the earlier ones, and I am very grateful to them for their assistance and courtesy. I especially want to thank Karl Yambert, my present editor at Westview, particularly for his patience and understanding when I had to postpone work on this edition for a significant length of time due to illness. Without his encouragement, I'm sure I would not have completed the revision. I also especially want to thank Sandra Beris, the project editor, for her very helpful assistance in preparing the manuscript for publication, and Katherine Streckfus for her superb work as copyeditor.

I am indebted to my colleagues in the International Association for the Philosophy of Sport, who have always been encouraging about my work. Their astute critiques have often inspired me to improve my arguments. Although I am sure I have not responded satisfactorily to all their suggestions, my work would be immeasurably poorer without their interest and support.

As always, I also express my special appreciation to my wife, Joy, not only for her critical help with the manuscript, or for putting up with an abnormal number of fits of abstraction ("Earth calling Bob" became, once again, one of the phrases used most often at our dinner table) during the writing of all the editions of the book, but also and especially for her support and encouragement, which were crucial during my treatment for prostate cancer in 1998–1999 and for a recurrence in 2008. (She has also been a devoted spectator at numerous golf tournaments in which I have played, rarely successfully, and in spite of past performance is *usually* encouraging about the next competition.) Sports have been one of the major activities my family and I have shared, so I hope they enjoy reading the finished product as much as I enjoyed writing it.

Finally, without the participants in sports who demonstrate the kind of quest for excellence discussed in Chapter 2, much of the subject matter of philosophy of sport would be empty abstraction. I thank past and present staff and players in both the Hamilton College men's and women's basketball programs, not only for getting me away from my computer (in view of my attendance at basketball games, many colleagues will find it miraculous that I was able to complete this project) but also for making the harsh upstate New York winter one of the most exciting and pleasurable times of year. I would like to thank my former players on the Hamilton men's golf team, during the years I was their coach as well as more recent team members, for some wonderful experiences with intercollegiate athletics, to say nothing of not teasing me too much when they outdrive me by 75 yards!

Robert L. Simon
Clinton, New York

ONE

INTRODUCTION
The Ethics of Sport

I would like to think that this book began on an unfortunately not atypical cold and rainy late October day in upstate New York. I had been discussing some of my generally unsuccessful efforts in local golf tournaments with colleagues in the philosophy department and let drop what I thought was an innocuous remark to the effect that although winning isn't everything, it sure beats losing. Much to my surprise, my colleagues objected vehemently, asserting that winning means nothing. In their view, the recreational aspects of sport, such as having fun and trying to improve—not defeating an opponent—are all that should matter. I soon found myself backed into a corner by this usually unthreatening but now fully aroused assortment of philosophers. Fortunately for me, another colleague entered the office just at the right moment. Struck by the vehemence of the argument, although he had no idea what it was about, he looked at my opponents and remarked, "You folks sure are trying to *win* this argument."

This incident illustrates two important aspects of a philosophical examination of sports. First, issues arise in sports that are not simply empirical questions of psychology, sociology, or some other discipline. Empirical surveys can tell us whether people think winning is important, but they cannot tell us whether that is what people ought to think or whether winning really ought to be regarded as a primary goal of athletics. Second, the incident illustrated that logic could be applied to issues in the philosophy of sport. Thus, at least on the surface, it appeared that my colleagues were in the logically embarrassing position of trying hard to win an argument to the effect that winning is unimportant. (Of course, they might reply that their goal was not winning but the pursuit of truth, but athletes might similarly argue that winning is important because it is a sign of achieving their true goal, excellence.)

We will return to the issue of whether winning is important in Chapter 2. For now, let us consider further what philosophical inquiry might contribute to our understanding of sports.

ETHICAL ISSUES IN SPORT

Sports play a major, if sometimes unappreciated, role in the lives of Americans. Most of us are exposed to them as children. As a result of our childhood experiences, many of us become participants or fans for life. Others are appalled by their early exposure to sports and avoid them like the plague later in life. They may have been embarrassed by failures in front of peers and parents or humiliated by an insensitive physical education instructor. They may just find sports less interesting than other activities, such as participation in the arts, reading, and writing, and less valuable than social service. Girls may have received less encouragement to participate than boys. Others may just find sports boring.

Many of us, however, retain some affiliation with sports for life, even if only as spectators.[1] Athletes and fans devote so much time and effort to sports at all levels that their involvement is surely one of their most personally significant activities. The situation is not unique to the United States. Intense interest in sports is virtually a global phenomenon. Whether it is ice hockey in Russia or soccer in Europe, South America, and Africa, sports play a major role worldwide. Sports were valued by the ancient Greeks, by the Romans, and by Native Americans. Indeed, participation in sports, and the related activity of play, is characteristic of most, if not all, human societies.

Although there is a tendency to regard sports as trivial, it is not clear that such a view is justified. Those critical of sports or bored by athletic competition must admit that sports play a significant role in our lives, even if they believe that dominance is misguided or even harmful. At the very least, it is surely worth discovering what it is about sports that calls forth a favorable response among so many people from so many different cultures.

Reflection upon sports raises issues that not only have intrinsic interest but also go beyond the bounds of sport itself. For example, reflection on the value of competition in athletics and the emphasis on winning in much of organized sports may shed light on the ethics of competition in other areas, such as the marketplace. Inquiry into the nature of fair play in sports can also help our understanding of fairness in a wider social setting. Indeed, because many of our basic values, such as playing fairly, are often absorbed through involvement in athletic competition, inquiry into values in sports is likely not only to prove interesting in its own right but also to have implications of more general concern.

Sports raise many kinds of philosophical issues. For example, what is a sport? Football, baseball, and soccer clearly are sports. But some have doubts about golf. What about chess and auto racing? How are sports related to games? Is participation in sport always a form of play? Questions such as these raise issues that go well beyond looking up words in a dictionary. To settle them, we will need to rely on a theory of what makes something a game, a sport, or an instance of play. Dictionary definitions often presuppose such theories. But the theories presupposed by the definition may be unclear; they may leave open how borderline cases are to be thought of; or they may just be wrong. For example, one dictionary account of games classifies them as competitive activities. But must all games be competitive? "Playing house" arguably is a game, but is it competitive? What about playing catch?

Some of the most important kinds of philosophical issues that arise in sport are ethical or moral ones; these are the kinds of issues about which this book will be primarily concerned. Some moral issues in sport concern specific actions, often by athletes. For example, in the championship game of the 1999 World Cup, the American women's soccer team completed regulation and overtime play against China with the score tied. The championship, viewed throughout the world by millions of fans, many of them young American girls captivated by the success of the American women, was to be settled by penalty kicks in a game-ending shootout.[2] The American goalkeeper, Briana Scurry, decided that one of the Chinese shooters, Liu Ying, lacked confidence. When Liu made her move, Scurry took two quick steps forward, in violation of a rule of soccer, to cut off Liu's shooting angle. The tactic worked. Scurry deflected Liu's shot, and the Americans won. But did Scurry cheat by violating a rule? Was Scurry simply doing what any goalkeeper would do in such a situation: namely, conforming to a convention of the game tacitly accepted by all players? Or was the American victory tainted by unethical behavior in a deliberate violation of the rules?[3]

Other kinds of ethical issues in sport involve the assessment of rules or policies—for example, the prohibition by many sports organizations of the use of performance-enhancing drugs by competitive athletes. What justifies this prohibition? Is it because performance-enhancing drugs such as steroids often have harmful side effects? But why shouldn't athletes, especially competent adult athletes, be free to take risks with their bodies? After all, many of us would reject the kind of paternalism that constantly interferes with the pursuit of our goals whenever risky behavior is involved. Think of the dangers inherent in a typical American diet, which contains a high proportion of unhealthy fat and sugar.

Or should performance-enhancing drugs be prohibited because they provide unfair advantages to some of the competitors? Are the advantages any different from those conferred by the legal use of technologically advanced equipment? Moreover, would the advantages still be unfair if all competitors had access to the drug? Defenders of baseball slugger Barry Bonds, who is alleged to have achieved his home run records in part with the assistance of performance-enhancing drugs, claim that some opposing pitchers undoubtedly also used performance enhancers, thus equalizing the competition.

Questions of marketing, sports administration, and the formulation of rules also involve moral issues, although the moral character of the questions raised may not always be obvious. For example, consider whether a rule change ought to be instituted that might make a sport more attractive to fans at the professional or college levels yet diminish the skill or strategy needed to play the game. Some would argue that the designated-hitter rule in American League baseball, which allows teams to replace their usually weak-hitting pitcher with a designated hitter in the batting order, is such a case. The rule may make the game more exciting to the casual fan, who values an explosive offense. However, it may also remove various subtleties from the game, such as the decision about when to remove the pitcher from the game for a pinch hitter, or the value of the sacrifice bunt, which weak-hitting pitchers might be capable of executing. Although this is not as obvious a moral issue as some of the other examples cited, it does have a moral, or at least evaluative, component. It raises questions about the purposes or goals of sports, what social functions they ought to serve, and whether sports have an integrity that ought to be preserved. Similar issues may arise when we consider when technological innovations ought to be permitted in sport, and when they ought to be prohibited for making a sport too easy.

At a more abstract level, other ethical issues concern the values central to competitive sport itself. Is competition in sport ethically permissible, or even desirable, or does it create a kind of selfishness, perhaps an analog of a narrow form of nationalism that says "My team, right or wrong?" Does the single-minded pursuit of winning, which is apparently central to competition in sport, help promote violent behavior in fans? Does it teach competitors to regard opponents as mere obstacles to be overcome and not as fellow human beings? Is it related to the anger shown by many parents of participants in youth sports, which culminated in 2001 in the killing of a hockey coach by an enraged parent? What kind of competition in sport can be defended morally, and how great an emphasis on winning is too much?

Questions such as these raise basic issues about the kinds of moral values involved in sports. They are not only about what people think about sports or about what values they hold; rather, they are about what people *ought* to think. They require the identification of defensible ethical standards and their application to sport. Critical inquiry into the philosophy of sport consists in formulating and rationally evaluating such standards as well as testing them by seeing how they apply to concrete issues in sports and athletics.

SPORT, PHILOSOPHY, AND MORAL VALUES

Just what does philosophy have to contribute to reflection about sports and moral values? It is evident even to a casual observer of our society that sports in the United States are undergoing intense moral scrutiny. How can philosophy contribute to this endeavor?

Philosophy of Sport

Misconceptions about the nature of philosophy are widespread. According to one story, a philosopher on a domestic flight was asked by his seatmate what he did for a living. He replied, perhaps foolishly, "I'm a philosopher," a statement that is one of the greatest conversation-stoppers known to the human race. The seatmate, apparently stupefied by the reply, was silent for several minutes. Finally, he turned to the philosopher and remarked, "Oh, and what are some of your sayings?"[4]

The image of the philosopher as the author of wise sayings can perhaps be forgiven, for the word "philosophy" has its roots in the Greek expression meaning "love of wisdom." But wisdom is not necessarily encapsulated in brief sayings that we might memorize before breakfast. The ancient Greek philosopher Socrates provides a different model of philosophic inquiry.

Socrates, who lived in the fifth century B.C., did not leave a body of written works behind him; however, we know a great deal about his life and thought, primarily through the works of his most influential pupil, Plato. As a young man, Socrates, seeking a mentor from whom to learn, set out to find the wisest man in Greece. According to the story, he decided to ask a religious figure, the oracle at Delphi, the identity of the man he was seeking. Much to Socrates' surprise, the oracle informed him that he, Socrates, was the wisest man in Greece. "How can that be?" Socrates must have wondered; after all, he was searching for a wise teacher precisely because he was ignorant.

However, looking at the oracle's answer in light of Plato's presentation of Socrates, we can discern what the oracle meant. In the early Platonic dialogues, such as the *Euthyphro*, Socrates questioned important figures of the day about the nature of piety or the essence of knowledge. Those questioned purported to be experts in the subject under investigation, but their claim to expertise was discredited by Socrates' logical analysis. These experts not only failed in what they claimed to know but also seemed to have accepted views that they had never exposed to critical examination.

Perhaps in calling Socrates the wisest man in Greece the oracle was suggesting that Socrates alone was willing to expose beliefs and principles to critical examination. He did not claim to know what he did not know, but he was willing to learn. He was also not willing to take popular opinion for granted but was prepared to question it.

This Socratic model suggests that the role of philosophy is to examine our beliefs, clarify the principles on which they rest, and subject them to critical examination. For example, in science, the role of philosophy is not to compete in formulating and testing empirical hypotheses in biology, chemistry, and physics. Rather, philosophers might try to understand in what sense science provides objective knowledge and then examine claims that all knowledge must be scientific. If we adopt such a view of philosophy, the task of the philosophy of sport would be to clarify, systematize, and evaluate the principles that we believe should govern the world of sports. This task might involve a conceptual analysis of such terms as "sport" and "game," an inquiry into the nature of excellence in sports, an ethical evaluation of such principles as "winning should be the only concern of the serious athlete," and an application of ethical analysis to concrete issues, such as disagreement over whether athletes should be permitted to take performance-enhancing drugs.

This book is concerned primarily with the ethical evaluation of principles that many people apply to sports and the application of the analysis to specific issues. Its major focus is the nature of principles and values that should apply to sports. Thus, its concern is predominantly normative rather than descriptive—assessing what ought to be rather than describing what is. Perhaps only a few people think of sports as activities that raise serious moral issues. They see sports either as mere instruments for gaining fame and fortune or as play, something relatively trivial that we do for fun and recreation. However, as the headlines of our daily newspapers show all too frequently, serious moral issues do arise in sports.

But can moral issues be critically examined? Is rational argument even possible in ethics? Aren't moral views just matters of opinion? Can moral principles be rationally evaluated and defended, or are they mere expressions of personal feelings that are not even the sorts of things that can be rationally evaluated or examined?

Ethics and Moral Reasoning

If reasoned ethical discourse is impossible, rational inquiry into ethical issues in sports is impossible. Although we cannot consider all possible reasons for skepticism about whether rationally justifiable moral positions can be developed, one widely cited reason for doubting the objectivity of ethics is relativism. Because relativism is so widely suggested as a basis for skepticism about the role of reason in ethics, a brief discussion of it will prove helpful. The remainder of this book attempts to consider moral issues in sports rationally. Clearly, if this attempt succeeds, it counts as an example of reasoned inquiry in ethics.

Relativism

Perhaps the most widely cited position that rejects the rationality and objectivity of ethical discourse is relativism. In his best-selling book, *The Closing of the American Mind*, Allen Bloom blames relativism for much of what he sees as the moral and educational decay infecting American universities. According to Bloom, "There is one thing a professor can be absolutely certain of: Almost every student entering the university believes, or says he believes, that truth is relative."[5] Relativism is so widely supported, according to Bloom, because its opposite is (incorrectly, as we will see) identified with a kind of intolerant and dogmatic absolutism. The price we pay for this misidentification is our inability to formulate, articulate, and defend standards we think are correct. But just what is relativism in ethics?

Actually, no one position has a unique claim to the title of relativism.[6] Rather, relativism is more like a family of related positions that share such features as the rejection of a universal outlook or perspective and the suspicion of principles that claim to be true or justifiable for all. According to *descriptive* relativism, the moral judgments people make and the values they hold arise from or are relative to their culture, socioeconomic state, or ethnic and religious background. For example, secular culture in the West tends to be permissive of sexual contact between consenting adults, but such contacts have been much more strictly regulated at other times and in other places. In the world of sports, some cultures may place more value than others on winning and less on, say, the aesthetic appeal of play. Different sports communities may recognize different conceptions of fair play. In golf, for example, players are expected to call penalties on themselves and are open to criticism if they do not, whereas in basketball, players defer to the calls of officials. This form of relativism is descriptive in that it is making a factual claim about the origin or empirical basis of our values. It claims to tell us where *in fact* our values originate, or describes the practices to which they are thought to apply rather than what we *ought* to think about them.

What does descriptive relativism have to do with whether our moral beliefs and judgments are or can be rationally justified? It is sometimes argued that if descriptive relativism is true, there cannot be objectivity or rationality in ethics. No one's ethical judgments would be any more justifiable or correct than anyone else's. Rather, people's ethical judgments would be mere subjective claims based on their distinct and different backgrounds. In this view, our moral values are the prejudices we absorbed as children. Perhaps they were presented to us as self-evident truths. In reality, they are only the blinders of our particular culture or group.

Accordingly, it is sometimes claimed that skepticism about the rationality and objectivity of ethics follows from descriptive relativism. Skepticism denies that we can know whether ethical beliefs or claims are justified or whether some are more reasonable and more defensible than others. This kind of philosophical skepticism needs to be distinguished from an ordinary and perhaps healthy kind of skepticism in ordinary life that cautions us not to accept the opinions of others at face value but to examine whether they are well supported. Philosophical skepticism of the kind at issue here denies that our ethical or moral views ever can be well supported, or that we can know which moral views are rationally warranted and which are not. Ordinary skepticism cautions us to look for evidence for our views, but philosophical skepticism questions whether it is even possible, even in principle, to provide evidence or rational support for our ethical views.

Others have suggested that descriptive relativism implies not skepticism but ethical (value) relativism. Ethical relativism is the view that each culture's moral code is right for that culture. For example, according to ethical relativism, repressive sexual practices are morally right for cultures that have such practices embedded in their moral codes but not for more liberal cultures or groups. Applied to sports, such ethical relativism might assert that we ought to follow the values of our own sports communities: If we are golfers we should call the penalties on ourselves, but if we are basketball players, we should leave it to the referees (even if they make a terrible call in our favor that enables us to win a game). Ethical relativism differs from skepticism in that skepticism denies that any ethical perspective is more justifiable or reasonable than any other (or denies that we can *know* which perspectives are more justifiable than others), whereas ethical relativism endorses an ethical view—namely, what is right for you to do is what your culture or community says is right.

What is the significance of these views for the ethical analysis of sports? If skepticism is correct, it follows that we cannot justify any position on questions of ethics that arise in sports, since skepticism denies that any ethical perspective is more justified than any other. For example, we could not justify either the claim that the use of anabolic steroids to enhance performance is warranted or the claim that it is unwarranted. However, if ethical relativism is correct, what is morally justifiable depends on the group to which one belongs. Perhaps the use of performance-enhancing drugs is permissible for cultures that find it permissible but not for those that find it impermissible.

Does descriptive relativism really have the skeptical implications examined above? Is relativism acceptable in the forms discussed above?

A Critique of Relativism

First, consider the argument that because the thesis of descriptive relativism—that moral codes of different cultures and groups conflict—is true, therefore moral skepticism is true. To evaluate this argument, we need to consider what general conditions an argument must meet to be acceptable. If the premises of an argument are to justify a conclusion, two fundamental requirements must be satisfied. (1) The premises must be true. False statements cannot be acceptable evidence for the truth of a conclusion. (2) The premises must be logically relevant to the conclusion; otherwise, the conclusion could not follow from the premises because they would be irrelevant to it. For example, we would not accept the conclusion that "The major goal of competitive sports is winning" on the basis of the claim that "Washington, D.C., is the capital of the United States." Even though the latter claim is true, it has nothing to do with the former claim and so cannot support it.

Consider again the argument that because the moral codes of different cultures and groups conflict, no set of moral judgments or principles can be correct, reasonable, or justified. First, the argument assumes that descriptive relativism is true, but is it? If descriptive relativism claims no more than that the moral codes, principles, and judgments accepted in different societies sometimes conflict, it may well be true. But it leaves open the possibility that, behind the apparent disagreement, there is deeper agreement on some morally fundamental values. The area of agreement might constitute the basis of cross-cultural universal values that some investigators have claimed to detect. For example, people from a wide variety of cultural, ethnic, socioeconomic, and religious backgrounds condemn incest, torture, and the random killing of members of one's community. Protests against Communist regimes in China and the old Soviet Union and, more recently, against rigid forms of Islamic fundamentalism that deny women fundamental rights, or against the murder and rape of non-Arabs, amounting to genocide in the view of many observers, in Darfur, are evidence for the broad appeal of values such as liberty and human rights.

This point can be taken further. Apparent surface disagreement can disguise deeper agreement in values. For instance, consider a dispute between a basketball coach and her assistant before a big game. The head coach wants to use a pressure defense to take advantage of her team's agility and the opponent's lack of speed. The assistant argues against this strategy because it may cause overanxious and inexperienced defensive players to commit too many fouls. In this example, there is disagreement over which tactics to follow. But behind the disagreement is a common value or principle shared by both coaches. Each is trying to select the strategy that will lead to victory.

A parallel situation is possible in ethics. Suppose culture A believes that old people should be separated from the group and left to die when they can no longer contribute to the general welfare, but culture B disagrees. Clearly, there is a disagreement here, but both cultures might share deeper fundamental values as well. For one thing, the circumstances of each culture might differ. Culture A may barely be surviving at the subsistence level; culture B may be affluent and therefore able to care for its older members. Perhaps culture A consists of nomadic bands that must move fast to keep up with game. Arguably, each culture may accept the same basic principle of promoting the greater good for the greater number, but the principle might apply differently in the different circumstances in which each group finds itself. Accordingly, although the descriptive relativist is undoubtedly correct in pointing to moral disagreement among groups, it remains controversial whether there is fundamental disagreement about all values or whether underneath the surface disagreement most societies have a deeper acceptance of fundamental core values.

Suppose, however, that we concede for the sake of argument that there are no universally accepted values or moral principles. The greatest weakness of the relativist argument is that, even if this point is conceded, moral skepticism does not follow. The premise of descriptive relativism is logically irrelevant to supporting moral skepticism. If cultures or groups disagree about moral problems, this does not mean that there are no correct or justifiable resolutions to the dispute. That certain values are not accepted does not mean they are not acceptable or justifiable. Similarly, some cultures believe the world is flat and others believe it is round, but this does not by itself establish that there is no correct answer concerning the shape of the earth.[7] Whether a justifiable resolution of a dispute is possible depends on whether justifiable modes of ethical (or scientific) inquiry can be applied to it. Moral disagreement can arise just as much from ignorance of such modes of inquiry, misapplication of them, or factual disagreement (as when one group of athletes denies and one asserts that steroids cause harmful side effects) as it can from the impossibility of distinguishing reasonable moral claims from those that are less reasonable.

Disagreement alone is not sufficient to show that no rational modes of inquiry exist, let alone that they are insufficient to resolve the issue at hand. Whether moral claims can be justifiable depends on the reasons or evidence that might support them. The mere fact of disagreement on an ethical issue between two sides does not show that both have equally good reasons for their view. Similarly, moral agreement that some values are justified does not establish by itself that they are justifiable; that, too, depends on the reasons that can be provided in their support. In disagreement or agreement, justification depends on the kinds of *reasons* that can be provided to support our moral views, not simply on whether others share our values.

Of course, the failure of descriptive relativism to establish moral skepticism doesn't show that there is a correct resolution to moral controversies, only that the presence of cultural or group diversity does not rule out such a resolution in advance of inquiry.

Does descriptive relativism do any better in establishing ethical relativism— the thesis that what your group or culture says is right or wrong for you is really right or wrong for you? For example, is it morally right to take anabolic steroids to enhance your performance in sports just because your peer group or even your culture says it is right?

Once again, no such implication follows. For reasons similar to those outlined above, just because groups may disagree on ethical issues does not show that each group's moral views are right for its members. One might just as well argue that if your culture believes the earth is flat, you ought to believe the earth is flat as well. If such an absurd view were correct, we would never be justified in trying to correct or change the view of our culture or peer group even if we had strong reasons for thinking their views were unfounded. Ethical relativism has the unacceptable implication that the views of our culture or of other groups to which we belong are acceptable just as they are. But surely, even if our peer group does advocate the use of performance-enhancing drugs in sports, they are not automatically correct to do so. We need to engage in ethical inquiry and argument to see whether the best reasons that can be given to support this view actually do support it, rather than accepting it merely because it is the view of the group to which we belong.[8]

Therefore, moral disagreement among cultures, or other kinds of groups, should not deter us from engaging in a moral inquiry designed to subject moral claims in sports or elsewhere to rational criticism and evaluation. Moreover, such a view does not make us dogmatic or intolerant of the views of others. Indeed, tolerance and the avoidance of dogmatism are themselves values, and many think they have objective support. If moral skepticism were justified, there would be no rational basis for tolerance itself if cultures disagreed about its value. Accordingly, commitment to rational inquiry in ethics does not make us arrogant dogmatists; if anything, it makes us open to the insights of those who may be different from us so long as we are willing to subject their views as well as our own to the test of reasoned inquiry in ethics. Thus, commitment to moral inquiry can help free us from insular prejudices and allow us to test our views by seeing whether they can stand up to the reasoned criticism of others.

Absolutophobia: The Seductive Appeal of Crude Relativism

In spite of such serious intellectual weaknesses, crude forms of relativism and skepticism appeal to many, especially to some college students. This subgroup of students seems unwilling to make moral judgments and views those who do as opinionated or "judgmental." I saw an extreme version of such an attitude some years ago when one of my own students wrote on an examination, "Of course I don't like the Nazis, but who am I to say they are wrong?"[9]

Why do so many people, particularly students, believe that some of the greatest crimes in human history, including genocide and slavery, should not be morally condemned, or, perhaps more understandably, that there are no rational grounds for such condemnation? I doubt there is one root cause of such attitudes, but I do suggest that certain intellectual errors contribute to such an attitude.

First, moral language is sometimes misused to bully or intimidate people into accepting the speaker's position. Moreover, moral positions that are held fanatically and asserted dogmatically leave no room for reasonable response. Morality may then be seen as a refuge for dogmatists who assert but never question their own absolutes and use the fear of being labeled immoral or unfair to force people to adopt favored views. Part of the reaction against "political correctness" on college campuses perhaps reflects resentment against ardent activists trying to impose their views on others. Religious zealots and extreme right-wing politicians, as well as those on the extreme left, sometimes use moral language as a weapon to stifle dissent.

However, such misuse of moral language does not imply that moral judgments cannot be justified. Indeed, to favor tolerance, judiciousness, and appeal to reason over dogmatism and zealotry is to favor one set of values over another and therefore makes a moral judgment. Respect for the views of others and willingness to reason with them about values is as much a moral outlook as dogmatism and fanaticism are.

Second, many people reject "absolutes." But moral judgments about what is right or wrong, fair or unfair, or just or unjust seem to presuppose the very absolutes we are told do not exist. The first thing to note about rejecting absolutes is that we don't really know what an "absolute" is supposed to be. If an absolute is a simple rule that is self-evident and immune from rational scrutiny, it is far from clear that moral judgments can be absolutes. But if an absolute is a reasonable claim well supported by evidence, surely we are all committed to absolutes. (The denial that absolutes exist in this sense seems itself to be one, since presumably it purports to be reasonable, well supported, and true.) Whether moral claims can be supported by critical rational inquiry can best be seen by exploring moral issues and not by dismissing moral claims through fear of committing an absolute (absolutophobia), no matter how murky that concept may be. In any case, the key point is that even if no moral judgments can be self-evident or immune from critical scrutiny, some moral judgments may still be reasonable, well supported, and justifiable.

Perhaps another reason for reluctance to make moral judgments is an interpretation (or misinterpretation) of multiculturalism. Although "multiculturalism" stands for a family of related positions, not just one central doctrine, most multiculturalists hold that we should learn to understand and respect cultures other than our own. But sophisticated multiculturalists ought not to blur this claim by asserting that we should not criticize the moral views of others. This second claim would prohibit them from criticizing opponents' views of multiculturalism, or from objecting to intolerance of others. Since multiculturalists want to assert that their approaches are morally more acceptable than those they reject, they would undermine themselves by embracing extreme forms of moral relativism and skepticism.

I suggest that many who express skepticism about morality are not true skeptics or relativists but instead hold a disguised morality that tolerates and respects diversity. But by denying the moral basis to condemn evils such as the Holocaust, slavery, and racial oppression, such people are unable to condemn any wrongdoing; they cannot even defend the values that lead them to tolerate and respect diversity to begin with. If the legitimate desire to avoid moral fanaticism drives us to see the condemnation of any evil, however great, as an unwarranted intellectual arrogance, then the truly arrogant and the truly fanatical will never fear moral censure, no matter what evil they choose to inflict.

Moral Reasoning

Dogmatism and fanaticism can be avoided if we base our moral views on reasoning and encourage critical examination of them. But how are we to distinguish cogent from weak or incorrect moral reasoning? Philosophers and ethicists have not agreed that any one theory of moral reasoning is the correct one or even whether theories of moral reasoning are morally neutral or are themselves part of a substantive code of ethics. Some philosophers have serious doubts about the objectivity of moral judgments, although not on the crude grounds criticized in earlier sections. Perhaps the best way to determine whether moral judgments can be rationally assessed is to examine moral issues in detail. We will do that, in connection with sport, in subsequent chapters. The following comments may be helpful in assessing moral judgment and argument.

At a minimum, it is doubtful that one can evaluate moral arguments with the precision and rigor appropriate to mathematics. This does not mean that we cannot recognize the difference between well-supported and poorly supported positions. As Aristotle suggested, we should "look for precision in each class of things just so far as the nature of the subject admits; it is evidently equally foolish to accept probable reasoning from a mathematician and to demand from a rhetorician scientific proofs."[10] This does not mean that ethical reasoning must be imprecise; it may resemble a sound case made by a skilled judicial scholar rather than strict mathematical proof.

Although good moral reasoning cannot be totally uncontroversial, the following three criteria will prove especially helpful. First, moral reasoning must be impartial. In evaluating a moral issue, we are not asking, "What's in it for me?" We want to see what position is supported by the best reasons, impartially considered. Moral deliberation has a broader perspective than self-interest. Thus, we cannot justify the claim that "the use of steroids by Olympic athletes to enhance their performance is morally legitimate" simply by claiming that "the use of steroids will help me gain a gold medal in the Olympics." The latter claim may show that the use of steroids is in the speaker's interest, but it does nothing to show that personal interest is the only relevant moral factor.

Philosophers have proposed various models or theories of impartial reasoning. For example, R. M. Hare has suggested that impartial moral reasoning requires that we imagine ourselves in the place of all those affected by the action or policy being evaluated, giving no special weight to any one perspective.[11] John Rawls of Harvard, author of the important book *A Theory of Justice*, has suggested that in thinking of social justice we must reason as if we were behind a veil of ignorance that hides from us the knowledge of our individual characteristics or social circumstances.[12] Thus, impartiality prohibits us from arbitrarily assigning special privileges to our own race or ethnic group, because it would be irrational to do so if we had to consider such a policy impartially from the perspective of all affected, as Hare requires, or in ignorance of our own group membership, as Rawls suggests.

Some theorists regard some theories of impartiality, such as those of Rawls and Hare, as too abstract to apply or to work with. Can we truly reason as if we did not know our place in society, as Rawls suggested, or fully grasp the perspective of others, as Hare's approach seemingly requires? Don't such theories commit us to taking an impossible "view from nowhere," and shouldn't we therefore abandon the notion of impartiality as a philosophical fiction?

These criticisms may overstate the difficulties. After all, in ordinary disputes, we may say to the other party, "You wouldn't hold such a view if you didn't benefit from it." And we often do try to understand things from the point of view of others and encourage others to do the same. Thus, in evaluating whether the women's athletic program at a university is being treated fairly when compared to the men's program, we may ask ourselves if we would find both programs equally acceptable regardless of the one in which we participated.

The core idea of impartiality, which is what the theories of philosophers such as Hare and Rawls try to capture, is that we are prohibited from arbitrarily assigning special weight to our own position or interests. Thus, a referee in a basketball game, to be impartial, must make calls in accord with the rules, not in accord with the team he or she likes better. Whatever the best theory of impartiality, impartiality plays an important and justifiable role in our ordinary moral thinking. Why otherwise insist that rules officials, judges, and professors grading papers be impartial? The core idea is not that they necessarily must adopt a view from nowhere (or any particular theory of impartiality), but that they must apply appropriate standards fairly, reasonably, and equally.

Second, in addition to satisfying the requirement of impartiality, the positions we take must be systematically consistent. For example, if one holds that it is wrong to assault another person but that it is permissible for a professional hockey player to assault another player during a game, one's position appears inconsistent. Unless one can show that the two situations are relevantly dissimilar, one or the other position must be given up. If the two situations are similar in the relevant moral respects, assault in one cannot be permissible and assault in the other impermissible because there would be no difference between them to justify the difference in judgment made about them.

Third, the principles one uses in making moral decisions must account for reflective judgments about clear moral examples. For example, in golf, we start with a firm conviction that competitors in a tournament should not lie about their scores.

But let's say that a particular golfer believed that it was permissible to turn in a wrong score merely to benefit himself. Reflective judgment about this example would reveal that turning in the wrong score was a case of lying about the score. The principle that competitors should not lie can be applied to the example of this particular golfer and would normally be grounds for rejecting, or at least questioning, the individual golfer's belief. After all, if golfers could lie about their scores, the whole point of a golf tournament, to find out who played best, would be undermined.

Of course, and this is what makes our third criterion controversial, we must be sure that our reactions to situations are critical and reflective, not merely unanalyzed, culturally conditioned responses. It is all too easy to be influenced by cultural, social, and even biologically based presuppositions. For example, our initial reaction that it is permissible for hometown fans to boo and wave while an opposing basketball player shoots a crucial foul shot may simply be a prejudice we share with other hometown fans. However, some of our judgments about particular situations may be reflective and unbiased and therefore allow us to check our principles.

Thus, our reflective reaction to actual and hypothetical examples may be a useful guide for moral inquiry; without such consideration, our principles would be empty abstractions. Conversely, we can criticize an abstract principle by showing that its application would lead to unacceptable consequences for concrete action.

The more an ethical theory survives counterexample and criticism, the more confidence we would seem to be entitled to place in it. Just as we expose our scientific theories to test, so we should test our moral perspectives by exposing them to the criticism of others. It may make us feel good to cling to our entrenched moral views by never exposing them to opposing views. The price we pay for such a policy is to prevent ourselves from discovering errors that might be recognized by others. We also lose opportunities for confirming our views when we refute the objections of our critics. Just as a scientific theory gains credibility by surviving tests, so may a moral view gain credibility by surviving criticism in the crucible of moral debate.

From a critical perspective, a moral view can be undermined by at least three strategies. We can argue that such a view would not be held if impartially considered, that its various parts are inconsistent or inharmonious, or that the view has unacceptable implications for action. Nothing said so far implies that only one moral perspective, code of ethics, or set of principles will survive moral criticism. It is possible that all who go through an extended process of moral inquiry will hold the same moral view; it is equally possible that a kind of moral pluralism will flourish. However, it is unlikely that serious and extended moral inquiry will rate all moral perspectives as equally justified. Many will be rejected as inconsistent, biased, vulnerable to counterexample, or deficient on some other appropriate ground. Thus, although there is no guarantee that our criteria of moral reasoning are the only defensible ones or that they will yield strictly determinate results for all investigators, they at least provide guidance in the rational evaluation of moral issues. By applying them, we employ reason in ethics.

Let us turn now to moral issues in sports. The discussion will ask us to make and evaluate moral judgments about controversial cases; hence the importance of the discussion about the justifiability of moral judgment. The challenge will be to develop positions that we can impartially affirm, that are consistent with our views in related areas, and that rely on principles whose consequences for action are acceptable. We will begin by examining a fundamental issue: the importance that should be assigned to competition and winning in sports.

TWO

COMPETITION IN ATHLETICS
Is It Morally Defensible?

"Winning is not the most important thing; it's the only thing." This widely cited claim, often attributed (perhaps falsely) to the late Vince Lombardi, famous former coach of the Green Bay Packers, raises a host of issues that are central to the moral evaluation of sports.[1] What importance should be assigned to winning in athletic competition? Consider sportswriter Grantland Rice's declaration, "For when the One Great Scorer comes to mark against your name, / He writes—not that you won or lost—but how you played the Game," and the rejoinder by coach Forest Evashevski that one might as well say of a surgeon that it matters not whether his patient lives or dies but only how he makes the cut.[2]

Questions about the importance of winning are closely tied to but not identical with questions about the value of competition. Should we be concerned primarily with winning or with competing well? Is competition in sport a good thing, or can it be harmful or even immoral? Should winning be the most important goal of an athlete? What degree of emphasis should be placed on competitive success and winning in athletics?

COMPETITION IN SPORTS

At first glance, competition seems to be the very nature of sports. We speak of sporting events as competitions or contests, evaluate athletes as good or bad competitors, and refer to other teams as opponents. But perhaps the connection between sports and competition is far looser than these habits suggest. Thus, someone can play golf or run a marathon just for the enjoyment of the activity. Indeed, all sports can be played noncompetitively. Men and women may participate for exercise, to forget about work, to enjoy the company of friends, and to enjoy the outdoors. Another goal of participation might be improvement. Such players, often described as competing with themselves, aim not at defeating opponents but at improving their own performances. Still others may have the aesthetic goal of performing the movements of their sport with skill and grace. For example, play-ground basketball players may value outstanding moves more than defeating their opponents. A leading amateur golfer of her generation, after years of hard practice, remarked that she wanted "to make a swing that you know is as close to perfection as you can get. And you say, 'Boy, look at what I did.' That's all it is."[3]

But just because a player does not aim for competitive success or is not moti-vated by it, it doesn't follow that competition isn't part of the sport. A group of people may play softball just to interact with friends, but the point of the game, as defined by the rules, is to score more runs than the opponent. Even if the principal desire of the participants is to get exercise, they are doing so by trying to achieve the goals of the game as prescribed by the rules. An outfielder who is playing soft-ball primarily to escape from the pressures of work still tries to catch a fly ball rather than just letting it drop, and the reason is that a successful catch may prevent the opponent from scoring. We need to distinguish, then, between two different kinds of questions. First, should the principal goal or motives of participants in sport be competitive, and, if so, to what degree? Second, do sports, insofar as they are games, structurally involve a competitive element?

Critics of competition in sports do not object so much to games that have an internal competitive element; rather, as we will see, they object to the defeat of an opponent as a main desire or goal. Critics also object to institutionalizing this attitude and to making competition in sports a social practice.

Competition in sports in the fullest sense can be thought of as participation in sports contests with the intent or major goal of defeating an opponent. In such clear cases, competition seems to be a zero-sum game. Because not all competitors can defeat an opponent, defeat by one precludes a like attainment by the other in the same contest.

Further, the clearest examples of athletic competition involve structured games such as baseball, football, basketball, and tennis, all of which are governed by a set of rules defining permissible moves. For example, the rules of basketball that stipulate what it is to score, foul, or travel are *constitutive* rules. If players were unaware of such rules or made no attempt to follow them, they could not be play-ing basketball (although minimal modifications might be acceptable in informal play). Constitutive rules should be distinguished from rules of strategy, such as "Dribble only if there is no faster way of advancing the ball up court." Rules of strategy are general suggestions about how to play the game well; constitutive rules determine what counts as a permissible move within the game itself.

Accordingly, competition in sports is the attempt to secure victory within the framework set by the constitutive rules. Some philosophers of sport, as we will see in Chapter 3, argue that cheaters cannot really win, since when they cheat they go outside the constitutive rules that define the game, and therefore they do not even play the game. In this chapter, we will explore the ethics of playing to win. Can a morally acceptable defense of competitive sports be developed? If such an ideal of competitive sports can be defended, we will be able to separate instances of competition in sports that are ethically defensible from those that are not; this knowledge can be applied in later chapters to concrete issues in sport.

The Critique of Competition in Sports

Why is it even necessary to make a moral evaluation of competition in sports? Isn't it enough to say simply that participants and spectators alike enjoy such competition? To critics of competition in sports, that is not enough. They argue that such competition is either inherently immoral or that it reinforces other social values that are undesirable. Many persons, including some professional athletes, who have criticized competition and overemphasis on winning have proposed a more relaxed attitude toward sports, at least at most levels of amateur play, than the one sanctioned by the competitive creed.

Proponents of competition in sports, in contrast, have argued for its moral value. General Douglas MacArthur, an American hero of World War II, may have overstated the case when he maintained that participation in competitive sports was "a vital character builder" that "molds the youth of our country for their roles as custodians of the republic."[4] Overstated or not, that view is widely shared.

A moral evaluation of competition in sports is necessary if we are to make a rational assessment of such conflicting views. It is not enough to assume uncritically that competition in athletics must be morally permissible simply because many people enjoy it. After all, a racist majority may enjoy terrorizing members of the minority racial group, but that doesn't make it right. Perhaps competition in sports is harmful or unjust in ways not acknowledged by many of its proponents; for this reason, we must subject the critics' views to rational examination.

It will be useful to divide the arguments about the morality of competition in sports into two kinds. The first is concerned with the good or bad consequences of competitive practices, either to competitors themselves or society at large. The second is concerned not with the effects of competition but with its intrinsic character.

The Consequences of Competition

One way of evaluating competition in sports is to assess its consequences. Surely, whether a practice has good or bad effects on other people is relevant to moral evaluation. Yet, although the strategy of evaluating consequences is sound, acting on it may be more difficult.

First, are we to look only at the effects upon ourselves or our team, or are we to look more broadly at the consequences for all participants, or for everyone affected by athletic competition, including long-term social effects on society at large? The important ethical theory known as utilitarianism holds that an action or practice is morally justified only if it has better consequences for all affected than the alternatives.[5]

Utilitarianism sounds like a relatively simple approach to ethics. Just do a cost-benefit analysis on the effects of the act or practice being evaluated, and you have your answer about whether something is ethical. But utilitarianism raises complex issues of theory and practice before it can even be applied to a problem. For example, what are we to count as a good or bad consequence? In economic analysis, costs and benefits can often be measured in monetary profits and losses, but what is to count as a cost or benefit in ethics? Should pleasure and pain be the criteria, as classical utilitarians such as Jeremy Bentham and John Stuart Mill suggested? Are there other criteria, such as excellence in performance, achievement, or knowledge, that should also count? For example, is a well-played game of greater intrinsic value than a poorly played game, and is this so even if the participants of both games experience the same levels of pleasure and pain? If we say that only pleasure and pain count, our theory may be too narrow. If we add other goods, such as excellence of performance, how are we to aggregate them with pleasure and pain to reach an overall total?

Moreover, even if we can agree on criteria of good and bad consequences, they may admit of different interpretations. For example, should we identify benefits with what actual participants seem to want or with what they would want if they were better informed and more rational? Suppose, for example, that Jones, who sees herself as a potential superstar, despises practices because of her coach's emphasis on teamwork, but would value the practices if she were better informed about the benefits of teamwork and more honest about her own abilities. Are the practices beneficial to Jones or not?

None of this totally discredits utilitarianism. We all sometimes assess the consequences of behavior on our own lives and others. An ethical theory that ignored the consequences of actions or practices on human life would be hard to defend. How many of us, for example, would advocate an action, however noble, knowing that one of its consequences would be the painful death of millions? But even though any satisfactory ethic must give some weight to the effects of acts or policies on human life, the choice of what framework we should adopt for evaluating the consequences will often be controversial.

In addition, if we are to evaluate the effects of competition in sports, another problem arises. Just what practices are we evaluating? Competition in sports can range from professional athletic contests to interscholastic competition to backyard contests among friends. Moreover, it is important to distinguish competition as it is practiced and as it ought to be practiced. Thus, even if competitive practices often have bad consequences, we should not necessarily conclude that competition in sports is morally indefensible. Perhaps competition in sports as carried out has harmful consequences that could be avoided if sports were properly conducted.

Accordingly, any utilitarian evaluation of competition in sports will rest on sometimes unstated and often controversial assumptions. In assessing a utilitarian evaluation's significance, we should identify just what presuppositions have been employed. For example, suppose a study shows that participation in sports has little positive effect on character development. To evaluate the significance of the study, we would need to know what traits of character the researchers considered positive, what forms of competition they studied, and whether they considered only competition as actually practiced, or included—or even focused exclusively on—competition as it should be practiced from the moral point of view.

An exhaustive analysis of the consequences of competition in sports is beyond the scope of this study, but it is important to remember the philosophical and methodological assumptions underlying such work. Given that the presuppositions of any utilitarian analysis are likely to be controversial, utilitarianism by itself probably cannot provide a decisive evaluation of competition in sports.

For example, we know that proponents of competitive sports claim that participation promotes loyalty, discipline, commitment, a concern for excellence, and a "never say die" attitude. These views are often expressed by well-known slogans, sometimes posted on locker-room walls, such as "A winner never quits, a quitter never wins" and "When the going gets tough, the tough get going." That athletics offer unique opportunities for character development is a common general assertion.

However, such claims are difficult to document. Thus, with regard to altruism, one early but influential study concluded: "Most athletes indicate low interest in receiving support and concern from others, low need to take care of others, and low need for affiliation. Such a personality seems necessary to achieve victory over others." More generally, the authors reported: "We found no empirical support for the tradition that sport builds character. . . . It seems that the personality of the ideal athlete is not the result of the molding process, but comes out of the ruthless selection process that occurs at all levels of sport. . . . Horatio Alger success—in sport or elsewhere—comes only to those who already are mentally fit, resilient, and strong."[6]

Although no study is by itself decisive, and conclusions such as the one quoted above will be challenged later in this book, this study does have significant methodological implications. In particular, even if participants in competitive sports do manifest desirable character traits to an unusual degree, it does not follow that participation in sports caused these traits to develop; they may have been there all along. Correlation should not be confused with causation.

This point is forcefully made in a widely discussed study by officers of the prestigious Mellon Foundation called *The Game of Life*. The authors, James L. Shulman and William G. Bowen, rely on an extensive database that allowed them to compare student athletes from highly selective colleges and universities with other students from the same institutions. Shulman and Bowen argued that although athletes may well show especially high levels of teamwork and ability to cooperate with others to achieve a common goal, the athletes had tended to exhibit these traits before participating in college athletics. Therefore, the preexisting character traits of athletes help to account for their athletic success rather than being created by participation in sports.[7]

However, the claim that preselection fully explains the virtues exhibited by many athletes can cut in different directions. For one thing, it can also be used to discount some of the consequentialist *criticism* of competitive sports. For example, competitive athletics may not promote selfishness or cheating, as critics of competitive sport may claim; rather, some successful athletes may already be selfish and predisposed to cheating before becoming successful in sport. There may be no causal effect, only correlation.

Thus, it is important not to confuse a factor associated or correlated with intense athletic competition with something caused by such competition. To take another example, it has been suggested that "athletes whose sense of identity and self-worth is entirely linked to athletic achievement often experience an identity crisis when the athletic career has ended, and it becomes necessary to move on to something else."[8] This statement may be true generally of hard-driving individuals who face significant career changes in fields other than sport, and so say little of significance about participation in competitive athletics itself. Would anyone be surprised by the claim that "executives whose sense of identity and self-worth is entirely linked to achievement in business often experience an identity crisis when their careers end and it becomes necessary to move on to something else"?

Perhaps anyone sincerely committed to a worthy endeavor would feel a sense of loss over change, which is not necessarily a bad thing. If so, participation in sports does not cause athletes to have an identity crisis when changing careers; instead, individuals who already are committed to achievement and dedicated to their careers are vulnerable to such episodes whether they are participants in athletics, business, medicine, law, academia, theater, or any other endeavor that demands a high level of commitment from successful participants. Accordingly, if critics of competitive sports are right to explain away evidence that participation in sports develops virtues as simply the result of preselection, they cannot also consistently claim that participation in sports causes all the vices or harms involving athletes. If preselection is plausible at all, it applies to both the good qualities and the bad qualities associated with sports participation. It should not be used to dismiss the possibility of sports causing the good qualities while asserting that sports must cause the bad qualities.

But is the preselection theory plausible, even if applied consistently? In fact, even though there may be no direct and demonstrable connection between participation in competitive sports and desirable character development, there may be more subtle and indirect connections. Harry Edwards, while acknowledging that competitive sports do not build character from scratch, suggests that participation may reinforce and encourage the development of preexisting character traits.[9]

True, it is not easy to show that participation does or does not promote specific character traits. Similarly, it is not easy to show that a liberal arts education affects the values of students. We do not conclude, however, that there are no effects. Do the alumni of the highly selective colleges and universities studied in *The Game of Life* tend to succeed in their careers because of their fine education? Or do the colleges and universities in question merely preselect those applicants whom anyone would predict as the most likely to succeed? We surely need to be careful about a double standard in attributing the positive character traits of athletes to preselection while refusing to apply the same argument to our own favorite social and educational practices. Professors are rightly reluctant to assume that they have no real influence on their students whose virtues, intellectual or moral, are entirely due to preselection. But then, why not be equally reluctant to assume that all the good qualities exhibited by some athletes are entirely the result of preselection, rather than at least partially the result of their participation in sports?

The commonsense position suggested by Edwards surely has force. Why assume that development and growth in either athletics or academics at the college level are entirely the result of preselecting those who already have the traits necessary for success? Although it is true that both college coaches and admissions officers at selective schools recruit students who have already demonstrated a capacity for success, these individuals also may develop significantly because of the influence of coaches and professors. Surely the most intuitively plausible model is one of interaction: Experiences at college, whether in the classroom or on the playing field, often promote the development of students, although the students selected to study and play sports at the institutions in question have already demonstrated some potential for success. The "add-ons" that college provides, whether in studies or in sports, in all likelihood make the educational experience valuable.

What should we conclude, then, about the consequentialist thesis that participation in athletics may promote moral and intellectual growth? For one thing, we have learned that whether the thesis is true or false is not an issue easily settled and raises many complex questions. Much will depend on context. On one hand, if athletics are conducted in an unethical manner, and if winning at all costs is the only goal that is emphasized, then participation may impede moral development rather than advancing it. On the other hand, if what is emphasized is the pursuit of excellence, if winning is considered an important goal but not the only goal, if respect for opponents and the best values of sport are emphasized, and if athletes are taught to think critically and reflectively about their performance, then participation might well have beneficial effects on participants and spectators alike. Surely much will depend on how sports are conducted in specific contexts.

Finally, and of great importance, even if competitive sports have less impact on character development than many have claimed (for example, if the preselection theory is justifiable after all), they still may play a major role in expressing and illustrating our values and even help to justify them; we might call these the expressive and the justificatory functions of sports.[10] For example, athletic competition may illustrate the value of dedication and teamwork by publicly manifesting the excellence attained through the cultivation of those traits. Close contests can bring out courage and loyalty. By welcoming challenges in sports, participants and spectators can affirm and exhibit such virtues.

Similarly, a highly talented team that never plays to its potential because its players are too selfish to work together, or who cannot put aside their differences to cooperate in a common cause, may provide justificatory support to those who affirm the importance of teamwork and solidarity with others. It is significant in this respect that prominent social scientist James Q. Wilson identified athletic teams as one of the few American institutions that often combined a significant degree of diversity with trust among participants, pointing out that they thus illustrated and perhaps helped to justify the thesis that diversity and social unity could be truly compatible.

In summary, we have seen that evaluating the social practice of competitive athletics by seeing whether its consequences are harmful or beneficial raises such complex issues that a decisive and uncontroversial consequential analysis is currently unavailable. However, we have also seen that those who are skeptical about the beneficial consequences of participation in competitive athletics have not necessarily won the day. On the contrary, there is much that believers in the benefits of sports participation can say in reply to the skeptic.

Moreover, although our assessment of consequentialist approaches may not admit of a decisive conclusion, consequentialism itself may not be the most significant part of the ethical story. Competition, the critics contend, cannot satisfy legitimate ethical requirements that are nonconsequential in character. Are they right? Maybe if we look beyond consequences (especially if we construe "consequences" narrowly) to other sorts of principles, ones that regard factors other than consequences as morally significant, we can come to a defensible moral assessment of competitive sports.

COMPETITION AS A MUTUAL QUEST FOR EXCELLENCE

Competition, Selfishness, and the Quest for Excellence

Perhaps the most important criticism of the moral worth of competition is that it is inherently selfish and egoistic. Because competitive activities are zero-sum games, one person's victory is another's defeat. As we have seen, the internal goal of competition is to defeat an opponent and win the contest. The point of this criticism is not that the consequences of competition are undesirable, but that competition by its very nature is imbued with values that we should reject.

Thus, some critics of competition throughout society, among them political theorist John Schaar, see the competitive society as a very unattractive place. It reduces human interaction to "a contest in which each man competes with his fellows for scarce goods, a contest in which there is never enough for everybody, and where one man's gain is usually another's loss."[11] Michael Fielding identifies competition with "working against others in a spirit of selfishness."[12]

The critics argue, then, that the goal of competition is to enhance the position of one competitor (or one small group of competitors, such as a team) at the expense of others. Thus, by its very nature, competition is selfish. Since selfish concern for oneself at the expense of others is immoral, it follows that competition is immoral as well.

These nonconsequentialist critics of competitive sports do not argue only against debased forms of competition, such as cheating. After all, virtually everyone acknowledges that competitive sports are morally objectionable when players are taught to cheat to win, to bribe officials, or to intentionally injure opponents to get them off the field of play. The critics, however, object to competitive sports at their best. Even supposing that the participants are playing fairly, is competition in sports still not selfish and egoistic?

The argument that competitive sports are selfish by their very nature is not without some intuitive force, because, in athletic competition, if X wins, Y loses. If they are good competitors, X and Y each try to win. Nevertheless, even if the argument that competition is essentially selfish is justifiable when applied to economic competition in the market, which is hardly self-evident, it faces special difficulties when applied to athletics.

For one thing, the idea of competition in sports as an unrestricted war of all against all seems grossly inaccurate. Even though team sports involve competition between opponents, they also involve cooperation among team members. In many sports, even at the professional level, it is common for opponents to encourage and even instruct each other in the off-season or between contests. Critics might reply that such examples show that even professional athletes find it morally impossible to live according to a strict competitive ethic. But, as we will see, such cooperative behavior can be regarded as part of a defensible competitive ethic that is based not on the idea of a war of all against all but on the value of meeting the challenges provided by competition in sports.

Indeed, competition in sports takes place within a context of binding constitutive rules. Constitutive rules are those that define what counts as a legitimate move within the game and what counts as winning and losing. Thus, running with the ball is prohibited in basketball because the constitutive or defining rules of the game require that the ball be advanced only through such allowed techniques as passing or dribbling. Good competition requires competitors to forgo breaking the constitutive rules for momentary advantages. Commitment to this ideal is perhaps best illustrated by the behavior of athletes in individual sports, from weekend tennis players to professional golfers, who call penalties on themselves in the heat of competition, sometimes at great financial cost. In many sports, rules are enforced by officials. But although it is legitimate to question the calls of officials, no one believes they ought not to apply the rules at all, or that they should apply them selectively.

In addition to obligations to obey the constitutive rules of the sport, there are obligations of competitive fairness that also restrict selfishness in sports. Thus, competitive success seems insignificant, or even unethical, if it is obtained by stacking the deck against one side—say, by bribing an official, or by scheduling vastly inferior opponents for all or much of one's season.

Finally, selfishness in competitive sports is often criticized. The basketball player who is overly concerned with how many points she scores rather than with whether her team wins is criticized for being selfish; coaches often tell such players that they must become team players instead of trying to be the star. This response would make no sense if selfishness was the norm in competitive athletics.

At this point, critics might concede that normative restrictions apply to selfish behavior in athletic competition, although they might still argue that, just as limited war is still war, so minimally constrained selfishness is still selfishness. To answer this point, we need a fuller account of competition in sports. Let us begin by considering a Yale-Princeton football game played in 1895. Princeton was winning 16–10, but Yale was right on the Princeton goal line with a chance to turn the tide on the very last play of the game:

> The clamor ceased once absolutely, and the silence was even more impressive than the tumult that had preceded it. . . . While they [the Yale players] were lining up for that last effort the cheering died away, yells both measured and inarticulate stopped and the place was so still . . . you could hear the telegraph instruments chirping like crickets from the side. Yale scored to win the game on a brilliant run. It is not possible to describe that run. It would be as easy to explain how a snake disappears through the grass, or an eel slips from your fingers, or to say how a flash of linked lightning wriggles across the sky.[13]

Is the important point here simply that Yale won and that Princeton lost? Edwin Delattre, former president of St. John's College of Annapolis, Maryland, has drawn a different lesson from this episode and the many like it that take place in all seasons and at all levels of competition:

Such moments are what make the game worth the candle. Whether amidst the soft lights and sparkling balls of a billiard table, or the rolling terrain of a lush fairway, or in the violent and crashing pits where linemen struggle, it is the moments where no letup is possible, when there is virtually no tolerance for error, which make up the game. The best and most satisfying contests maximize these moments and minimize respite from pressure.[14]

According to Delattre, these moments of testing rather than victory or defeat are the source of the value of competition in sports:

The testing of one's mettle in competitive athletics is a form of self-discovery. . . . The claim of competitive athletics to importance rests squarely on their providing us opportunities for self-discovery which might otherwise have been missed. . . . They provide opportunities for self-discovery, for concentration and intensity of involvement, for being carried away by the demands of the contest . . . with a frequency seldom matched elsewhere. . . . This is why it is a far greater success in competitive athletics to have played well under pressure of a truly worthwhile opponent and lost than to have defeated a less worthy or unworthy one where no demands were made.[15]

Delattre's comments suggest that although it is essential to good competition that the competitors try as hard as they can to achieve victory, the principal value of athletic competition lies not in winning but in overcoming the challenge presented by a worthy opponent. On this view, good competition presupposes a *cooperative* effort by competitors to generate the best possible challenge to each other. Each has the obligation to the other to try his or her best. Although one wins the contest and the other loses, each gains by trying to meet the challenge.

If this view has force, competition in sports should be regarded and engaged in not as a zero-sum game but as *a mutually acceptable quest for excellence through challenge.* Underlying the good sports contest, in effect, is an implicit social contract under which both competitors accept the obligation to provide a challenge for opponents according to the rules of the sport. Competition in sports is ethically defensible, in this view, when it is engaged in voluntarily as part of this mutual quest.

This does not mean that all competition in sports is ethically defensible; actual practice may not satisfy the requirements of the mutual quest for excellence. It does say, however, that competition in sports is ethically defensible when it satisfies such requirements.

Competitive sports as a mutual quest for excellence not only emphasizes the cooperative side of athletic contests and the acceptance of the challenge from the point of view of all the competitors but also explains much of our society's fascination with competitive sports. A. Bartlett Giamatti, former president of Yale and commissioner of baseball, emphasized the quest for excellence:

> When . . . a person on the field or fairway, rink, floor, or track, performs an act that surpasses—despite his or her evident mortality, his or her humanness—whatever we have seen or heard of or could conceive of doing ourselves, then we have witnessed . . . an instant of complete coherence. In that instant, pulled to our feet, we are pulled out of ourselves. We feel what we saw, became what we perceived. The memory of that moment is deep enough to send us all out again and again, to reenact the ceremony, made of all the minor ceremonies to which spectator and player devote themselves, in the hopes that the moment will be summoned again and made again palpable.[16]

Now critics of competition in sports may become impatient. Sports events, conceived as part of a mutually acceptable quest for excellence, may indeed be ethically defensible, they might reply, but such a view does not justify competition in sports. Rather, they might claim, it replaces competitive sports with something else. What has been done is a verbal trick. "Competition" has been so redefined that it no longer refers to true competition at all, but rather to the quest for excellence, self-improvement, and self-knowledge through exposure to challenge. By emphasizing the quest for excellence, we have changed the aim of the sports contest from that of defeating opponents to the quest for self-development and achievement. The aim is no longer to defeat opponents but to reach certain standards of performance or to gain self-knowledge and development through trying to satisfy those standards. Competition in sports has been replaced by so-called "competition with oneself." Is this charge correct? Let us consider the issue further.

Self-Development and Competition with Self

"Competition with self" suggests that athletes play against ghostly images of their earlier selves. Because there are no ghostly images and no presently existing earlier selves with whom to compete, this expression is potentially misleading. It is perhaps less paradoxical to speak of individuals as striving for self-development or self-improvement than to speak of individuals competing against earlier versions of themselves.

Should participants in sports strive mainly for self-development or personal improvement? Is such improvement a more important or more ethically defensible goal than the goal of attaining competitive success? After considering such questions, we will explore whether competition, conceived of as a mutual quest for excellence, really is only a disguised way of talking about the quest for self-improvement.

The claim that improvement is an ethically better or more defensible goal than competitive success in sports presupposes, first, that an ethically relevant difference exists between the two and, second, that the difference contributes to the ethical superiority of the improvement model. What might that difference be? Perhaps the difference is that in aiming for improvement, we do not necessarily aim to beat others. We can all improve together, so the element of the zero-sum game is missing. Since all can improve together, to aim at improvement does not appear selfish. Intending to beat others seems selfish, at least to the critics, because it seems to value success of the self (or of one's team) without regard to the interests of others.

There are two defenses against such an approach. The first, as we have seen, is that competition thought of as a mutual quest for excellence is not necessarily selfish or a total zero-sum game. Although only one party can win, each cooperates in providing a mutually acceptable challenge to the other. Although not all competitors can win, there is a sense, as we will see, in which all the competitors in a well-played contest can meet the challenge and achieve excellence.

Second, and perhaps most important, we can question the degree to which the quest for self-improvement differs from competitive sports in an ethically important way. At the very least, the two approaches share some central features. For one thing, an especially significant criterion of improvement is change in one's competitive standing when measured against the performance of others. Perhaps the best way of judging one's progress is to see whether one is doing better against opponents now than in the past.

Doing better against opponents is not merely a contingent sign of improvement; often, what counts as playing well is logically determined by what counts as an appropriate competitive response to the moves of opponents. For example, it would be incorrect to say that Susan is playing good tennis if Susan is hitting crisp ground shots when intelligent play calls for charging the net. Similarly, it would be incorrect to say that she is improving if she continues to make such competitively inappropriate moves in match after match.

The conceptual point, then, is that achievement, improvement, or development cannot easily be divorced from comparison with the performance of others. Robert Nozick provided a pertinent illustration: "A man living in an isolated mountain village can sink 15 jump shots with a basketball out of 150 tries. Everyone else in the village can sink only one jump shot out of 150 tries. He thinks (as do the others) that he's very good at it. One day along comes Jerry West."[17] (West was an All American for West Virginia University and one of the great professional players of all time in the NBA where he played from 1960 to 1974.)

The example illustrates that what counts as a significant achievement requires reference to the performance of others. It further suggests that judgments about what counts as a significant improvement also presuppose comparative evaluations about the performance of others. Before the arrival of a great professional basketball player such as Jerry West, the village star may have thought that improving his average to 17 out of 150 shots would constitute significant improvement. After the visit, even if it is acknowledged that no villager can ever match West's skill, the very criterion of significant improvement would have radically changed. At the very least, the more expert villagers should expect that, after reasonable practice, they should make at least 50 shots out of 150 tries. Before the visit, the "30-shot barrier" must have seemed as impossible to reach as breaking the 4-minute mile must have seemed to runners of an earlier era.

Does this imply that an athlete seeking to improve really is implicitly competing with others? Such an athlete is striving to reach standards set by an appropriate reference group of others, at least if the improvement is thought of as an achievement. Thus, success or failure is partially determined by how others perform. Accordingly, those who value "competition with self" because it seems not to involve (possibly negative) comparisons with the performance of others may need to rethink their position. Although differences may remain, the quest for improvement and the quest for victory both share an element of comparison with the performance of others. That is why the rhetoric of competition with self can be misleading; the appropriate reference group is not only an earlier self but also a reference class of fellow competitors. Even in judging our own performance, we are evaluating it by how it compares to a group with whom we believe it appropriate to compare ourselves.[18]

And yet, there are important differences between striving for improvement and striving for competitive success. In particular, the significant improvement of some participants does not preclude the improvement of others and may even facilitate it, as when the whole group improves. The attainment of victory by some, however, does preclude its attainment by the opposition. Although this difference may not be as important as critics allege, since everyone can meet the challenge of competition, it is true that although all participants can improve, not all participants can win. Competition emphasizes meeting the challenge set by an opponent, whereas improvement emphasizes the development of one's own skills. Even if one can measure development only by examining competitive performance, the two goals are conceptually different. One can meet an opponent's challenge without improving one's past performance, and one can improve one's past performance while continuing to lose to a more skilled competitor.

Our discussion suggests three conclusions. First, although the quest for improvement and the quest to achieve competitive success by defeating opponents are different in important ways, they also have much in common. In particular, the attempt to improve involves the performances of fellow athletes, and so reaches beyond the self. It is true that the idea of competition as a mutual quest for excellence sees excellence achieved by meeting the challenge presented by an opponent, and that therefore it differs from the notion of simply trying to improve. However, since what counts as improvement often is determined by how one reacts to the moves and strategies of opponents, trying to meet the challenge of competition and trying to improve also have a great deal in common.

Second, and perhaps more important, the defense of competition as a mutual quest for excellence avoids many of the objections to competitive excess that may have made "competition with self" seem more attractive than competition against others. As we have seen, athletic competition, conceived of as a mutual quest for excellence, is significantly cooperative; each competitor freely agrees (if only implicitly) to provide a challenge to the opponent, and each opponent can meet the challenge by playing well even though only one can win. So even though the goal or intent of the competitors may be to win, each can meet the challenge by playing well.

But consider a third point. Suppose dancers were given the following advice: "It's unimportant whether you are good or bad dancers. Just try to get better and better every day." Surely it is important that dancers improve their performance, but isn't the level of achievement they have attained also important? In the dance, we appreciate personal development, but we also value achievement and a skilled performance. If athletic performance is regarded as significant, skilled performance is important in sports as well. Competition is the mechanism by which achievement is measured and determined. Improvement is a desirable goal, but achievement is no less important or noble. Improvement, then, is a worthy goal toward which all competitors ought to strive. But it is not the only goal; high achievement in athletics can be equally worthy, and sometimes inspiring, and, as Giametti has suggested, even ennobling as well.[19]

Competition, Selfishness, and Inequality

Let us return to the critics' arguments. Their major charge is that competitive sports are inherently selfish, a criticism that seems to ignore the kind of cooperation involved in the mutual quest for excellence through challenge. According to this conception, opponents cooperate in generating mutually acceptable challenges.

It is true that winning will normally be in a competitor's self-interest, but even if victory is in one's *self-interest*, it does not follow that the pursuit of victory is *selfish*. If we define selfish behavior as self-interested behavior, then the trivial pursuit of victory is selfish because we have stipulated it to be so by definition. But is such a definition or characterization of selfishness acceptable?

Consider the following examples.

1. Jones is playing in a touch football game with friends. Jones says, "I'll be the quarterback." The others declare that they, too, want to be quarterbacks

and suggest the position be shared. Jones replies, "It's my football! If you don't let me play quarterback, I'll take my ball and go home!"
2. Jones is in a spelling contest between two teams in his fifth-grade class. He correctly spells a difficult word. As a result, his team wins and the other team loses.

The concept of selfishness is stretched too far if it is applied to both scenarios. Isn't there a significant difference between the first, in which Jones disregards the interests of others in favor of his own, and the second, in which each student is given a fair chance to succeed? Similarly, an important difference exists between trying to defeat an opponent within a mutually acceptable framework of rules and simply disregarding the interests of others. Thus, there is a significant, ethically relevant difference between athletic competition and selfishness.

To summarize the discussion of competition and selfishness, the charge that competition is intrinsically selfish faces several weighty objections. It does not take into account cooperation in competition, and it does not appreciate the ethical significance of competition conceived of as a mutual quest for excellence. It also rests on a far too broad conception of selfishness. Accordingly, unless the critics can reply satisfactorily to these objections, we may reject the claim that competition in sports is just another example of selfishness and greed. This is not to deny that competitors sometimes behave selfishly; rather, it is to deny that action within competitive sports must be selfish because of the nature of the activity.

Even if competition in sports is not intrinsically selfish, another feature may worry critics. Competitive sports, according to this second critical view, generate inequalities. We become winners and losers, successes and failures, stars and scrubs. Many of us are all too familiar with the slogans that equate losing with failure, and that virtually assign "losers" to an inferior branch of the human race.

In practice, competition is too often used for making invidious distinctions. Making an error in a crucial game or situation is equated with a lack of drive or courage. One of the sadder features of organized sports for children is the emphasis that some parents and coaches sometimes place on winning. As a result, young players often become more concerned with avoiding errors, and the criticism and even ridicule that follows, than with enjoying the competition or developing fundamental skills. Thus, there is something to the claim that competitive sports generate inequalities and that these are sometimes harmful or unethical. But before we accept too broad a version of the criticism, some considerations must be examined.

First, we need to distinguish between whether a rule or practice generates a factual inequality or difference and whether that difference is unethical, unfair, or inequitable. Some inequalities may well be fair or equitable, as when an instructor gives a high grade to an excellent paper and a low grade to a poor paper. Whether inequalities or differences exist is one thing; whether they are morally defensible is quite another. Accordingly, it doesn't follow that every inequality generated by competitive sports is unethical, unfair, or inequitable.

On one hand, then, it should be acknowledged that competitive sports generate inequalities, and even that some of these inequalities, such as those generated by excessive emphasis on winning and losing in children's sports, are ethically objectionable. On the other hand, many inequalities generated by competitive sports may not be ethically objectionable.

Consider the distinction made by legal scholar Ronald Dworkin between the right to equal treatment, "which is the right to an equal distribution of some opportunity of resource or burden," and the right to treatment as an equal, which is the right "to be treated with the same respect and concern as anyone else."[20] Unlike equal treatment, equal respect and concern do not require the identical distribution of a good, such as playing time on a basketball team. Thus, if one of my children is ill and the other isn't, treatment as an equal does not require that I divide the sick child's medicine in half. Rather, giving all the medicine to the sick child is compatible with and may even be required by equal respect and concern for both children.[21] This suggests, as Dworkin maintained, that the right to treatment as an equal, or the right to equal respect and concern, is more fundamental ethically than the right to equal treatment. This is because factual inequalities in distribution, or what Dworkin called unequal treatment, may or may not be defensible depending upon whether they are compatible with the showing of equal respect and concern to all affected.

This distinction suggests that even though competition in sports may lead to unequal treatment, such as different assignments of playing time to better and worse players on a team, this is not sufficient to show that competition in sports is inequitable or unjust. Thus, critics of competition in sport must show not just that a distinction between winners and losers is accorded significance, but that this distinction violates the right to treatment as an equal or that it is unjustified in some different but equally fundamental moral way.

It is plausible to conclude that if people are treated with equal concern and respect, justified inequalities in distribution will emerge naturally. This is because part of treating persons with respect surely is treating them as beings "who are capable of forming and acting on intelligent conceptions of how their lives should be lived."[22] But people will have different conceptions of how their lives should be lived and make their choices accordingly. For example, if critics prefer one novel to another, the author of the first novel may make more money than the author of the second novel. But how can such an inequality be avoided without prohibiting persons from making and acting upon their critical judgments? Inequalities of outcome can be avoided only by failing to treat and respect others as the persons capable of critical choice that they are.[23]

A similar point can be made about many of the inequalities of result that emerge from competitive sports. For one thing, most participants want to compete. They find the challenge posed by competitors worth trying to meet and the competitive sport they play worth their commitment. If respect for persons requires that we respect their conception of how they should lead their lives, the inequalities generated by competition in sports seem no less justified than the inequalities arising from the autonomous choices of those involved in other areas.

Critics might object that treating people as equals involves more than simply respecting their choices. The choices must be reasonably informed and competent; they must not be made if mental illness, depression, or mood-altering drugs are influences. For example, suppose Jones chooses to humiliate himself to gain Smith's affections. Surely, Smith does not treat Jones with respect if she heaps extreme humiliation upon Jones, even though he chooses to leave himself open to such treatment. Rather, Jones is degrading himself, and Smith is contributing to that degradation. Similarly, just because participants in sports agree to compete, it doesn't follow that their choice ought to be respected. It must be shown that the competitive relationship itself is not inherently degrading or incompatible in some other way with respect for persons as equals.

Indeed, competitive relationships are often characterized in derogatory terms. Competitors are often seen merely as obstacles to be overcome. They are to be "destroyed," "humiliated," and "run off the court." Persons are reduced to mere things or barriers standing in the way of competitive success.

For example, in a major college football game, a star running back, playing again for the first time after experiencing a serious knee injury, reported that during a pileup, he felt the opposing players trying to twist his injured knee. Thinking quickly, he yelled out, "You've got the wrong knee! You've got the wrong knee!"[24]

It would clearly be ethically indefensible if competition required that we win by deliberately injuring our opponents. We already know that the ethics of good competition prohibits the intentional infliction of injury. Indeed, if competition is understood as a mutual quest for excellence, competitors should want their opponents to be at their peak so they can present the best possible challenge. Noted golfer and 2001 British Open Champion David Duval expressed how a good competitor should view opponents when he discussed the possibility of contending against Tiger Woods in a major championship: "One of the great things about golf is that you don't have to have any ill-will in this game. If I come head-to-head against him at say, the U.S. Open, I want him to be playing as good as he can play because I want to beat him when he's playing his best. It would be a heck of a lot better, if you know he gave you all he's got, and you beat him."[25]

Significant victory requires outplaying worthy opponents, not deliberately injuring them to prevent them from competing.

In evaluating competition in sports, it is crucial that the features that are central to competition be distinguished from those that are not. Many features of competitive sports that are ethically objectionable are not necessarily part of competitive sports. In particular, the reduction of opponents to mere things, although too often a part of high-pressure athletics, is not a central element of competitive sports and can consistently be condemned by proponents of a defensible competitive ethic.

Inequalities generated by competitive sports, then, need not be ethically indefensible. Participants in competitive sports presumably prefer a life that includes competition, with the possibility of winning or losing, to a life that does not. If treating individuals as equals requires us to react appropriately to the life plans of persons—to treat them as agents "capable of forming and acting on an intelligent conception of how their lives should be led"—then inequalities that arise from their decisions in athletics are presumptively fair and equitable.

An even stronger conclusion is supported by our discussion. Each competitor in an athletic contest must respond and react to the choices and actions of fellow competitors, actions manifesting the skills the participants have chosen to develop and the decisions they have made during play. Therefore, competition in sport conceived along lines of a mutual quest for excellence is a paradigm case of an activity in which the participants treat each other as equals. The good competitor does not see the opponent merely as an obstacle to be overcome but as a person whose activity calls for an appropriate response. Rather than being incompatible with equal respect for persons, competition in athletics, at its best, may presuppose it.

Is Winning Important?

If we view competitive sports as a mutual quest for excellence in the face of challenge, what importance should be assigned to winning? Is simply playing well in an attempt to meet the opponent's challenge all we should strive for? Why should who wins or loses matter at all?

Can't it be argued that winning is significant precisely because it is a criterion of meeting the challenge? To lose is to fail to meet the challenge; to win is to succeed. If competition in sports is justified by attempts to meet challenges, it is surely important whether or not we succeed in meeting them. After all, isn't the principal point of deliberately attempting a difficult task to see whether we can accomplish it?

Although there is much to this position, perhaps it is overstated. Winning is not necessarily a sign of competitive success, and losing is not necessarily a sign of competitive failure. If winning were the only criterion of success, it would be sensible to take pride in consistently defeating far weaker opponents by wide margins. Conversely, if losing were necessarily a sign of competitive failure, a weaker opponent would have no cause for pride after having extended a far superior opponent to the limit before going down to defeat. Moreover, as Nicholas Dixon has pointed out, winning can result from factors other than athletic excellence, such as a bad call by an official or a fluke of luck.[26]

This line of argument suggests that winning, while an important criterion of athletic success, is far from everything in competitive sports. Not everyone can win, but each competitor may well meet the challenge set by an opponent, although one wins and one loses. But it is not unimportant who wins or loses. If winning is not everything, it is something. For one thing, if the competition is not one sided, winning will certainly be an important criterion, sometimes the criterion, of having met the challenge of the opposition. Because one is trying to meet the challenge set by the opponent, it seems appropriate to feel elated at victory or disappointed at defeat. Even when opponents are mismatched, pride in victory may be appropriate: The victors rightly may be proud that they played to their potential without the incentive of strong opposition.

Finally, we should remember that playing well in some aesthetic sense is not necessarily playing well in the sense of meeting the competitive challenge presented by an opponent. Remember the earlier example of the tennis player who hit ground strokes with beautiful form yet lost because the competitive situation called for aggressive play at the net. Similarly, a 3-point shot from 20 feet may look good but may make no competitive sense if the team with the ball has a 2-point lead and 15 seconds left on the clock. What may look like good play from an aesthetic standpoint may be poor play given the competitive situation.

Indeed, as sports philosopher Scott Kretchmar recently pointed out, winning requires the development and use of certain skills that are key elements of the challenge of sports. Such qualities as "knowing how to hold a lead," "employing the proper strategy for the moment," "knowing how to weather a cold spell," and "knowing how to make a run from behind" are key qualities exhibited by top competitors.[27] In other words, winning, as opposed to playing well in some aesthetic sense, requires utilization of a set of abilities and skills that are central elements in the quest for athletic excellence through challenge.

Therefore, although winning may not be a necessary criterion of competitive success, it is often the most reliable indicator of it. In many competitive contexts, it won't do to separate winning and losing from how well one played the game, because the outcome of the game is an especially significant indicator of how well one actually played.

But why should success and failure matter at all? After all, "It's only a game." Isn't concern for competitive success overemphasized, given the nature of the activity?

There is no question that competitive success can be overemphasized, especially at the level of children's sports. And on one hand, certainly, if the slogan "It's only a game" means that extreme depression, abusiveness to others, extended withdrawal from family and friends, spouse beating, and existential anxiety are inappropriate responses to losing, it surely is correct. On the other hand, if that slogan means that success in competitive athletics shouldn't matter at all, it is far more dubious.

Competitive sports provide a context in which we can stretch our bodily skills and capacities to the limits in the pursuit of excellence. The pursuit of excellence in the use of the body is hardly trivial; on the contrary, for athletes, meeting the demands of the sport often involves beauty, courage, dedication, and passion. If these things don't matter, what does? Would the critics say to the artist who botches a significant painting, a musician who misses key notes during a concert, or the dancer who performs poorly in a major performance, "Well, it's only art!" Concern for success and the pursuit of excellence in athletics seems no more deserving of criticism than concern for success and the pursuit of excellence in other areas of human endeavor.

Our conclusions do not imply that all sporting activity should always be intensely competitive. Not everyone wants or needs a challenge all the time. At many levels of play, the trick for coaches and educators is to balance an emphasis on achievement and competitive success with participation and instruction in developmental skills. But insofar as an activity is a sport, then, even if played with little emphasis on competition, it will involve a degree of competitive challenge. The goal of the participants, as players, will be to make correct moves or plays, which in turn will be defined by the moves of the opposing players. If standards of good and bad performance did not apply, the participants would merely be exercising, not engaging in sports.

This point suggests that critics of overemphasis on winning and competitive success may take their points too far by ignoring the perhaps equally deleterious effects of underemphasis. Thus, if participants normally are told that "it doesn't matter how you do, just go out and have fun," the subtle message being conveyed may be that doing well is unimportant. If participation in competitive sports can be a form of human excellence, if it can contribute to self-development and self-expression, and perhaps reinforce desirable character traits, performance may well matter after all. As William Bennett has observed: "Serious playing and watching . . . are rarely if ever doing nothing, for sports is a way to scorn indifference, and occasionally, indeed, one can even discern in competition those elements of grace, skill, beauty, and courage that mirror the greatest affirmations of human spirit and passion."[28]

Bennett suggested that competitive sports, at their best, involve applying standards of excellence to challenges that people regard as worthwhile in themselves. This idea should be taken seriously. If competitive sports are understood on the model of a mutual quest for excellence through challenge, they not only can be activities of beauty and skill but can represent a striving for human excellence, and in so doing they can be a paradigmatic way of respecting each other as persons—of taking our status as persons seriously.

SUMMARY

This chapter suggests that competition in the context of sports is most defensible ethically when understood as a mutual quest for excellence in the intelligent and directed use of athletic skills in the face of challenge. Athletic competition of this sort, under appropriate conditions, may have such beneficial consequences as expressing important values and reinforcing the development of desirable character traits. Perhaps more important, competition in sports may have intrinsic worth as a framework within which we express ourselves as persons and respond to others as persons in the mutual pursuit of excellence. Although other such frameworks also exist, few are as universally accessible and involve us so fully as agents who must intelligently use our bodies to meet challenges we have chosen for ourselves.

Competition as the mutual quest for excellence, it must be emphasized, is an ideal. Actual practices may not conform to its requirements. In the real world, winning may be overemphasized, rules may be broken, athletes may be exploited, and unfair conditions for competition may preclude genuine challenge. If so, the ideal provides grounds for the moral criticism of serious deviations from it. In the remainder of this book, the ideal will be applied to the moral evaluation of actual practices in sports.

THREE

SPORTSMANSHIP, FAIRNESS, AND COMPETITION IN SPORT

The victory of the U.S. women's team in the 1999 World Cup Soccer matches was one of the most exciting events in sports in the last decade of the twentieth century. Not only were the contests leading to this triumph hotly contested, the final game being decided in a shoot-out, but the team was also taken by many to symbolize the emergence of women into the center of attention in athletic competition. The team's stars, popular and highly skilled players such as Mia Hamm and Brandy Chastain, were heroes to many young girls who played in soccer leagues across the country, as well as to adults throughout the United States.

However, as noted in Chapter 1, the final plays of the world championship game, in which the Americans defeated China, became the center of an important ethical controversy. Regular and overtime play had ended in a tie, and the game was to be decided by a shoot-out in which players from each team would go one-on-one against the opposing goalie. The team that scored the most goals after a set number of attempts would win the game. Under the rules, which prevented the goalkeeper from moving forward to cut off the shooter's angle until a shot was launched, the offensive player had a major advantage.

So the world championship was on the line while the offensive players matched each other goal for goal as the shoot-out progressed. The American goalkeeper, Briana Scurry, decided that one of the remaining Chinese players, Liu Ying, seemed to lack confidence. When Liu made her move against Scurry, the American goalie decided on a controversial tactic to stop the shot. As the Chinese player made her move, Scurry, by stepping forward in violation of the rule limiting the movement of goalies in such circumstances, attempted to deprive Liu of the angle she would need to score. The tactic worked, Scurry blocked the shot, and the Americans won. But did they win fairly?

As one view has it, "It's only cheating if you get caught." A more sophisticated and surely more defensible modification of that view is that it is the referee's job to call the game, and as long as the player is willing to accept the penalty if detected, no unethical behavior is involved. As another prominent goalkeeper put it, "What Briana did was perfectly normal. She took a step and the referee didn't call it. I don't call that cheating."[1]

Is it cheating to commit what we will call a strategic foul, an intentional violation of the rules designed to secure a tactical advantage? What if it is done openly and with willingness to accept the penalty if the referee calls the fouls? What if it is a common practice, known about and accepted by the players, as is fouling at the end of a basketball game to stop the clock? Scurry's move in the World Cup has been defended on exactly such grounds; all goalkeepers do it, players know that goalkeepers do it, and a penalty is prescribed under the rules if the violation is detected. After all, it is not as if Scurry was trying to hide her move from the referee or claim an advantage for herself that she would not accord to other goalies as well. But what happens to sport as a rule-governed activity if players decide for themselves when to obey the rules and are encouraged to test referees to see what they can get away with? Do we have a true sports contest if each team plays only by the rules it feels are useful to obey at a given moment?

Consider a second example that also raises issues of ethics in competition. In early October 1990, the highly regarded University of Colorado Buffaloes played a home football contest against the University of Missouri. Top national ranking was at stake. The final seconds saw Colorado trailing 31–27 but driving toward the Missouri goal line. Somehow, in the confusion on the field, the seven officials on the field, the "chain gang" working the sideline markers, and the scoreboard operator all lost track of the downs. On what should have been the fourth and deciding down, Colorado failed to score, in part because the Colorado quarterback, mistakenly thinking he had another play left, intentionally grounded a pass. In fact, the officials signaled that Colorado had another chance, unaware that the Buffaloes already had used the four chances to score allowed by the rules. Colorado scored on the illegal but unnoticed fifth down to eke out a 33–31 "victory."

Did Colorado really win? Should the final score have been allowed to stand? It was decided that the officials' mistake was not the sort of error that can be overruled. But should the University of Colorado have accepted the victory? Is such a "win" meaningful in an important ethical sense?

Consider a third example. A championship basketball game is tied, and only a few seconds remain. A player on the defensive team steals the ball and breaks away for the winning basket. Only one player can catch the streaking guard heading for the winning bucket. The defender realizes she cannot block the shot, but she also knows the opponent is her team's worst foul shooter. She pretends to go for the ball but in fact deliberately fouls her opponent. Is deliberate fouling to gain a strategic advantage ethical? After all, fouling is against the rules. But is that sufficient to make it unethical?

These examples raise questions not about the general issue we examined in Chapter 2, of whether competition in sports is ever ethical, but about how to conduct competition ethically. They raise issues of sportsmanship and fair play. By examining them, we can better understand the values that may be used in assessing the behavior of competitors within the athletic contest itself.

SPORTSMANSHIP AND FAIRNESS
IN THE PURSUIT OF VICTORY

What values ought to govern the behavior of competitors in athletic competition? Sportsmanship is one value that is often appealed to in such contexts. Sportsmanship has received relatively little attention by moral thinkers, and probably suffers today because of associations with the morality of an elite upper crust, and perhaps by concerns that a male bias is built into the meaning of the term.[2] Nevertheless, sportsmanship is a value frequently cited by coaches, players, and commentators on sports. It should not be simply dismissed as out of date or only for the socially or economically elite without first trying to understand what it might involve.

But what is sportsmanship? Does it apply equally to intense athletic competition and informal games among friends?

James W. Keating provided a particularly interesting analysis of sportsmanship. Keating properly warned, first of all, that we must not make our account of sportsmanship so broad as to make it virtually identical with virtue. Not every virtue is an instance of sportsmanship, and not every vice is unsportsmanlike. Keating observed that a formal code of sportsmanship promulgated earlier in this century included such diverse injunctions as "Keep yourself fit," "Keep your temper," and "Keep a sound soul and a clean mind in a healthy body." The trouble with such broad accounts of sportsmanship is that they do no specific work. We cannot say conduct is ethical because it is sportsmanlike, for "sportsmanlike" has just become another way of saying "ethical." The idea of sportsmanship has been characterized so broadly that there is no particular aspect of morality that is its specific concern.[3]

Keating argued that a more useful account of sportsmanship would develop the rather vague suggestion of the dictionary about behavior expected of a sportsman or sportswoman. To develop this idea, he introduced a crucial distinction between sports and athletics: "In essence, sport is a kind of diversion which has for its direct and immediate end fun, pleasure, and delight and which is dominated by a spirit of moderation and generosity. Athletics, on the other hand, is essentially a competitive activity, which has for its end victory in the contest and which is characterized by a spirit of dedication, sacrifice, and intensity."[4]

Sportsmanship, then, is the kind of attitude toward opponents that best promotes the goal of sports as defined by Keating—namely, friendly, mutually

satisfactory relationships among the players. "Its purpose is to protect and culti-
vate the festive mood proper to an activity whose primary purpose is pleasant
diversion, amusement, joy."[5] In Keating's view, the supreme principle of sportsmanship was an injunction to "always conduct yourself in such a manner that you
will increase rather than detract from the pleasure found in the activity, both your
own and that of your fellow participant."[6]

Sportsmanship, Keating said, was a virtue that applied to the recreational activity of sports, as he understood it, but not to the more serious and competitive
activity of athletics. To Keating, sportsmanship and athletics did not fit together
easily: "The strange paradox of sportsmanship as applied to athletics is that it asks
the athlete, locked in a deadly serious and emotionally charged situation, to act
outwardly as if he was engaged in some pleasant diversion."[7]

On Keating's theory, sportsmanship only applies to athletics in an attenuated
way involving adherence to the value of fair play, which to Keating implies adherence to the letter and spirit of equality before the rules. Since the athletic contest is
designed to determine which competitor meets the challenge best, fair play requires
that competitors not intentionally disregard or circumvent the rules. Broadly understood, perhaps more broadly than Keating would recommend, fair play requires
that victory be honorable. So fair play can be expected of the serious athlete in intense competition, but to also require sportsmanship—the attempt to increase the
pleasure of the opponent in the contest—normally is to ask too much.

But what is honorable behavior in competitive sport? Is it ethically required?
Do we act wrongly, in a way that is morally prohibited, if we behave dishonorably,
or do we just fail to live up to an ideal that is above and beyond the call of duty?
And what is fair play? Does it mean simply following the rules, or does it require
more than that? Did Scurry act unfairly in the decisive play in the World Cup
championship game? What precisely is the relationship between unfair and unsportsmanlike conduct? Did the University of Colorado act dishonorably in accepting its disputed victory over Missouri? Even if it didn't, is honorable behavior
too much to expect at elite levels of competitive athletics? Finally, is the line between sports and athletics as sharp and as ethically significant as Keating's account suggests?[8]

To answer these questions, and to clarify the relationship between fair play and
sportsmanship, we need to say more about how sport is to be understood and the
implications of such an understanding for ethics and fair play. For example, if sports
are understood principally as rule-governed activities, and fair play is thought of
simply as conformity to the rules, any deviation from the rules may be considered
unethical. But if common social understandings and conventions accepted in practice by participants are ethically relevant, a more permissive account of ethically acceptable behavior in sport may emerge.

SPORTS AND GAMES: THE ANALYSIS OF BERNARD SUITS

Perhaps the best way to begin our discussion is by considering the nature of sport itself. One plausible approach is to suggest that all sports are games of physical skill. This suggestion would cover clear cases of sports such as baseball, golf, soccer, and football. But while running marathons is a sport, are marathons games? Is skiing a game? Let us consider further.

If the thesis we are examining is that sports are games of physical skill, we may need to clarify the notion of "game." The great twentieth-century philosopher Ludwig Wittgenstein suggested that while we can clarify such concepts as "game," we cannot strictly define them. Wittgenstein, although not generally known to the general public, was extraordinarily influential in philosophy, in part because in his later work he stressed understanding the use we make of philosophically puzzling concepts in our ordinary discourse.

In particular, Wittgenstein called into question that the concepts we use always have an essence or set of necessary and sufficient defining characteristics. In raising this issue, he questioned the Platonic search for the form that lies behind our conceptual scheme—the form we search for when we ask such questions as "What is beauty?" "What is truth?" and "What is justice?" Thus, in a passage about games, Wittgenstein wrote:

> Consider for example the proceedings we call "games." . . . What is common to them all?—Don't say: "There *must* be something common or they would not be called 'games'—but *look and see* whether there is anything common to all.—For if you look at them you will not see something common to *all*, but similarities, relationships, and a whole series of them at that. To repeat: don't think but look!"[9]

Wittgenstein suggested that games resembled each other as family members did: in a plurality of overlapping ways but without any one characteristic or set of characteristics that each and every family member had. For this reason, many theorists influenced by Wittgenstein have regarded "game" as a "family resemblance concept" and denied that any precise definition of "game" can be provided.

Was Wittgenstein right about games? In a series of influential works, another philosopher, Bernard Suits, has raised doubts about Wittgenstein's challenge and proposed another important account of games. Indeed, Suits's book *The Grasshopper: Games, Life and Utopia* is a thesis on the nature and point of games.[10] Besides being analytically acute, it is also humorous and just plain fun to read. In any case, if Suits was correct, we can define "game" and then go on to understand sports as games of physical skill.

Games, Suits pointed out, are governed by constitutive rules that define what counts as winning and losing and distinguish moves that are permissible within a game from those that are impermissible. Thus, dribbling is a permissible way of advancing the ball in basketball, but running with the ball is not, precisely because the former is allowed by the constitutive rules and the latter is not. Dribbling too much can be bad strategy and violate what might be called strategic rules for playing well, but still, dribbling is allowed in a way that running with the ball is not.

However, many activities, such as taking an examination in a course, are governed by constitutive rules but are not games. Suits therefore introduced additional criteria to distinguish games from other practices defined by constitutive rules. In particular, the rules of games create challenges by setting up what Suits called unnecessary obstacles to achieving the goals that the players must pursue. Thus, it is a simple matter to put a ball into a hole, but it becomes exceedingly difficult to put a ball into a hole when, in golf, it must be done with what former British prime minister Winston Churchill called "implements ill-designed for the purpose." In other words, the constitutive rules of games create unnecessary challenges that make accomplishing an ordinary task (putting a ball into a hole), which Suits called the *pre-lusory goal*, into a challenging game (golf) that requires a legitimate golf score, the *lusory goal*.

In a game, moreover, we accept the constitutive rules simply in order to try to meet the challenge of the game. Suits called this the "lusory attitude." Thus, to return to our earlier example, although taking an examination in a college course may have constitutive rules (for example, that students may not refer to notes or texts during the examination period), taking a test is not a game, because tests are normally taken to get grades that enable participants to get jobs or secure entrance to graduate and professional school.

Consider, then, the suggestion, based on this rough summary of Suits's account, that a game is defined by: (1) constitutive rules that set up unnecessary obstacles to achieving a particular goal by defining permissible and impermissible ways of achieving it; and (2) the rules are accepted just to allow participants to attempt to meet the challenges so created. As Suits aptly said when summarizing his view, a game is "a voluntary attempt to meet unnecessary obstacles." Sports, then, would be, as already suggested, games of physical skill.

Should we accept Suits's account? Of course, there are difficulties with it. First, it may be objected, participants may accept the rules for a variety of reasons other than the lusory attitude—for example, to get exercise, to socialize and make friends, or, in the case of professionals, to make money. However, a proponent of Suits's definition might reply, with a good deal of plausibility, that although these may be motives of the participants, they still get exercise or make friends or make money by trying to meet the obstacles set by the rules. In fact, professional athletes achieve fame and fortune precisely by overcoming the challenges of the game. Tiger Woods has been considered the best golfer because he does better than anyone else at shooting low scores within the rules of the game. Thus, professional athletics are *parasitic* on the lusory attitude precisely because spectators are willing to pay to see the performance of professionals in what we called in Chapter 2 the mutual quest for excellence through competition.

Whether Suits's definition is completely successful remains debatable by philosophers of sport. Many questions remain to be examined. Thus, a marathon seems to be a sporting event, but we do not commonly call marathons "games." A "game of marathon" might be something played by children in imitation of a genuine marathon. (Suits might reply, however, that this is just a fault of ordinary language; a marathon has the structure of a game whether it is *called* one or not.) Suits himself at one time raised questions about whether sports like gymnastics or synchronized swimming are more like performances than games, and his account of games continues to be interpreted, debated, and evaluated within the professional literature.

Whether or not Suits has identified the essence of games, his account can illuminate the following discussion of the ethics of sport in two ways. First, his account certainly seems to fit paradigmatic instances of sports such as baseball, lacrosse, football, soccer, golf, and many other clear instances of sporting activity. Second, his emphasis on the role that constitutive rules play in setting up unnecessary obstacles calls attention to the notion of games as activities undertaken and valued fundamentally because of the challenge created by the rules. Indeed, in *The Grasshopper* Suits suggested that meeting the challenges of games is an intrinsically valuable human activity, and that a life of game playing might be what constitutes utopia. Even if we don't fully accept this last point, we can acknowledge the intrinsic interest athletes have in meeting challenges for their own sake, which, as should be clear, has enormously influenced the account of competitive sport as a mutual quest for excellence developed in the last chapter.

Keeping Suits's account in mind, let us see if it can help to illuminate our discussion of sportsmanship and fair play within competitive athletics.

INTERNALISM, EXTERNALISM, AND THE ETHICS OF SPORT

In this section, the view that sport has a kind of internal morality that is tightly (perhaps conceptually) connected with the structural features of athletic competition will be examined. The results then will be applied to the examples cited at the beginning of the chapter. We'll begin by considering two approaches to the connection between competitive sports and moral values.

Externalism denies that sports are a fundamental source or basis of ethical principles or values, although sophisticated externalists acknowledge, and even emphasize, that sports play a significant role in reinforcing values already extant in the culture and in socializing participants and spectators to accept those values as their own. On this view, the values that sports promote either express or simply mirror, reflect, or reinforce the values dominant in the wider society. Thus, to take one example, in a predominantly capitalist society sports may emphasize such capitalist values as intense competition and rivalry, whereas in more communal and less individualistic societies more emphasis may be given to teamwork and the role of opposing players as facilitators who help make good competition possible.

Internalism, in contrast, holds that sports are themselves sometimes significant sources of or bases for ethical principles and values. Internalists emphasize that sports can have a significant degree of autonomy from the wider society and that they can support, stand for, and express sets of values of their own that in particular contexts may conflict with the values dominant in the broader society. Thus, in his important work entitled *Leftist Theories of Sport*, William J. Morgan defended the idea of a "gratuitous logic" of sports, positing that sports do not merely mirror or reinforce the values dominant elsewhere.[11]

Internalism need not, and in my view should not, be taken to mean that the internal values of sport are entirely unique or have no basis in broader ethical principles such as respect for persons and fairness.[12] Rather, it claims, first, that key values in sport are not mere reflections of values popular or dominant in the society and, second, that these values are related to and can at least in part be supported by ethically defensible conceptions or interpretations of competition in sports.

Why is this distinction between externalism and internalism important for the concrete problems we raised earlier, such as the ethics of rule breaking for strategic purposes? Perhaps it is this. If internalism is correct, then the ethical principles embedded in or implied by central features of athletic competition may provide a morally relevant framework for adjudicating difficult moral issues that arise in athletic competition. Of course, just because some values or moral principles are internal to sport does not mean they are justifiable or well supported by reasons. Nevertheless, they may provide a useful starting point for analysis. Let us begin by considering one form of internalism and the critical response to it.

Formalism

"Formalism" is the name given to a family of positions that characterizes games, such central elements of games as winning and losing, and allowable moves within the activity, primarily in their formal structures and particularly in their constitutive rules. Formalism reflects Suits's emphasis on the constitutive rules of sports as the formal structure of sports. (The rules of a sport would constitute its structure, whereas the particular skills and strategies tested in the sport would be its substance.) Thus, in a narrow sense, formalism has been characterized as the view that such game derivative notions as "a move or play within a game" and "winning a game" are definable by reference to the constitutive rules of the game.

In a broader sense, formalism is the view that games (and sports to the extent that sports are games of physical skill) can be defined primarily by reference to constitutive rules. The goals or obstacles of the sport are defined by those rules and are unintelligible outside the context of the rules. A move within a game is what is permitted or required by the constitutive rules, and what counts as winning a game also is defined by such rules. For example, using a tank during a football game to run over the opposing team's defensive players is not a move within the sport, since such moves may be made only in accord with the constitutive rules. There are different versions of formalism, so "formalism" might best be regarded as an umbrella term covering a family of positions that, although closely related, sometimes differ on points of varying degrees of significance.

Formalism not only is a theory about the nature of games but also has normative implications. Perhaps the best known is the incompatibility thesis: Cheaters violate the rules by failing to make moves within the sport and therefore fail to play it. One can win the game only by playing it, and since cheaters do not play, cheaters can't win.

The emphasis of formalists on the constitutive rules of the game has helped us understand the nature of games. However, formalism lacks the normative resources to address many of the moral problems that arise in connection with sports. (To be fair, many versions of formalism were developed to define the notions of "game" and "sport" rather than to resolve ethical issues arising in games and sports.)

Issues of sportsmanship, for example, often go beyond conformity to the formal rules of a sport. Thus, consider the case of clubless Josie, a top amateur golfer who arrives at a national amateur golf championship without her clubs. Clubless Josie has lost her clubs not because she is clueless but because her airline was careless. Josie's chief rival, Annika, has a spare set of clubs virtually identical to those Josie has lost. Should Annika lend poor clubless but not clueless Josie the spare set of clubs so that Josie can compete in the tournament? Because Josie's problem does not concern the application of rules, it is unclear that formalism addresses this question.[13]

Some formalists might reply that their view, sympathetically interpreted, supports lending the clubs to Josie. If we correctly understand the *spirit* or *point* of the rules, which is to promote competition, we should do what enhances competition. However, in appealing to the spirit of the rules or their underlying point, formalists go beyond a narrow version of formalism and ask *how* we are to understand the spirit of the rules or their underlying point. We will consider this broader form of internalism below.

A second criticism of formalism is that it suggests an implausible account of the ethics of strategic rule violations in certain situations. A strategic foul, as we noted when considering Briana Scurry's behavior during the World Cup, is a rule violation designed to secure an advantage within the sporting contest to the team or individual who fouls. Another widely discussed example is the strategic foul at the end of a basketball game, where the losing team fouls as a strategy to stop the clock and force the team in the lead to make foul shots to maintain its advantage. According to critics of this practice, whom I suggest are influenced by the formalist emphasis on the rules as central to the game, such fouls are intentional violations of the rules and therefore are not legitimate moves within the game. In particular, according to many formalists, they violate the understanding or implicit contract that must hold between opponents to play the game by the rules. On this analysis, strategic fouling is a form of cheating.[14]

However, virtually all practitioners of many sports, especially basketball, consider strategic fouling an established part of the game and deny that it is a form of cheating. And some goalkeepers in soccer maintain that Scurry's behavior reflected common practice within the game. These participants might just be wrong, of course, but if their view can be defended, formalism may not be adequate, even on what seems to be its strongest ground where violating the central rules of the game is concerned.

Formalism also has problems with the ethics of rule changes and rule formation. How are proposed changes in the rules, or sets of rules for new sports and games, to be assessed? Formalists might point out that the rules of many sports include what legal philosopher H. L. A. Hart called "rules of change." A rule of change for golf might state that a proposal becomes a rule of golf if, and only if, it is accepted through established procedures by the governing golf organizations of an area, such as the United States Golf Association (USGA) in the United States and the Royal and Ancient in Britain. But although such rules of change might establish when a rule change becomes official, they do not establish whether the change is good or bad for the game.

Consider, for example, the proposed rule that anyone who commits a strategic foul in the last four minutes of a basketball game is thrown out of the game and the opposing team is awarded thirty straight foul shots. Because it is so penal, such a rule might eliminate strategic fouling. But is it a good rule? Is basketball a better or worse game if fouling late in the game to stop the clock is recognized as a legitimate tactic? Similar questions might be raised about the designated-hitter rule in baseball or proposals to give the goalkeeper more freedom of movement during shoot-outs in soccer. Although formalists are quite right to emphasize the formal structure of games, it is not clear how their theory might apply to ethical questions in sport that are not necessarily resolvable by formal or structural features alone.

Conventionalism

Many theorists argue that in emphasizing the formal constitutive rules of given sports, the formalists have ignored the implicit conventions that apply to the sports in question. These conventions are sometimes referred to as the "ethos of the game."[15] For example, with respect to strategic fouling in basketball, conventionalists argue that a convention in basketball permits such fouls as a legitimate strategic move within the game. Since the players all accept the convention, and since each team knows the other team will strategically foul at appropriate points in a contest, no team has a special advantage over others. Therefore, strategic fouling is not cheating, but is justified by practice and the widely accepted social conventions within that practice.

But can social conventions be a source of value in sports? Conventionalists have made a contribution to our understanding of sporting practice by exploring the role of the ethos and cultural context of games. But does the ethos have normative force? Do the conventions express what *ought* to take place as well as describe what *does* take place in sporting practice?

Consider clubless Josie. For one thing, if such a dilemma were highly unusual, there might be no applicable convention. Conventionalism, like formalism, would not tell us what should be done. But suppose there was an applicable convention under which players were not supposed to lend equipment to fellow competitors. Would that settle the issue, or would it simply raise the deeper issue of whether that convention was ethical or reflected appropriate standards of fair play? Thus, one major problem with conventionalism is the ethical status of the conventions themselves.

This is true even where conventionalism is plausible—namely, its analysis of strategic fouls in sports such as basketball. But even in basketball, it is unclear that the mere existence of conventions settles the issue of strategic fouling. The critics of strategic fouling acknowledge that they are opposing a widely accepted practice, as well as the conventional understandings upon which that practice is based, but they argue that appeal to central values implicit in the logic of sports requires the reform of existing conventional behavior. Unless we are to immunize conventions from criticism, and, in effect, always choose to preserve the existing understandings of sport, challenges to existing conventions cannot be dismissed simply because they counter our present conventional understandings of sporting practice.

It also is unclear whether conventionalism can respond any better than strict formalism can to the evaluation of proposed changes in the rules or conventions of a sport. When is a change for the better? How are we to evaluate a proposed change to the conventions of basketball, for example, to the effect that players on a losing basketball team should not foul simply to gain a strategic advantage? Just as appeal to the existing rules alone cannot settle the issue of whether a proposed rule change is or is not an improvement, so appeal to existing conventions cannot be the sole basis for evaluating proposals for reform. Arguments for and against the proposed changes, either in the rules or in the conventions, would have to come from elsewhere. But from where?

So far, then, the discussion suggests that both pure formalism, understood as a narrow version of internalism, and conventionalism, which can be either externalist or internalist depending on whether the conventions are imported from outside sport or arise within it, lack the intellectual resources to deal with the important ethical issues that arise in sport. It is hard to see how emphasizing either existing formal rules or social conventions can resolve fundamental moral issues in sport or provide the moral and educational development that many expect sport to provide. Perhaps a third position, which we can call "broad internalism," can do better.

Broad Internalism: Expanding the Formalist Approach

In a series of writings in jurisprudence, noted legal scholar Ronald Dworkin has criticized legal positivists, particularly the highly influential legal philosopher H. L. A. Hart, for holding too narrow a view of the nature of law. Because legal positivists, particularly Hart, tend to identify law with a formal structure of rules, their views resemble the formalist approach to the analysis of games and sport. According to Dworkin, the legal positivists have identified law with a model of formal rules. One of Hart's major contributions is to show the diverse rules that make up law; these include criminal sanctions, rules of change and adjudication, and the Rule of Recognition, which identifies the rules of the legal system and distinguishes them from non-legal rules, such as rules of etiquette, which normally have no juridical standing. Dworkin has argued that in addition to rules, there are legal principles, which have normative force within the legal system. What makes these principles legal ones, rather than simply moral principles imported from beyond the law and applied according to the particular political and ethical commitments of individual judges, is that they are either presupposed by the legal system or provide a logical basis for some of its key elements. In other words, the principles either are presupposed by the legal system or must be presupposed in order for us to arrive at the most comprehensive, coherent, and morally acceptable account of the law itself, the best interpretation of the legal system. In fact, a principle is not justified as a "legal principle" unless it meets this condition.[16]

An analogous position in the philosophy of sport has been developing for some time.[17] Although many writers are sympathetic to various aspects of formalism, or may even view themselves as formalists, they go beyond narrow versions of formalism in developing resources for the ethical assessment of behavior that can be distinguished from rules without being mere conventions. The considerations they point to seem to be presuppositions of sporting practice in the sense that they must be accepted if our sporting practice is to make sense, or perhaps make the *best* sense. Before developing this view, which we will call broad internalism (those who see it as a version of formalism may prefer to call it "interpretive formalism"), let us consider some examples.

In "Fair Play as Respect for the Game," Robert Butcher and Angela Schneider maintained that "if one honors or esteems one's sport, ... one will have a coherent conceptual framework for arbitrating between competing claims regarding the fairness ... of actions."[18] Where does this conceptual framework come from? Butcher and Schneider suggested that sports themselves have interests; athletes show respect for the game when they make its internal interests their own. Thus, the authors claimed that "the idea of the interests of the game provides a means for judging one's own action in relation to the sport. ... Taking the interests of the game seriously means that we ask ourselves whether or not some action we are contemplating would be good for the game concerned, if everyone did that."[19]

Butcher and Schneider illustrated their position by applying it to poor clubless Josie (who in earlier versions of the example is a racquetless squash player rather than a clubless but not clueless golfer):

> The notion of respect for the game provides ample reason for lending Josie the racquet. At the personal level ... you would forgo a valuable experience and personal test if you decline to play Josie. At a more general level, the sport of squash is enhanced by people playing and competing at their best whenever possible. Squash at the institutional level would not be served by neglecting to play a ... scheduled match. You should want to lend Josie your racquet.[20]

This is an example of broad internalism because appeal is being made to norms or principles internal to the idea of sport. These principles are not mere social conventions; rather, they might even provide a basis for criticizing existing social conventions that would support requiring Josie to forfeit the match. Neither are they formal rules of the game. Although broad internalists might well want to avoid the metaphysical complications attached to the notion of games having interests— games may not even be the sort of entities that can have their own interests— perhaps all that internalists need to say to make their point succinctly is that the point of playing competitive golf would best be made if the match was played.

A second and very instructive example of broad internalism was provided by J. S. Russell in an article entitled "Are Rules All an Umpire Has to Work With?"[21] Russell, appealing explicitly to Dworkin's views in jurisprudence, argued against the view that rules are all an umpire has to work with. He discussed various games from American baseball that call on umpires and officials to extend, change, or interpret rules that, by themselves, may be indeterminate when applied to hard cases.

For example, in an 1887 American Association game between Louisville and Brooklyn, a Louisville player named Reddy Mack, who had just scored, jostled the Brooklyn catcher, thereby interfering with him, and allowed another Louisville player to score as a result. At that time, the rules of baseball stated that no base-runner could interfere with a fielder, but the Louisville player might have reasoned that when he crossed home plate, he was no longer a base runner. The umpire, Wesley Curry, called Mack out for interfering with the catcher. As the rule technically did not apply once Mack had crossed home plate and ceased to be a base runner, did Curry make the right decision?

Russell pointed out that Curry's decision "was not explicitly covered by the rules, but his actions seem irreproachable, were not overturned, and were the basis for a subsequent rule change. . . . Any other decision would have invited a nine-inning . . . wrestling match."[22]

Russell was going beyond explicit formal rules here and offering what might be called an interpretation of baseball. Thus, following Dworkin's suggestions in legal philosophy, Russell suggested that "we might try to understand and interpret the rules of a game, say, baseball, . . . to generate a coherent and principled account of the point and purposes that underlie the game, attempting to show the game in its best light."[23] Russell cited, as an example of a principle that might underlie such competitive sports as baseball, the injunction that "rules should be interpreted in such a manner that the excellences embodied in achieving the lusory goal of the game are not undermined but are maintained and fostered."[24]

Broad internalism, or interpretivism, then, is the view that in addition to the constitutive rules of sport, there are other resources connected closely—perhaps conceptually—to sport that are neither social conventions nor moral principles merely mirroring the dominant morality in society. These resources can be used to adjudicate moral issues in sports and athletics. In William J. Morgan's terms, sport has an independent "gratuitous logic" of its own that makes it more than a mirror reflecting the values of society.[25] This underlying logic may be helpful in analyzing concrete ethical issues that arise within competitive sports.

FAIR PLAY IN COMPETITIVE SPORTS

The argument of Chapter 2 suggested that competitive athletics are justified morally when conducted as a mutual quest for excellence through challenge. On this view, competitive sport is best understood as a place where we freely test ourselves and attempt to develop excellence at overcoming the obstacles allowed by the rules. On the broad internalist view, this approach to sport is an interpretive theory that attempts to make the best sense out of sporting practice and provide principles for appropriate sporting behavior. This theory, or interpretation, has implications for the cases we discussed earlier.

Consider again the dilemma of Annika and clubless Josie. Surely Butcher and Schneider were correct to argue that Annika should lend the clubs to Josie. Sporting contests are designed to be tests, and competitors should not avoid a worthy opponent. However, this suggests that Keating's distinction between sports and athletics was, at the very least, overdrawn. Even if the event in question is at an elite level of golfing competition, Annika still should lend the clubs to Josie (although, to give Keating his due, it may be less blameworthy for Annika to refuse to lend the clubs and accept the forfeit at the professional level than, say, at the level of youth sports).

Although Annika should be encouraged to lend the clubs to Josie, and may be subject to moral criticism on the basis of poor sportsmanship for not doing so, it is controversial whether she is morally required to make the clubs available to Josie and should be formally punished or penalized for failing to do so, at least at the professional or top amateur level. Failing to lend her opponent the clubs arguably is in a different moral category than, say, trying deliberately to disable an opponent or bribing an official. The latter forms of external interference with competitors make it impossible for the good sports contest to occur and undermine the very point of competitive sports. However, the idea that competitors must take positive steps to promote good play on the part of opponents, although worthy, is open-ended and not so clearly essential to the good sports contest. What level of support should be provided, and in what contexts? Attempts to draw the line somewhere would no doubt involve controversy. Suppose, for example, Josie needed a golf lesson from Annika just five minutes before teeing off. It would also be unclear when noncompliance was worthy of punishment. We would need to distinguish between prohibited behavior that ought to be penalized or sanctioned, on the one hand, and desirable behavior that should be encouraged, but for which nonperformance was not necessarily sanctionable or punishable, on the other.

Competition as a mutual quest for excellence also suggests the attitudes competitors should have toward each other. Although every participant at some time probably hopes for an easy victory in an important contest, reflective participants should acknowledge that such an attitude should not be prevalent among competitors. Rather, competitors normally should hope to meet worthy opponents who can provide a true test of the abilities required in the sport being played. After all, as we have seen, if victory is the primary goal, one need simply schedule vastly inferior opponents. (At the time of writing this sentence I am the best basketball player on my street; but, as all the other players are less than eight years old and most cannot even reach the basket, is that anything to take pride in?)

The appropriate attitude toward fellow competitors is well expressed by professional golfer David Duval in talking about the prospects of going head-to-head with Tiger Woods in the last round of a major championship. In a passage also quoted in Chapter 2, Duval makes this remark: "If I come head-to-head against him at say, the U.S. Open, I want him to be playing as good as he can play because I want to beat him when he's playing his best."[26] Duval's attitude seems to be the one that best fits with the conception of sport as a mutual quest for excellence through challenge. Good competitors want to be challenged by worthy opponents. Given that, good competitors should want to promote conditions under which other athletes can play their best. As we have noted, it is unclear just how stringent such a requirement should be; however, from the perspective of broad internalism, there seems to be enough support for it to say that athletes should be encouraged to follow it as an ideal. Whether they also should adopt it as a moral rule they have a duty to obey, and if so, to what extent they should be obligated, is much more controversial.

Broad internalism also suggests that sport presupposes an at least partial conception of the good life for human beings. According to this conception, a significant segment of the good life consists of seeking out and trying to meet interesting challenges, including physical ones. Thus some activities, such as participation in sport, are worth doing not because of external rewards, but because of the nature of the activity itself.

Of course, some athletes compete for fame, trophies, and incredibly large salaries. But although many professional players may not be motivated by the ideal of meeting challenges for their own sake, their large salaries are still parasitic on that ideal, as we noted in our discussion of Bernard Suits's account of games. If the players did not try to meet the challenges set by the rules of the sport, but instead tried to win through such external means as deliberately injuring opponents or bribing referees, they would undermine the structure of their own practice and perhaps even destroy it. Thus, regardless of the personal motivations of the players, they must meet the challenge set by the sport on its own terms and will be rewarded to the extent that they do so.

CHEATING, BREAKING THE RULES, AND TAINTED VICTORIES

Let us now consider how our discussion can help us with the ethical issues raised by behavior such as Briana Scurry's during the World Cup or deliberate fouling by a losing basketball team to stop the clock toward the end of a game; that is, the intentional breaking of rules for strategic advantage.

Cheating

What is cheating, and what makes it wrong in athletic competition? Can cheating ever be allowed by the ethic of the mutual quest for excellence as developed so far in this book?

Although moral skeptics often appeal to disagreement on controversial moral issues, not all moral issues are controversial. Thus, most people agree that straight-forward cheating in sports is to be condemned. And although cheating might be hard to define, sometimes we know it when we see it: For example, a golfer who deliberately fails to count all her strokes in an important tournament clearly is cheating, as is a basketball coach who, in the confusion of a last-second foul call, intentionally deceives referees and opponents by directing his best foul shooter to go to the line, even though it was another player, a particularly poor foul shooter, who was fouled.

What makes these examples paradigm cases of cheating? Since rules can be broken by accident or ignorance, cheating cannot mean simply breaking the rules; it must have other components. Sometimes, for example, cheating is identified with deception, as when an unfaithful spouse deceives his or her partner, or when a basketball team sends its best foul shooter to the line even when she was not the player who was fouled. Or it could involve breaking an explicit or implicit promise, as when someone consciously violates an agreement made with others, as in sports when a tennis player dishonestly calls out a shot by an opponent after having agreed before the match to make accurate calls.

However, as philosopher Bernard Gert has pointed out in a perspicuous analysis, cheating does not necessarily involve either deception or promise breaking.[27] For example, an athlete who has power over her competitors might cheat quite openly, or an athlete might deny that he ever promised to obey a particular rule. The latter would be like, say, a revolutionary who cheated on a civil service examination to attain a powerful position, but who then denied that he had ever promised, even implicitly, to obey the rules laid down by the government he despised. More generally, the idea of an "implicit" promise may be too vague to support charges of cheating.

Cheating, Gert suggested, is best identified with the intentional violation of a public system of rules to secure the goals of that system for oneself or for those for whom one is concerned.[28] Cheating is normally wrong, but not only because it usually deceives or violates a promise, although these may contribute to its wrongness. The distinctive element in the general presumption that cheating is wrong is that the cheater behaves in a way that no one could rationally or impartially recommend that everyone in the activity emulate. Thus, cheaters make arbitrary exceptions of themselves in order to gain advantages over others, in effect treating those others as mere means to their own ends or their own well-being.

Cheaters, in other words, fail to respect their opponents as persons, as agents with purposes of their own, by violating the public system of rules that others may reasonably expect to govern the activity in question. A golf tournament would not truly be an athletic contest if everyone cheated, nor would it determine who the best player was. The rules of golf are the public system under which it can reasonably be presumed the participants expect to compete. It may be difficult to say what is or is not cheating in borderline cases, but in paradigm cases, cheaters arbitrarily subordinate the interests and purposes of others to their own, and so violate the fundamental moral norm of respect for persons.

Thus, cheating, at least in paradigm cases, involves violating a public system of rules that every participant in an activity may reasonably assume will govern the activity in question in order to obtain benefits for oneself, one's teammates, or others for whom one cares. The cheating is wrong because it could not be reasonably accepted by other participants in the activity. Cheaters disregard the legitimate interest that other competitors have in a fair contest and may use other competitors as mere means to an end or tools for their own benefit. Cheating is not normally done openly because the cheater usually does not want to be caught, and it may involve the breaking of an implicit or explicit promise to obey the rules, although, in exceptional cases, no promise need be involved.

If our suggestion that cheating normally takes unfair advantage of other competitors is sound, then cheating is morally prohibited. But what if there are sometimes weightier conflicting factors involved? Could there be cases where engaging in cheating might be morally justifiable? For example, if gamblers have kidnapped your family and will kill them unless your team wins, you would seem to be morally justified, or at least excused, if you cheated to ensure the victory and save their lives.

It has been suggested that cheating is not always wrong in sports. On this view, cheating may undermine fair play, but it still might make for good sports. As one commentator has maintained:

> Many competitions . . . would be more interesting if cheating takes place within it or if several players try to stretch the rules. Such deviant behavior adds a new dimension to the game which can also add to its interest. . . . Insofar as the contest is one of wits as well as one of skill and strategy, it can be exciting to compete with and against someone who uses his wits to try to cheat and it can be exciting for an audience to observe such intelligent behavior.[29]

For example, what about the use of the illegal spitball pitch in baseball? If, when it is used by a Major League pitcher such as Gaylord Perry, who was well known for throwing spitballs, it can make the game more fascinating and exciting, isn't its use justified?

This position seems open to the objection that cheating undermines the idea of the sports contest as a test of skill, a mutual quest for excellence by the participants. Sports do, however, serve other purposes in our society, such as providing entertainment and giving professional players an opportunity to secure financial gains. But these other purposes are parasitic in that what ought to be entertaining about our sports, and what makes them sometimes worth paying to see, is the test of excellence they provide. Pitchers who throw the illegal spitball are taking an advantage for themselves that is unavailable to competitors who play by the rules, and they are therefore undermining the idea of competition as a fair quest for excellence.

Perhaps, however, what is being endorsed is not solitary acts of cheating that deceive opponents, or that in some other way violate the public system of rules that players are entitled to have apply to the game. Thus, "if . . . cheating is recognized as an option which both sides may morally take up, then in general the principles of equality and justice are not affected."[30] Perhaps the practice of strategic fouling in basketball fits such a description, in that players expect other players to foul strategically in appropriate situations.

But if the practice is acknowledged and expected and engaged in by all sides, it is far from clear that it is cheating at all. If all players acknowledge that other competitors will engage in the action at issue, and if the rules contain just compensation for violation, why is the act one of cheating? The difficulty for those who believe that cheating in sports is sometimes justified because it makes for better sports is to find behavior that clearly is cheating and that is also morally permissible.

On one hand, insofar as such activity is acknowledged to fall under the rules, as interpreted by morally acceptable conventions known by participants and officials, it arguably is not cheating, especially when it is done openly and with willingness to take the penalty. On the other hand, if the behavior does not fall under such rules, as interpreted by morally acceptable conventions known by participants and officials, and is not done openly with willingness to accept the penalty, it arguably is not permissible. Rather, as in the case of throwing the spitball, it is not an acceptable violation of the public rules that all participants may reasonably expect to govern the game. In such a case we do not find an instance of behavior that is both cheating and morally acceptable. Hence, our conclusion that cheating is not a morally acceptable form of behavior in athletic competition still stands. Let us test this thesis by considering the ethics of strategic fouling.

Strategic Fouling

Strategic fouling is an example of the intentional violation of the rules of a sport for a competitive advantage. Specific instances of strategic fouling already mentioned include Scurry's save at the World Cup, an intentional foul by the losing team to stop the clock in the last minutes of a basketball game, and a football team that deliberately incurs a delay of game penalty to get a better angle for an attempt at a field goal. Is strategic fouling a case of cheating, though? If it is not, is it unethical in some other fashion?

The debate about the ethics of strategic fouling is not just a narrow controversy that is of interest to only a few "purists" who fail to understand the practice of competitive athletics. Rather, the critics of strategic fouling are implying that we have become so consumed by the pursuit of victory in sports that we embrace even highly questionable tactics in trying to win. The prevalence of strategic fouling, on this view, is evidence not of smart play but of the corruption of athletic competition by the cult of achieving victory by whatever means necessary.

Some philosophers would unequivocally assert that strategic fouling is unethical and perhaps a form of cheating. For example, in an early discussion of the issue, Warren Fraleigh analyzed the basketball example by maintaining that "intentional holding, tripping, and so on are not part of the game or within the rules of basketball. . . . [Therefore] the 'good' foul is a violation of the agreement which all participants know that all participants make when they agree to play basketball, namely, that all will pursue the . . . goal of basketball by the necessary and allowable skills and tactics and will avoid use of proscribed skills and tactics."[31] In a similar vein, Kathleen Pearson wrote that strategic fouling "destroys the vital framework of agreement which makes sport possible."[32] These comments reflect the central emphasis of the formalists on the rules. Indeed, one might go further and argue that cheaters aren't even really playing the game, since the game is constituted by the rules. Be that as it may, the remarks of Fraleigh and Pearson suggest that strategic fouling is a form of cheating because it intentionally violates the framework of rules that make the game possible and that the participants have agreed (either implicitly of explicitly) to obey.

If the analysis of cheating presented earlier is on the right track, this formalist approach to strategic fouling may be seriously questioned. One criticism is that the formalist approach does not give sufficient weight to the conventions associated with specific sports that have sometimes been called the "ethos" of the game. Thus, in basketball, players understand that losing teams will foul at the end of the game to stop the clock. Virtually all players expect the losing team to foul to stop the clock when such behavior is strategically appropriate; the players expect it of themselves and of their opponents. Similarly, in soccer the goalies generally try to move into position a bit more quickly than the rules allow in order to cut down the shooter's angle, so it can be argued that Scurry's action in the World Cup conformed to a convention widely accepted among participants.

Just because such behavior is conventional does not make it morally right or in the best interests of the game. But if cheating means violating a public set of norms to gain an advantage for oneself or one's team, and these norms include conventions as well as rules, then strategic fouling is not always a form of cheating. This is in part because conventions exist that sometimes make such behavior normal and expected. But, more important, it is also because the strategic fouler acknowledges that such behavior is appropriate for all participants, including opponents. This is quite a different situation from that of the cheater who, say, wants to get an advantage by falsifying the scorebook, behavior that could not possibly

be made universal without destroying the game itself. In addition, strategic fouling, at least in basketball, normally is done openly. The fouler in fact wants the
referee to call the infraction, stop the clock, and award compensatory foul shots to
the other team.

Theorists such as Fraleigh and Pearson could object that conventions, unlike
rules, are too vague to form a basis of the common understanding presupposed
by players who commit themselves to respecting the game. For example, is there
really a convention or common understanding in international soccer that goalkeepers can bend the rules as Scurry did in the World Cup? How are we to tell?

Sigmund Loland and Mike McNamee provided an example of just such a difference in understanding. In a major soccer competition in England between Arsenal FC and Sheffield United, when an Arsenal player became injured, a Sheffield
United player deliberately kicked the ball out of bounds so that during the ensu-
ing pause in play the injured player could receive medical treatment. This is one of
the conventions of soccer: that when an injury appears to have occurred, an out-
of-bounds kick be performed in order to create the pause necessary for the medical personnel to attend to the injured player. According to the convention, once
the ball is back in play, the receiving team, in this game Arsenal, would turn the
ball over to the opposition so that Sheffield would suffer no competitive disadvantage for following the convention. But this time, according to Loland and
McNamee, an Arsenal player, a recent recruit from another continent (and presumably a different cultural setting) "intercepted the ball, crossed it to one of his
teammates, who instinctively (so it is said) . . . scored."[33] Apparently, the understanding of the convention was not common to all players.

Conventions, unlike rules, are not usually in written form, and often they are
not explicitly taught or discussed. Thus, the new player did not know the convention. Indeed, the possibility of misunderstanding conventions may be more common in international competition, or when competitors come from different sport
cultures. In the women's World Cup situation, for example, perhaps Scurry's strategy was not understood in the same way by the Americans, the Chinese, and the
World Cup officials. If that is the case, then her decision to use the strategy would
seem ethically questionable, whereas it would seem more appropriate if all these
participants shared the same view of it as an example of a convention that was
commonly accepted.

Fraleigh and Pearson's rejoinder that conventions are too vague to form the basis of a common understanding surely has force. Nevertheless, the idea that strategic fouls are different from paradigm examples of cheating still seems plausible.
Strategic foulers are conforming to a general practice that they are willing to con-
done even when it works against them, whereas cheaters are violating rules in ways
they do not want others to emulate. Moreover, they could not reasonably want
such violations to be part of the public system of rules governing the sport.[34] How

could anyone reasonably advocate a rule allowing falsification of the scorebook, for example, since this would destroy the ability for anyone to see who really won the contest?

But even if strategic fouling is not a form of cheating, it may be morally unacceptable on other grounds. After all, just because behavior is conventional does not mean it is ethical. Strategic fouling may be unethical because it is unsportsmanlike or because it shows disrespect for principles that should govern conduct in competition. Let us explore these possibilities more fully.

Penalties as Sanctions and as Prices

The remarks of Fraleigh and Pearson suggest that players and teams committing strategic fouls violate an implicit social contract according to which players agree to play by the rules. As we have seen, one possible reply is that the game is defined by conventions as well as rules, and that conventions sometimes permit strategic fouling. But this reply may not be fully satisfactory, because the conventions themselves may be vague or not understood the same way by all, and because the ethical status of the conventions may be questioned.

Perhaps a stronger moral defense of strategic fouling is that such behavior really does not violate the rules to begin with. For example, in basketball, one could argue, the strategic foul is part of the game because an explicit penalty—foul shots—is provided for in the rules.

Pearson has considered this rejoinder and pointed out that "the obvious rebuttal to this position is that penalties for breaking the law are contained within the law books, but no sensible person concludes, therefore, that all acts are within the law."[35] For example, we surely would not say that murder is allowed by law simply because penalties for murder are prescribed by law. Similarly, we should not say that the strategic foul is allowed by the rules of basketball simply because the penalty is prescribed in the rule book.

But is this reply decisive? The parallel drawn between sanctions in law, such as punishment for criminals, and penalties for strategic fouls needs closer examination. In particular, some penalties in sports do not play a role analogous to criminal sanctions in law. A jail sentence for a crime should not be thought of as the price the law charges for a particular act, such as a felony. That would make the felony a permissible option for those criminals who were willing to bear the cost of a jail sentence if caught. Rather, a felony is a prohibited act, and a jail sentence is not the price for allowable commission of the act, but rather a punishment for committing it.

However, not all penalties in sports are punishments or sanctions for prohibited acts. For example, in golf, when balls come to rest in a position from which players judge no shot is possible, as when a ball comes to rest up against a tree, golfers may invoke the "unplayable lie rule." According to this rule, the player may either replay the shot from the original location, hit a new shot from two club lengths from either side of the location of the unplayable ball, or hit a new shot from as far behind the location of the ball as the player chooses. The penalty for exercising any of these options is one shot. Here, the penalty clearly is not intended to punish. Rather, the options are there for the player to use. The penalty in this example is the price of exercising the option rather than a sanction for doing what is forbidden.[36] Of course, invoking the unplayable lie option is unlike strategic fouling, in that the latter violates a rule and the former is permitted by a rule.[37] The point of the example is not to say the two are totally analogous but only to illustrate the difference between the two functions penalties may have: They may be punishments or sanctions for impermissible acts, or they may be the price to be paid for exercising a strategic option.

But are the penalties for strategic fouls punishments or prices? If the penalties for the fouls in at least some contexts can be regarded as prices for exercising a strategy rather than sanctions for violating a rule, then strategic fouling, in those cases, rather than being unethical, would be a permissible strategy of play.

Although it is sometimes difficult to tell whether a penalty should be regarded as a sanction or a price, the notion of a fair price might help us distinguish the two. The intuitive idea here is that if a pricing penalty is fair in sports, then violating the rule should invoke a fair penalty for the infraction. The penalty for intentional fouling in basketball is probably best regarded as a price rather than as a sanction if the foul shots awarded are fair compensation for the violation. Sports authorities can more clearly distinguish sanctions from prices by making the penalty for prohibited acts more severe than mere fair compensation would require. Recent rule changes in college and high-school basketball awarding extra foul shots and possession of the ball to the team that is intentionally fouled can be regarded as a step toward making intentional fouling prohibited rather than a strategy with a price.

This analysis of strategic fouling in basketball in effect rests on a (broad internalist) theory of the game that views foul shots as fair compensation for the team that was fouled for strategic reasons. A good team should be able to convert the foul shots and be no worse off than before the infraction was committed. Inability to convert the foul shots indicates a weakness that rightly puts that team's lead in jeopardy.

The strategic violation allegedly committed by Briana Scurry might be analyzed in a similar fashion, but arguably is more complex. The penalty for illegal movement by the goalkeeper allows the shooter to make another attempt to score if the original shot was missed (otherwise the goal stands), so the rules call for restoring the situation to what it was before the infraction was committed. But although this suggests that the prescribed penalty is a price rather than a sanction, it may not demonstrate it beyond reasonable doubt.

Another relevant factor is that officials seldom call the kind of infraction committed by Scurry. In the World Cup finals, the officials should have suspected that the goalkeepers would seek every edge in the shoot-out, but either they did not notice the infraction or deliberately ignored it. Do referees tend not to make this call because they believe the shoot-out is too heavily weighted in favor of the offense and that goalkeepers have no real chance to stop a shot without moving illegally? If so, the referees, by refraining from calling all but blatant violations by goalkeepers, may be trying to restore competitive balance to what they regard as an unfair restriction imposed by the rules. In fact, the reason an implicit convention allows goalkeepers to move forward in shoot-outs, even though this involves breaking a rule, is that competitors believe that the rule creates a significantly unbalanced competitive match-up. Goalkeepers have only the lowest probability of stopping a shot if they play within the rules. In other words, they believe the convention improves the game.

One might also wonder whether strategic fouling is less acceptable in a low-scoring game such as soccer than in a high-scoring one such as basketball, where one play has much less effect on the outcome. Clearly, there is much room for further discussion on the ethics of strategic fouling in different sports. Before leaving the topic of strategic fouling, however, we will consider a more recent argument by Fraleigh for the view that the practice is unethical.[38] This new argument relies on a distinction made by Cesar Torres between the basic, or constitutive, skills and the restorative skills of a sport.[39] Constitutive skills are the skills that the game is designed to test. In basketball, these would include dribbling, passing, rebounding, and shooting. Restorative skills are those that are used to restore the status quo after a rules infraction has been committed. These would include foul shooting in basketball and taking a penalty shot in soccer.

According to Torres, constitutive skills normally require a more complex set of abilities to execute and are more interesting than restorative skills. Thus, running a fast break in basketball is more complex, difficult, and interesting than shooting a foul shot; running the bases intelligently in baseball similarly is more complex, difficult, and interesting than being awarded a base as compensation for a fielder's interference with a runner.

Although Fraleigh's argument is complex, his basic point is that strategic fouling ruins the game by making the less complex and less difficult compensatory skills more central and the basic, constitutive skills less central to the outcome. It is perhaps for this reason that fans at a basketball game will feel that the game has been made boring or that it has been ruined by referees who are excessive in calling fouls. Such fans often will yell "Let them play," indicating that they do not regard foul shooting as being as interesting or as central to the game as the more complex basic skills exercised in the normal course of play. In addition, Fraleigh argued that strategic fouling often will deprive a player of an advantage earned through excellent use of basic skills, as when a hockey player, who has been fooled by the brilliant skating move of an opponent, trips the opponent from behind to prevent a break-away shot on the goal.

This new argument is an important one and is itself a version of broad inter-nalism. That is, it advances a theory about which skills are the most important skills in a sport and indicates why it is important to keep those skills at the center of play. On this view, strategic fouling, while certainly not cheating, shows a funda-mental disrespect for what is really valuable about athletic competition—the quest for excellence—and gives undue priority to winning even at the cost of harming the game.

Nevertheless, although Fraleigh's argument is an important one, it may not carry the day, or at least it may not apply to all cases of strategic fouling.[40] For one thing, not all exercises of restorative skills are routine or require less skill than constitutive skills require. Running a good power play in ice hockey clearly re-quires the use of both physical and mental abilities of a high order, but arguably it is restorative because it compensates an offended team for a rule violation by the opposition. Even shooting a foul shot in basketball, under pressure at the end of a close game, can test the composure and shooting ability of the player on the line.

More important, the assumption that team strategy should never make re-storative skills central to determining the outcome of contests is itself question-able. Let's say, for example, that Team A and Team B are meeting for the third time in the basketball season. Team A won the first game by 3 points, and Team B won the second by 4 points. So far, in the third and deciding contest, the teams are evenly matched. Suppose that it is evident from all three games that the two teams are evenly matched in constitutive skills. However, Team B is awful at foul shoot-ing, a restorative skill. Team B has possession of the ball and is ahead by 2 points, with 10 seconds to go.

Team A's coach realizes that his squad has little chance of stealing the ball and scoring in only 10 seconds. In fact, Team B is simply trying to hold the ball and run out the clock without even trying to score. He orders his team to strategically foul in order to stop the clock, reasoning that if the poor foul shooters on Team B miss, his team will have a chance to at least tie the game.

It is hard to regard this strategy as unethical or ruining the game. After all, if we are trying to find out which team is better, and they are roughly equal in con-stitutive skills, why shouldn't a difference in restorative skills then be relevant? If the teams are equally skilled at the constitutive level, but one team is clearly better at the restorative level, isn't that the better team? Moreover, it is hard to see how fouling at such a point in a close game ruins the game or makes it less interesting than simply letting the team with the ball hold it and run out the clock.

Of course, this example is an extreme case, but it does suggest the following thesis. According to what I suggest we call the Strategic Fouling Thesis, strategic fouling is presumptively permissible in a competitive athletic contest when the following four conditions are satisfied. First, the teams playing have demonstrated, perhaps by the closeness of the contest, that they are roughly equal or well matched in constitutive skills. Second, the team that strategically fouls has no other strategy based on the use of constitutive skills that gives it a reasonable chance to win. Third, it must be reasonable to regard the penalty for the strategic foul as a price rather than as a punishment. Last, the foul must not take away a major advantage earned by the use of constitutive skills, such as would be the case if a hockey player on a breakaway was tripped from behind.

This suggests that in close contests, particularly in high-scoring sports such as basketball, the judicious use of strategic fouls not only may be morally allowed but also may enhance the challenge of the athletic contest. Although the extent to which this argument applies to other sports needs to be debated case by case, I suggest that the distinction between judicious and indiscriminate use of strategic fouls is important. Thus, the Strategic Fouling Thesis might not justify a hockey team that was vastly inferior to its opponent in skating and shooting skills if it were constantly taking penalties designed to deprive the opponent of advantages earned through superior skills, or turning the game, in effect, into a wrestling match to prevent the opponent from demonstrating its constitutive superiority.

What, then, does our extended discussion suggest about the morality of strategic fouling? One conclusion is that strategic fouling often cannot be equated with paradigm cases or blatant examples of cheating. One reason is that it rests on implicit practices accepted by all the players, whereas in cheating, the cheater tries to gain an advantage through actions that could not reasonably be accepted by all players as a universal practice. Moreover, in many contexts in sport, strategic fouling may constitute a strategic option for which the rules exact a price rather than impose a sanction. It might even be argued that strategic fouling sometimes improves the game by creating interesting tactical choices or, as in the example of the movement at issue in the World Cup, even improves the competitiveness of the game. Finally, although strategic fouling in some circumstances can undermine the sports contest by making the exercise of constitutive skills secondary and restorative skills primary, this does not have to be the case. Although strategic fouling may sometimes be unethical, judicious use of strategic fouls not only may be morally acceptable but also may reinforce the idea of the sports contest as a worthy challenge or test of excellence.

The Fifth Down: A Tainted Victory?

There are many other situations in sports where it is unclear whether certain actions are cheating or are unethical in some other way. Although we cannot explore all these kinds of situations in this chapter, we can consider another of the examples with which we began the chapter. It involved a top-ranked university football team winning a game on a fifth-down play that was run because officials lost count and didn't notice that the allotted number of downs already had been used up. Should the winning team, the University of Colorado, have accepted the victory, or, as many critics of the university suggested, should it have refused to accept a tainted win?

Proponents of one view might begin by appealing to Keating's distinction between sports and athletics. They might argue, first, that since a major intercollegiate football game is clearly an example of athletics, neither team is under an obligation to make the experience pleasurable or enjoyable for the other. Generosity should not be expected, either; after all, if a referee had made an incorrect pass interference call in their favor, Missouri would not have been urged to refuse to accept the penalty. Second, Colorado did not cheat, as least as we have defined cheating. There was no intent to violate a public system of rules to gain an advantage. The Colorado team seemed unaware of the true situation. Tapes of the game reveal that on the fourth-down play, the Colorado quarterback looked to the sideline, noticed that the play was officially marked as a third down on the official scoreboard, and intentionally grounded a pass to stop the clock. Had the quarterback believed the play was his team's last down, he surely would have gambled by attempting a touchdown pass, perhaps successfully.

Although these arguments cannot just be dismissed, some may think they rest on an indefensible conception of ethics in competition. To begin with, they might reject Keating's distinction between sports and athletics as misleading. In particular, if it is taken as descriptive, it may set up a false dichotomy. Activities need not be classified exclusively as athletics or exclusively as sports but may share elements of each. Thus, to refer back to another previous example, Josie's opponent ought to lend her the clubs whether it's for a friendly match or a round of a major tournament.

Second, critics might maintain that sportsmanship, although certainly not an all-encompassing value, covers more than generosity toward opponents. In particular, if athletic contests ought to be regarded as mutual quests for excellence, along lines argued in Chapter 2, implications follow for sportsmanship. Thus, opponents ought to be regarded as engaged in a cooperative enterprise designed to test their abilities and skills, and, whether or not they are owed generous treatment, they should be treated as partners in the creation and execution of a fair test. To treat them differently is to reject the presuppositions of the very model of athletic competition that ought to be observed.

We can argue that the Missouri team was not treated in such a fashion. The play that won the game was not allowed by the rules of the game. Even though the officials were mistaken about how the rule applied, that does not alter the fact that Colorado did not win the test as defined by the rules. Moreover, there is no common convention acceptable to all participants that covers the situation. According to its critics, Colorado, by accepting the victory, did not treat its opponents as partners or facilitators in a common enterprise but instead treated them as a means for attaining the kind of external rewards that go with victory in big-time college games.

If this point has force, it suggests that the distinction between sportsmanship and fair play may not be as sharp as Keating's account suggests. If by "fair play" we mean adherence to criteria of fairness implied by the idea of a mutual quest for excellence, it is at best unclear whether Colorado's decision was truly fair. If its team did not truly demonstrate superiority by the public code of rules that all parties agree applied to the game, in what sense was the assignment of a victory fair?

In a famous game played forty years before the contest between Colorado and Missouri, a similar incident led to a dissimilar resolution. In the late fall of 1940, an undefeated Cornell team, also in contention for the national championship and a Rose Bowl bid, played a Dartmouth team that was hoping for a major upset. Although trailing late in the fourth quarter, Cornell apparently pulled out a victory with a scoring pass on the game's last play. But did Cornell really win? Film of the game indicated without a doubt that the referee, who admitted the error, had allowed Cornell a fifth down! The game should have ended a play earlier, and Dartmouth should have pulled off a major upset.

Although no rule required that Cornell forfeit the victory, soon after the game film's release "Cornell officials (including the Director of Athletics) telegraphed Hanover formally conceding the game to Dartmouth 'without reservation . . . with hearty congratulations . . . to the gallant Dartmouth team.' Another loss the following Saturday to Pennsylvania helped the Cornell team drop from second to 15th in the Associated Press polls, its season ruined but its pride intact."[41] Should Colorado take pride in its victory? Should Cornell be proud of its loss?

Our discussion so far suggests that some of the distinctions with which we began our discussion may need to be rethought. Suppose we take fair play as a central value to be articulated along lines suggested by a broadly internalist approach to sport that encompasses the principles of athletic competition as a mutual quest for excellence. On this interpretation, fair play would require treating opponents in a way fitting their status as partners in a partially cooperative enterprise—namely, the provision of a challenge so that skills and abilities may be tested.

Finally, we can question whether even intense competition at high levels of performance ought to be regarded as pure cases of athletics in Keating's sense. Although some activities, such as major intercollegiate and professional sports, might justifiably tend more in that direction, a strong argument can be made that sportsmanship and fair play should both apply, although perhaps with different emphases, at all levels of sports and athletics. We can argue that athletics, in Keating's sense, ought not to exist at all in its pure form because, unless fair play is understood broadly enough to encompass sportsmanship in the wider sense developed above, "athletics" and the ethic of the mutual quest for excellence are incompatible. Accordingly, the terms "sports" and "athletics" will be used interchangeably in what follows, unless otherwise indicated.

We also need to consider the role of officials and referees in sports. Should we conclude that since opponents in many forms of organized competition delegate responsibility for enforcement of the rules to officials in full knowledge that officials sometimes make mistakes, the decisions of officials should be accepted as ethically final? Alternately, do participants have obligations not to accept unearned benefits arising from particularly egregious official errors, especially those that involve misapplication of the rules rather than "judgment calls" about whether a rule was violated?

Although these questions do not admit of easy answers, an argument can be made that Colorado's victory was tainted. Although there was no intention to violate rules and therefore no cheating in a central sense, and although the referees bear heavy responsibility for what happened, Colorado still had to decide after the game was over whether or not to accept the victory. Although it may not have been morally required for Colorado to forfeit the game, as Cornell did in a perhaps more innocent era of intercollegiate sports, it seems just as clear that Colorado did not meet the test of defeating opponents within the rules. The Colorado victory was therefore less meaningful than it otherwise would have been. It would seem, then, that Colorado's reasons for wanting the full benefits of victory had more to do with securing the external benefits of a win, including national rankings and a bid to a bowl game, than to intrinsic pride in a well-earned victory. Be that as it may, it is at least questionable whether Colorado met the challenge set by its opponent, or that Missouri failed to meet it simply because the final score was in Colorado's favor.[42]

Among the tests of a principled ethical approach to sport are overall consistency and compatibility. Relevantly similar situations should be evaluated in similar ways, and responses to one set of issues should fit well with responses to others. Otherwise, the theory appears tailored to the sympathies of its proponents to rationalize the views they personally favor.

Does our discussion of the 1999 World Cup and our discussion of the Colorado-Missouri game fit together coherently? A critic might argue that the intentional rule-breaking by Scurry seems to have been condoned out of hand, while the Colorado football team's unintentional violation of a rule has been judged as tainting the team's victory. Are these responses compatible, or are they in conflict?

Arguably, there are relevant differences between the two. Scurry's movement to cut off the shooter can be viewed as a strategic foul with a set price rather than a prohibited act. Moreover, it falls under a convention recognized by the players, and perhaps by officials as well. Presumably, if the situation had been reversed, the Americans would have expected the Chinese goalkeeper to act in the same way and would have regarded her behavior as appropriate. And perhaps such movement by goalkeepers alters the competitive balance in the direction of fairness, since the shoot-out in soccer seems far too heavily weighted against the defense. In contrast, although the Colorado team surely did not cheat (players were unaware they had been awarded a fifth play), the rules infraction involved was not a strategic foul with a set price and so was not within the established framework of the game.

This reasoning might not convince all readers. Those who are not persuaded that the two accounts are mutually coherent have two options. The first is to come up with a better argument for the overall coherence of the discussion; the second, of course, is to either reject the conclusion that Scurry's act was not unethical or to reject the conclusion that Colorado's victory was tainted. Although these cases are controversial, trying to arrive at principled responses to them allows us to formulate and then test our ethical intuitions about specific cases by trying to place them within the context of an overall theoretical approach to the ethics of sport. Analysis of these cases is of theoretical as well as practical interest because different and sometimes competing factors must all be taken into account before a coherent response to both can be formulated and tested through reasoned dialogue.

Cases such as those discussed here are likely to be controversial, and discussion of them may generate disagreement, but it is important to remember that such disagreement occurs against a general background of deeper agreement on sports ethics. None of the parties to the discussion endorses cheating, blatant examples of unfair play, or unsportsmanlike behavior. Rather, the disagreement concerns "hard cases" that help us define the boundaries of the values we are exploring. Sometimes disagreement over controversial cases is used as a justification for overall moral skepticism, since a rational resolution may seem impossible. This overall drift to moral skepticism should be resisted, however, for often rational adjudication is possible (as application of the model of the mutual quest for excellence to our cases may suggest); or, if it is not, there still remains deeper agreement on the moral fundamentals that are not at stake in the controversies at issue.

The Actual and the Ideal in the Philosophy of Sport

Our discussion so far has been concerned with standards that should apply to sports. The attempt to find such standards is not only of philosophical interest but also of great practical importance. It is difficult to understand how we could even identify abuses in sports unless we had some grasp of the ethical principles that were being violated in the first place. Besides, without some standards to aim for, we would not know the proper recommendations to make for moral change.

Some of the cases we have examined are controversial, and reasonable people may disagree over their proper resolution. However, as noted earlier, hard cases are important because they force us to identify the relevant moral factors that bear upon them and also require us to see whether our responses to a diverse set of such cases can fit within a coherent and rationally defensible framework. Hard cases often presuppose a background of agreement on fundamentals. Disagreement may persist over how the University of Colorado should have responded to its victory over Missouri, but surely all parties to the discussion would acknowledge that a victory earned through blatant cheating is unearned and should be disallowed.

Our argument also suggests that athletes not only are morally prohibited from such practices as cheating but also may have positive moral duties, or at least be morally encouraged to promote good competition. Perhaps in addition to rules prohibiting certain acts, there are reasons for encouraging good behavior in sport, although it undoubtedly is controversial when failure to take encouraged positive action merits an actual penalty.

Although it may be difficult to define the extent of such positive duties, an example at a 2008 high-school state track championship in the state of Washington illustrated the kind of sportsmanship that is at least encouraged by the theory of competition as a mutually acceptable quest for excellence through challenge. A senior, Nicole Cochran, thought she had won the girl's 3,200-meter title but was disqualified by a highly questionable call by an official, who ruled she had stepped outside her lane once during the race. According to reports of the incident, even her competitors thought the judge had made an error, and the error was later confirmed by a video of the race.

As a result of the disqualification, the winner was sophomore Amanda Nelson of Spokane, who had finished second but then was moved up to first as a result of the disqualification. Nelson, however, thought this decision was unacceptable. As Nelson said, "It wasn't fair. She deserved it. She totally crushed everybody."[43] So when Nelson received the medal, she left the podium and placed the first-place medal around the neck of the person she regarded as the rightful winner, Cochran. Moreover, the other girls who placed all did the same thing, removing their medals and placing them around neck of the runner who would have placed ahead of them if Cochran had not been disqualified (e.g., the second-place finisher gave her medal to Amanda Nelson).

I hope our discussion in this chapter illustrates that while it sometimes is difficult to always draw the line between what sportsmanship and fair play permit and what they forbid, those values are not vacuous and do apply to the behavior of competitors in sports. A defensible sports ethic, one that respects participants as persons, should avoid the twin errors of, on one hand, leaving no room for such tactics as the judicious strategic foul or, on the other hand, assuming that any behavior that contributes to victory is morally acceptable.

FOUR

DRUGS, GENES, AND ENHANCING
PERFORMANCE IN SPORT

In the summer of 1998, Major League Baseball was abuzz with talk of the home-run race between Chicago Cubs star Sammy Sosa and Mark McGwire of the St. Louis Cardinals. McGwire would end up with seventy home runs and Sosa with sixty-six, both eclipsing the single-season record for home runs set in 1961 by Roger Maris, who had scored sixty-one. Maris had broken Babe Ruth's previous record of sixty homers in a single season, a record that itself had stood for forty years. Maris's record had stood for thirty-seven years. Yet McGwire's record was eclipsed just a few years later by Barry Bonds, who hit seventy-three home runs in 2001. Bonds went on to later eclipse Henry Aaron's record for career home runs.

The race between Sosa and McGwire attracted tremendous attention by baseball fans, but by the time Bonds set his career record, all of these figures in the game had become controversial, the significance of their records called into question. Increasingly, evidence suggested that their achievements were not due entirely to skill but also to the use of performance-enhancing substances by the players themselves.[1]

Concern about the use of performance-enhancing drugs in sport is hardly new, but it perhaps first came into the public eye through allegations, since confirmed, of drug use by Olympic athletes, primarily the East German women's swimming team and other East German athletes in the 1960s, 1970s, and 1980s. But the use of performance-enhancing drugs was hardly restricted to East German swimmers, at least by the end of that period. A highly publicized incident took place in the 1988 Summer Olympics in Seoul, Korea, in a long-awaited track race between Canadian star Ben Johnson and American star Carl Lewis. In a hard-fought 100-meter race, Johnson defeated Lewis and apparently won the gold medal.

Urinalysis tests subsequently revealed that Johnson had been taking the steroid stanozolol to enhance his performance. To the shock of Canadians, to whom Johnson had become a national hero, and the rest of the sports world, Johnson was disqualified and had to forfeit his medals from the 1988 Olympics, including the medal he had been awarded for his race against Lewis.

Of course, it is now well known that a perhaps significant proportion of Olympic athletes, as well as professional athletes in many sports, have used performance-enhancing drugs. Testing programs to keep sports "clean," or drug free, have been instituted by most major sports associations. However, it is surely the use of steroids and other performance enhancers, such as the more difficult-to-detect human growth hormone, by some Major League Baseball stars that has attracted the most attention and generated the most discussion in the United States.

Assertions about the relatively widespread use of steroids in baseball that were made by star player Jose Canseco in his 2005 book, *Juiced: Wild Times, Rampant 'Roids, Smash Hits, and How Baseball Got Big*, were at first ridiculed by many. However, many of Canseco's claims were supported by subsequent revelations. Soon, admissions by players emerged in the face of various investigations, including inquiries by Congress. McGwire himself was observed with androstenedione, often called "Andro," in his locker during his sensational 1998 season. He was reticent and evasive, according to virtually all observers, during his testimony on the issue before Congress in 2005. However, in January 2010, McGwire acknowledged using steroids in 1998, when he set the then single-season record for home runs, although he denied the drugs were responsible for his achievements as a slugger.

Examples of admitted users include Canseco, 1996 National League MVP Ken Caminiti (who died prematurely in 2004, perhaps as a result of his use of performance enhancers), Jason Giambi of the Yankees, and McGwire. All acknowledged the use of performance enhancers at some point in their careers. Alex Rodriquez admitted being a user from 2001 to 2003 before he became a Yankee, and former San Francisco Giants slugger Barry Bonds and star pitcher Roger Clemens, seven-time winner of the Cy Young Award, are under heavy clouds of suspicion as well. According to an influential report for Major League Baseball authored by former senator and diplomat George Mitchell, anonymous tests conducted in 2003 found that 5 to 7 percent of Major League Baseball players were using anabolic steroids.[2] The actual figure of those using performance-enhancing drugs was probably much higher, however, as the tests employed were incapable of detecting human growth hormone.

Bonds, in particular, has been widely thought to have benefited from the use of steroids and other drugs, partly because of his involvement in the Bay Area Laboratory Cooperative (BALCO) scandal, described below, and partly because of the remarkable improvement in his home-run statistics at an age when most athletes in his sport are in decline.

According to many observers, Bonds may have started using performance-enhancing drugs before the 1999 season, perhaps, as some speculate, as a reaction to the record-setting seasons of McGwire and Sosa the year before.[3] He was thirty-four years old at the time, an age when most baseball players' performance starts to deteriorate. Yet four of his five best seasons came after he was thirty-five. During the 2001 season, he batted .318 and hit his record-setting seventy-three home runs. No other player in the history of baseball had done so well at that age or later; according to one analysis, "by what should have been the end of his baseball career, Bonds became a significantly better hitter than at any time in his life."[4]

In 2003 a team of federal and state law-enforcement agencies raided BALCO, which had been the subject of an investigation since 2002. BALCO was suspected of supplying several MLB players with performance-enhancing substances, and the raid turned up records showing that Bonds and other Major Leaguers had been supplied with substances designed to frustrate discovery through tests. Testimony by Bonds's trainer, Greg Anderson, to a grand jury is alleged to have also confirmed the hypothesis that Bonds used performance enhancers.[5] Bonds himself denied knowingly having used steroids, however, and Anderson has recanted some of his testimony before the California grand jury investigating BALCO—but it is also worth noting that in 2007 Bonds was indicted for committing perjury in his testimony.

Whether or not Bonds used performance-enhancing substances, subsequent revelations and admissions by players clearly indicated that the use of performance-enhancing drugs was a big problem for Major League Baseball. As a result of widespread concerns about the legitimacy of competition and of the records set during the so-called "steroid era," in 2004 Major League Baseball instituted random testing of players for drug use. It was one of the last major American professional sports organizations to adopt such a policy, and the organization, as well as the players' union, which for a long time opposed testing, has been widely criticized for not reacting more quickly.[6] However, MLB strengthened the penalties for violating the rules concerning banned substances in subsequent years and also instituted a policy of random in-season testing of players for the use of performance-enhancing substances.

Our major concern, however, is not primarily how many elite athletes use performance enhancers, or the extent of such use in Major League Baseball, but the ethics of such use. Many sports fans, commentators, and ethical theorists regard the use of performance enhancers as unethical or a form of cheating. Others, however, including some philosophers of sport, argue that prohibitions on the use of performance enhancers in sport are arbitrary and unjustified. Why shouldn't athletes be free to explore how far they can go in setting records and improving achievement in sport? Why is the use of performance enhancers unethical, but the use of new technology, such as graphite-shafted titanium golf clubs or oxygen chambers that simulate the beneficial effects of high-altitude training for runners, acceptable?

Is the use of performance-enhancing drugs in sports a form of cheating, or, if it is not cheating, is it unethical in some other way? Or are restrictions on the use of performance-enhancing drugs illegitimate restrictions on the freedom of athletes to pursue excellence in their own way? Are records set by users of performance-enhancing drugs legitimate, or should they be discounted? In the next section, we will pursue the ethical issues raised by performance-enhancing drugs in some depth. We will conclude the chapter by examining the issues raised by another form of enhancement: genetic enhancement of athletic abilities.

THE ETHICS OF USING
PERFORMANCE-ENHANCING DRUGS

Performance-Enhancing Drugs and the Quest for Excellence

A principal conclusion of Chapters 2 and 3 was that competition in sports is ethically defensible when it involves participants in a mutual quest for excellence through challenge. In effect, competitors should view themselves as under moral obligations to their opponents. Competitors are obligated to try their best so that opponents can develop their own skills through facing a significant test. In this view, sports are of interest and significance in large part because they fully involve our minds and bodies in meeting a challenge, one regarded as worth meeting for its own sake. Whether one is a recreational softball player imagining himself or herself as a Major Leaguer, or a hacker on the golf course who for once hits a perfect shot, participants in sports all take part in the quest for excellence, although with various degrees of intensity. In great part, what distinguishes the fun we have through sports from mere exercise is the presence of standards of excellence and the challenge presented by the play of others.

Many athletes at the most skilled levels of professional and amateur competition love the challenge provided by sports and seek constantly to improve their performance. Often they seem to compete as much for the love of competition as for financial reward. Some professional athletes—Michael Jordan during the peak of his career, and Tiger Woods, at least until highly publicized personal problems involving infidelity surfaced in late 2009, being especially prominent examples—seem to play as much for the love of the challenge and the desire to compete as for external rewards such as fame and fortune. Indeed, could anyone rise to the top in a highly competitive sport unless love of the game and dedication to excellence provided the motivation for the hours of practice, drills, and preparation that are required?

The danger, of course, is that the drive to win will lead some dedicated athletes to use dangerous and arguably unethical means to achieve success. Losing becomes identified with failure, and anything that promotes winning is also seen as promoting success. But is winning achieved by any means always a success worth having?

We need to ask how excellence might be achieved. In particular, is the use of drugs, such as anabolic steroids, an ethically permissible method for achieving excellence in sports, or, as most sports authorities argue, should the use of such drugs be prohibited in organized athletic competition?

Understanding the Problem

Anabolic steroids are a family of drugs that are synthetic derivatives of the hormone testosterone that stimulate muscle growth and repair injured tissue. They are among the most widely discussed performance-enhancing drugs. Although not everyone would agree that the controlled and medically supervised use of steroids to enhance performance is dangerous, the American College of Sports Medicine, as well as other major medical organizations, warns against serious side effects. Some of these are, at least in high doses, liver damage, arteriosclerosis, serious hypertension, a lowered sperm count in males, and development of masculine physical characteristics in women. The regular use of steroids is also asserted to produce such personality changes as increased aggressiveness and hostility.

What is particularly frightening is that world-class athletes are reported to be taking steroids at dosages so high that it would be illegal to administer them to human subjects in legitimate medical experiments. Some athletes are said to "stack" various forms of steroids along with other kinds of performance enhancers, such as human growth hormones, in attempts to find the most effective combinations. Moreover, many, perhaps most, athletes who use steroids do so without medical supervision. Such athletes are likely to ignore claims that steroids have little effect on performance when such claims are based on studies that administer only low doses of the relevant drugs.

WHAT IS A PERFORMANCE-ENHANCING DRUG?

Before we can turn to a discussion of the ethics of the use of performance-enhancing drugs in sports, we need to be clearer about what counts as a performance enhancer. Are vitamins performance-enhancing drugs? What about a cup of coffee that stimulates a sleepy athlete before a match? What about medication that alleviates allergy symptoms, thereby allowing an athlete to compete more effectively? If we want to forbid the use of performance enhancers, what defines these substances?

Unfortunately, there does not seem to be a clear and simple definition that distinguishes the kind of performance-enhancing drugs that officials of major sports organizations want to prohibit from the legitimate use of other substances such as vitamins or allergy medicine. The situation is complicated further by the fact that a substance that might enhance performance in one context or sport may fail to do so, or even harm performance, in another. Thus, moderate use of alcohol normally would affect performance adversely, but it can be a performance enhancer in such sports as archery and riflery. This is because alcohol is a depressant and therefore slows the heartbeat, which in turn allows for a steadier hand on the shooting range.

Moreover, it is of little help to say that athletes should be permitted to take only what is "natural"; steroids are derivatives of the hormone testosterone, which does occur naturally in the human body, whereas many legitimate medications that athletes ought to be allowed to take are synthetic and not present in a normal or natural diet. The term "natural" is too vague and open-textured to be of much help in this area. In addition, what of practices such as blood doping, where athletes inject stored samples of their own blood in an attempt to boost their oxygen-carrying capacity? It is doubtful whether one's own blood can be classified as "unnatural," yet major sports organizations regard blood doping as an unethical form of performance enhancement.

We might also try to distinguish those substances that merely restore normal function, such as taking aspirin for a headache, from those such as steroids that enhance performance. While this suggestion has promise, the line between restoratives and enhancers is not a sharp one, or at the very least is unlikely to be uncontroversial. What if a proponent of the use of steroids to enhance performance argued that steroids simply restore the ability to work out more intensely and recover sooner from workouts that imperfections in the human body subvert, just as a headache might subvert the ability to concentrate intensely?

Rather than search for a precise definition to distinguish the substances that we intuitively believe are illegitimate performance enhancers from those that are not, it seems more useful to examine anabolic steroids, prohibited by major sports organizations. We can then ask what factors, if any, morally justify this prohibition. If the prohibition is justified, and if we can isolate the moral reasons for it, then any other substances to which the same reasons apply should also be prohibited. Thus, rather than search for an abstract definition, we should first decide what ought or ought not to be allowed to affect athletic performance.

Evaluating the Use of Performance Enhancers

Various reasons are cited as justifications of the claim that competitive athletes ought not to use performance-enhancing steroids. Among the most frequently cited are the following: (1) use of steroids to enhance performance is harmful to athletes, who need to be protected; (2) use of steroids to enhance performance by some athletes coerces others into using steroids; (3) use of steroids to enhance performance is unfair, or a form of cheating; (4) use of steroids to enhance performance violates justifiable norms or ideals that ought to govern athletic competition; and (5) use of steroids demeans or cheapens achievement in sport—for example, by making home runs too common and too easy to hit in baseball. Let us examine each kind of justification in turn.

Paternalism, Informed Consent, and the Use of Steroids

Why shouldn't athletes be allowed to use performance-enhancing steroids? According to one argument, steroids, particularly at the high dosages believed necessary to enhance performance, can seriously harm those who use them. For example, according to the Mitchell Report, "steroid users place themselves at risk for psychiatric problems, cardiovascular and liver damage, drastic changes to their reproductive systems, musculoskeletal injuries, and other problems." The report adds that "users of human growth hormone risk cancer, harm to their reproductive health, cardiac and thyroid problems, and overgrowth of bone and connective tissue."[7] Let us accept the factual claim that steroids as performance enhancers can be seriously harmful and consider whether potential harm to the user justifies prohibiting their use.

The principal criticism of prohibiting steroid use to protect athletes from themselves is that it is unjustifiably paternalistic. Paternalistic interference prevents athletes from making decisions for themselves. After all, would any of us want to have our liberty interfered with whenever some outside agency felt that our personal decisions about how to live our lives were too risky? If widespread paternalism was practiced, third parties could prohibit us from eating foods that might be harmful, playing in sports that carried even slight risk of injury, or indulging in unhealthy lifestyles. Our lives would be monitored—for our own good, of course. The difficulty is that we might not conceive of our own good in the same way as the paternalist.

The trouble with paternalism, then, is that it restricts human liberty. We may believe, with John Stuart Mill, the great nineteenth-century defender of human freedom, "that the only purpose for which power can be rightfully exercised over any member of a civilized community, against his will, is to prevent harm to others. His own good, either physical or moral, is not a sufficient warrant."[8]

If each of us ought to be free to assume risks that we think are worth taking, shouldn't athletes have the same freedom? In particular, if athletes prefer the gains in performance allegedly provided by the use of steroids, along with the increased risk of harm, to the alternative of less risk and worse performance, what gives anyone else the right to interfere with their choice? After all, if we should not forbid smokers from risking their health by smoking, why should we prohibit track stars, baseball players, or weight lifters from taking risks with their health in pursuit of their goals?

Although these antipaternalistic considerations have great force, we cannot yet dismiss paternalism as a justification for prohibiting steroids as performance enhancers. First we must consider some difficulties with this view. Even Mill acknowledged that the kind of antipaternalism articulated in his Harm Principle (the principle stating that the only justification for limiting liberty is to prevent harm to others) had limits. Mill excluded children and young people below the age of maturity, as well as those, such as the mentally ill, who may require care by others. Moreover, Mill would surely exempt those who are misinformed or coerced from the immediate protection of the principle. To use one of his own examples, if you attempt to cross a bridge in the dark not knowing that the bridge has been washed away by a flood, I do not violate the Harm Principle by preventing you from attempting the crossing until I have explained the situation to you.[9]

In particular, before accepting the antipaternalistic argument, we need to decide whether athletes who use steroids to enhance performance really are making a free and informed choice. If behavior is not the result of free and informed choice, it is not really the action of a rational autonomous agent. If it is not informed, the person does not truly know what she is doing; but if the behavior is coerced, it is not what the agent wants to do in the first place.

Is there reason to believe that athletes who use steroids are either uninformed about the effects of the drug or that they are coerced or otherwise incompetent to make rational decisions?

First, those below the age of consent can legitimately be prevented from using performance-enhancing steroids on paternalistic grounds. In the same way that parents can prevent children from engaging in potentially harmful behavior, even if the children want to take their chances on getting hurt, so sports authorities can prohibit the use of harmful performance enhancers by those who are incompetent because of their age.

Moreover, elite athletes often are role models for younger athletes, who may strive to imitate their idols or hope to eventually achieve similar levels of success. When elite athletes use performance-enhancing drugs to better their own performance, their use may encourage noncompetent minors to use them as well. As the Mitchell Report points out, even if steroid use by high-school athletes is declining, as has been reported, and only 3 to 6 percent of such young people are using steroids, it still would be the case that hundreds of thousands of young people are using such drugs.[10] Therefore, instead of trying to justify restrictions on the use of performance-enhancing drugs by any need for paternalism toward competent adult athletes, we can justify the restrictions by the claim that we must fulfill our duty to protect noncompetent (or at least less competent) younger athletes from themselves.

A possible problem with this argument is that it is not completely consistent with our practices in other areas. We don't prevent adults from consuming alcohol, for example, even though adult drinkers may serve as models for abuse of alcohol by underage drinkers. Adults normally are not prohibited by law from being bad role models for young people. Why should we apply a double standard to athletes? This point suggests that while we cannot ignore the effects of steroid use by star adult athletes on young people, the claim that prohibitions on the use of performance enhancers by competent athletes can be justified solely on the basis of the need to protect younger, less competent individuals is dubious. Such a consideration may factor into the ultimate case against allowing steroid use, but it cannot bear the whole weight of the argument.

What about the requirement of informed consent? Are athletes who use steroids adequately informed about the serious potential side effects of the drug? Some athletes, particularly teenagers, may be uninformed or skeptical about the information available, but it is hard to believe that most adult users of steroids could be ignorant of the risks involved. Even if H. L. Mencken may not have been totally off the mark when he suggested that it was impossible to go broke by underestimating the intelligence of the American people, it is difficult to believe, in view of the amount of publicity devoted to the use of performance enhancers, that the majority of mature athletes could be unaware that steroid use can be dangerous. However, even if ignorance about the effects of steroids were widespread, antipaternalists still might argue that the remedy is better education, so that informed choice becomes possible, not simple prohibition.

Accordingly, paternalism alone probably does not provide a strong enough justification for prohibition of the use of harmful performance-enhancing drugs by competent athletes, although it does justify prohibitions on use by those below the age of consent. However, we should leave open the possibility that paternalism, when conjoined with other premises, may provide partial support for prohibition. For example, if steroid use by some people reasonably may be thought to threaten harm to others as well as to the users, and if it is less clear than suggested above that adult users give free consent to assuming the risk of use, then a limited kind of paternalism may play a supporting role in the prohibitionist argument. The argument for prohibiting steroids might then be similar to the argument for requiring automobile drivers to wear seatbelts: that we may justifiably require automobile drivers to wear seatbelts because it is for their own protection, because the decision not to buckle up may not result from thoughtful consideration of the dangers involved, and because of the high costs associated with collisions, which place a burden on the health-care system as well as on the taxpayers who support it.

Coercion and Freedom in Sports

What about the requirement of free choice? Are athletes really free to not use steroids? At least some analysts would argue that athletes are coerced into using steroids. Consider professional sports. The professional athlete's livelihood may depend on performing at the highest level. Athletes who are not among the best in the world may not be professionals for very long. Thus, as one writer concluded, "the onus is on the athlete to continue playing and to consent to things he or she would not otherwise consent to. . . . Coercion, however subtle, makes the athlete vulnerable. It also takes away the athlete's ability to act and choose freely with regard to informed consent."[11]

Although this point may not be without force in specific contexts, the use it makes of the term "coercion" seems questionable. After all, no one literally is forced to become (or remain) a professional athlete or to participate at elite levels in amateur athletics. If we want to use "coercion" so broadly, are we also committed, absurdly it seems, to saying that coaches coerce players into practicing or training hard? Do professors similarly "coerce" students into studying hard? Isn't it more plausible to say that although there are pressures on athletes to achieve peak physical condition, these no more amount to coercion than the pressures on law or medical students to study hard? Rather, the athletes (or the students) have *reasons* to try hard to achieve success; the pressures are self-imposed.

At best, it is unclear whether top athletes are coerced into using steroids or can freely decide that the gains of steroid use outweigh the risks. Surely we are not entitled to assume that professional athletes as a class are unable to give informed consent to steroid use unless we are willing to count similar pressures in other professions as forms of coercion as well. And if we use "coercion" that broadly, it becomes unclear who, if anybody, is left free.

Sometimes, however, in particular contexts, athletes may be victims of coercion. Perhaps an athlete who otherwise would not use steroids is threatened with dismissal by an owner who requires such use. Specific overt or even implied threats do imply coercion. Apart from such specific situations, however, it appears doubtful that a general desire by the athlete to be successful at his or her profession can by itself undermine the capacity for free choice.

But is this conclusion too hasty? A critic might point out that even if the athlete's own internal desires for success do not rule out free choice, coercion by other competitors could be present. That is, even if we agree that internal pressures generated by the athletes are not coercive, we might suspect that their competitors create external pressures that are. It is sometimes argued that even if some sophisticated athletes do give informed consent, their drug use may force others into taking steroids as well. Athletes who would prefer not to become users may believe that unless they take the drugs they will not be able to compete with those who do. Athletes may believe they are trapped because they are faced with a choice where neither option is attractive: Don't take steroids and lose, or take them and remain competitive.

Note that the argument here is no longer that we should interfere with athletes on paternalistic grounds—to prevent them from harming themselves—but that we should interfere with them to prevent them from coercing others. Such an argument is in accord with Mill's Harm Principle: Liberty is restricted, but only to prevent harm to others.

Do pressures generated by athletes who use drugs coerce other athletes into using performance enhancers too? One reason for doubting that they do is that it once again appears as if "coercion" is being used too broadly. One might just as well say that students who study harder than others "coerce" their classmates into studying harder in order to keep up, or that athletes who practice longer hours than others "coerce" their competitors into practicing longer hours as well. The problem with such claims is that all competitive pressure becomes "coercive." As a result, the term "coercion" is deprived of any moral force. Indeed, if all the competitive behaviors that were "coercive" in this way were put into a list, virtually no competitive behaviors would be left over that were not coercive.

Critics might reply that there is a difference between weight training and extra studying, on one hand, and steroid use, on the other. As one writer has pointed out, "Steroids place regard for enhancement of athletic performance above regard for the health of the athletes themselves."[12] Weight training should make athletes stronger and more resistant to injury; studying normally enhances the intellectual ability of students. But steroid use, even if it enhances athletic performance, also presents serious risk of harm to the user.

These differences are important and suggest that the use of steroids does present athletes with a difficult choice. But is this enough to show that a user coerces other athletes into also becoming users? Much depends upon how we understand the term "coercion."[13] If we understand coercion to mean imposing difficult choices on others when we have no right to do so, and if we assume the user has no right to impose the choice of using or not using on other athletes, then perhaps a strong form of the coercion argument can be defended.

But before any such argument can be made good, we need to consider whether steroid users do have a right to impose the choice of becoming a user on others. And even if they have such a right, would it be wrong for them to exercise it? Rather than engaging in a conceptual analysis of the notion of "coercion," perhaps it will be more profitable to consider directly whether it is morally wrong for athletes who use steroids to place other athletes in a situation where they must choose between becoming users themselves or becoming competitively disadvantaged.

Unethically Constrained Choice

The appeal to coercion as a justification for prohibiting the use of steroids is open to the charge that it uses the notion of coercion far too broadly. Perhaps the argument can be reconstructed or modified without unacceptably stretching the term "coercion."

Whatever the proper definition of "coercion," what seems to make coercion presumptively wrong is that it unduly, illegitimately, or in some other way improperly interferes with the freedom of another. Thus, if we are reluctant to say that the student who studies harder than his peers, or the athlete who trains harder than her competitors, is coercing them, perhaps it is because we do not think the student or the athlete is acting improperly to begin with. Both have a right to work harder, so their working harder does not coerce others to do the same; or, if it does, it does not do so improperly or wrongly. Accordingly, we have no reason to prohibit the behavior of the student or the athlete (and even have reason to encourage it because it leads to superior achievement). In fact, their hard work may be inspiring to others and so make a positive social contribution.

But consider another situation in which competitive pressures are imposed improperly. Suppose you work in a firm where young employees compete for promotions to higher levels. Up to a point, if some work harder than others, no ethical issue is involved, because it is not wrong and usually highly desirable for some workers to try to perform better than others. But now, suppose that some workers work all the time, including weekends. Everyone feels the pressure to keep up, and soon all the workers give up their holidays and evenings for fear that they will lose their jobs if they do not. In this situation, it looks a bit more plausible that the workers are coerced, or, if not "coerced," at least unjustifiably pressured into putting in many hours of overtime.

Let us go further. Suppose some of the workers start taking stimulants—drugs having harmful side effects—so they can work even harder. Other workers feel that, to keep up, they, too, must take the stimulants. They ask the employer to set limits on the amount of time they are expected to work because they are being coerced into taking the stimulant to keep their jobs.

In this example, it is unclear that the workers who take the stimulants are behaving properly. Arguably, they are putting undue pressure on other workers to risk harming themselves so they can keep their jobs. If so, the workers taking the stimulants are violating the freedom of their fellow workers, and their behavior may be regulated in the interests of protecting the freedom of all.

Is the practice of steroid use in competitive sports like that of our last example? Do users of dangerous performance-enhancing drugs behave improperly when they put pressure on others to keep up competitively? Some would say "No!" As one writer has argued, "the ingestion of steroids for competitive reasons cannot be distinguished from the other tortures, deprivations, and risks to which athletes subject themselves to achieve success. No one is coerced into world class competition.... If they find the costs excessive, they may withdraw."[14]

But although such a rejoinder has force, it may not be decisive. Although steroid use is not strictly "coercive," because athletes can always withdraw from the competition, the choice of either using a potentially harmful drug or being noncompetitive may be unethical if it is imposed on others. Perhaps a prohibition on steroids can be justified as a means of protecting athletes from being placed in a position where they have to make such a choice. To the extent that we think it is wrong or illegitimate to present athletes with such a dilemma, then to that extent we will find the argument from coercion to have a point. Whether or not we want to apply the term "coercion" in such a context, we need to consider whether it is morally wrong to insist that athletes risk harming themselves to compete. If so, a prohibition on steroid use may be justified as a means of protecting athletes against having such a choice imposed upon them and protecting them from competitive pressures that, if unregulated, are far too likely to get out of hand.

Such considerations may not satisfy those who think steroid use is permissible. They would reply that athletes are not considered unethical if they engage in demanding training and thereby impose hard choices on other competitors. How can we justifiably condemn the users of performance-enhancing drugs for confronting competitors with difficult choices when we do not make the same judgment in similar situations?

This rejoinder does need to be explored further, but it is far from decisive. Perhaps we can distinguish the risks inherent in stressful training programs from those inherent in the use of steroids. As M. Andrew Holowchak remarked in a passage quoted earlier, we might distinguish between steroid use, which can be harmful, and training, which, if done properly, promotes conditioning and reduces the chances of injury.

Although we have not arrived at an uncontroversial justification for prohibiting the use of steroids in organized athletic competition, we have discovered an argument that is well worth further examination. According to this argument, athletes who use steroids have no right to put other athletes in the position of either damaging their health or competing under a significant disadvantage. Whether it will survive the test of further critical discussion remains to be seen, but perhaps it is strong enough to create at least a presumption in favor of prohibiting steroids in athletic competition, especially when we also consider the effects of elite athletes using steroids on impressionable young athletes as an added reinforcing factor (i.e., the "role model" argument considered earlier). Perhaps this presumption can be strengthened when conjoined with another argument of a different, but not totally unrelated, kind.

Fairness, Cheating, and the Use of Performance Enhancers

Many of those who object to the use of performance-enhancing drugs in sports do so not (or not only) because they believe users coerce others into also becoming users, but (also) because they believe that using such drugs is cheating. What reasons, if any, can be given for regarding the use of drugs, such as steroids, as an unfair competitive practice?

Those who assert that users of performance-enhancing drugs are cheating their opponents mean more than that users are breaking existing rules. In fact, Major League Baseball did not have an explicit prohibition on the use of performance enhancers prior to 2004 (although, as the Mitchell Report notes, prohibition was implied by earlier regulations); nevertheless, many fans still thought users were cheating.[15]

Of course, if the existing rules prohibit the use of such drugs, then their use is cheating. Those who secretly violate the rules take unfair advantage of those who don't. The interesting philosophical issue is whether the rules prohibiting the use of performance-enhancing drugs should be adopted by sports organizations in the first place, or, if such rules already exist, they should be changed to allow the use of performance-enhancing drugs. Would allowing the use of performance-enhancing drugs be unfair even if such drugs were available to all participants in a sport?

Many of us share the feeling that use of performance enhancers provides an unfair advantage, but we need to ask whether this intuitive conclusion can be supported by good arguments. We also need to consider just where the unfairness lies. Roger Gardner made a perceptive distinction when he asked whether steroid use was unfair *to competitors* because of the advantage it provides or was unfair *to the game* because it made success too easy. It will be useful to keep this distinction in mind as we explore the topic further in what follows.[16]

One line of argument suggests an analogy with differences in the equipment available to competitors. For example, if one player in a golf tournament used golf balls that went significantly farther than balls used by opponents, even when struck with the same force, and the same ball was not available for others to use if they so desired, the tournament arguably would be unfair. One player would be able to avoid one of the major challenges of golf not through skill but by using a superior product. Perhaps the use of steroids provides a similar unfair advantage.

The problem with this argument is that it is, at best, unclear that such a golf tournament was unfair. If the ball was acceptable under the rules and available to other competitors, the user indeed would have an advantage over players who were using ordinary equipment, but what would make the advantage unfair? Other players could use the same brand of golf ball if they wished to do so. There are all sorts of differences in equipment, past experiences, training facilities, coaching, and diet that can affect athletic performance but are not regarded as unfair. Until we can say why the advantages provided by steroids are illegitimate and the advantages provided by other conditions are legitimate, the charge of unfairness must be dismissed for lack of support.[17]

A similar difficulty affects the view that performance enhancers make sports too easy. Thus, we might say that the trouble with the "hot" golf ball is not that it gives some competitors unfair advantages over others, but that it makes golf significantly less challenging than it would be otherwise. Similarly, perhaps the trouble with steroids, we might claim, is that they reduce the challenge of sports by making achievement the result of taking a pill rather than the result of skill. But, as Roger Gardner pointed out, the same claim can be made about equipment, such as perimeter-weighted golf clubs that expand their "sweet spot," thereby reducing the skill needed for a desirable shot, as well as about diets promoting carbohydrate loading, high-tech running shoes, streamlined designer swimsuits, and top-of-the-line practice facilities, all of which are regarded as acceptable parts of athletic competition.[18]

The difficulty, then, is that of finding a principled way of drawing the line between the illegitimate use of steroids and other performance enhancers, on one hand, and factors that provide legitimate competitive advantages, on the other.

After all, some advances in equipment can make the game too easy and should be prohibited in the interest of preserving the game's inherent challenge, but other innovations should be allowed. (We will return to this issue in Chapter 7 when we discuss the potential conflict of interest between equipment manufacturers and sports organizations whose role it is to safeguard the interest of the sport.) Perhaps steroid use is on one (prohibited) side of the line and effective dieting is on the other (permissible) side. The problem is to draw the line properly in the first place. Just when does an innovation make the game too easy?

Although a simple answer to such a question is unlikely to exist, the charge of unfairness should not be dismissed too quickly. Perhaps by expanding the considerations mentioned in our discussion of the potential coercive effects of steroid use we can develop a different analysis of the unfairness involved. This analysis may be able to help us develop a reasonable—although perhaps not conclusive—case that steroid use should be prohibited in competitive sports.

That steroid use by some athletes creates a situation of unpalatable choices for others was suggested earlier: Either use steroids and risk harm, or cease to be competitive (or at least assume a significant competitive disadvantage). In a sense, the steroid user, though perhaps not like the robber who demands your money or your life, at least creates a dilemma like that facing the workers who must use harmful stimulants to keep pace with the drug-induced, energetic colleagues. We may conclude that neither athletes nor workers should face such choices and that we should enact legislation to protect them from such a cruel dilemma.

Does a similar line of argument also suggest that the use of performance-enhancing steroids is *unfair*? Suppose we ask whether it would be rational for all athletes to support either the rule "Use of steroids should be prohibited in athletic competition" or the rule "Use of steroids should be permitted in athletic competition"? Let us stipulate one artificial but plausible and morally justifiable limitation on their choice: namely, the athletes vote as if in ignorance of how the use or nonuse of steroids would affect them personally, but with knowledge of the general properties of steroids. The use of this limited "veil of ignorance," suggested by

John Rawls's theory of justice, forces the athletes to be impartial and unbiased rather than to vote according to personal self-interest.[19] How would rational and impartial athletes vote?

Can it be established that a vote for the rule permitting steroid use would be irrational under such circumstances? One might argue for such a view by pointing out that all athletes would know of the general harmful effects of steroids, but, because of the requirement of limited ignorance, none would have any reason to believe that steroids would be especially beneficial to them personally. Widespread use would, at best, yield only minimal gains for any one competitor, since the advantages gained by some would be largely canceled out by roughly similar advantages gained by others. However, the risk of serious effects on health would be significant for all.

Under such circumstances, a rule allowing the general use of steroids seems collectively irrational. Why would rational individuals choose to run great risks for minimal gains, gains that, from behind the veil of ignorance, they have no reason to believe will benefit them rather than their competitors? It seems that significant competitive advantage can be secured only if some athletes use steroids covertly. Allowing steroid use would not be supported by the informed, impartial choice of all athletes and would provide only minimal gains relative to the risk of serious harm. The use of steroids as performance enhancers is unethical precisely because rational and impartial athletes would not agree to it as a universal practice.

Thus, steroid use may seem rational if users think only about themselves and hope to secure advantages over nonusers. But if they must think impartially about what is an acceptable universal practice, steroid use no longer seems rational. This is why the use of steroids seems to many to be a form of cheating. The user operates from principles that could not be consented to as principles applying to all.

In effect, this argument appeals to a hypothetical contract among rational and impartial athletes. It is hypothetical because it attempts to specify what would be agreed to under specified but not necessarily real or actual conditions of choice. Although it is hypothetical rather than actual, writers such as Rawls have suggested that such a contract nevertheless is binding on us in that the hypothetical conditions reflect considerations we think ought to apply to moral reasoning. The veil of ignorance, for example, reflects our belief that moral reasoning should be impartial rather than biased in our own favor and should not be unduly influenced by our social class, race, gender, religion, or genetic endowment.

Unfortunately for those who oppose the use of performance-enhancing steroids, this sort of argument is hardly free from criticism. In particular, it assumes, perhaps incorrectly, that the only outcomes athletes would consider behind the veil of ignorance would be risks to health versus competitive gains over other athletes. Some athletes might consider other issues: For example, some might believe that a universally higher level of competition generated by using steroids more than compensates for health risks. Others may value their greater strength as a result of steroid use, regardless of competitive gain over others.[20] Thus, it is not as uncontroversial as it first appeared to suppose that impartial and reasonable athletes would unanimously agree to prohibit steroid use; their deliberations behind the veil might even be indeterminate because of conflicting views.

This critique indicates that the contractual version of the argument from fairness is open to reasonable objection. However, further development of the argument may undermine some of the objections to it. For example, we might consider whether the official rule-making bodies of sports, such as the National Collegiate Athletic Association (NCAA) or the International Olympic Committee (IOC), are obligated to ignore the idiosyncratic values of individual athletes and simply consider steroid use from the standpoint of promoting good competition. If we can justifiably rule out the preferences of athletes who value increases in strength or in overall athletic achievement over risks to health, and only consider the issue from the standpoint of weighing competitive advantages and disadvantages (which arguably is the point of view that rule-making bodies should take), then our original conclusion seems to follow. From the standpoint of collective impartial choice about the conditions of competition, users of steroids are exempting themselves from rules to which they would not consent under conditions of free, impartial choice. Because they are making exceptions of themselves arbitrarily, their behavior may be regarded as unfair. Users who engage in a behavior they could not rationally endorse as a policy for others to follow treat their fellow athletes merely as a means to their own success.[21]

Sports organizations such as Major League Baseball or the IOC are justified in considering things from this perspective—and discounting the possible desires of those athletes who would like to see the overall level of play improve as a result of drug use—because their job as organizations is not to make play better and better but to regulate competition fairly. This conclusion, as we have seen, may not follow if, behind the veil of ignorance, we take into account the fact that athletes may take a point of view based on some value not directly connected to competitive success, such as raising the limits of human performance. However, because sports organizations regulate fairness in competition, it seems reasonable for them to ignore such idiosyncratic values when making regulations about steroid use.

Performance-Enhancing Drugs, Respect for Persons, and the Ethic of Competition

Even if the contractual version of the argument from fairness has force, it may seem to miss part of the issue raised by the use of performance enhancers. For one thing, it depends heavily on the harmful effects of prolonged steroid use to the user. But we may believe that the use of performance enhancers would be wrong even if the drugs were not harmful. If there were a "magic pill," which if taken properly would improve athletic ability without significant risks to health, would using such a pill be ethical? Doesn't the use of steroids run counter to the ethic of good competition outlined in earlier chapters, even if the potential dangers to the user are discounted?

To many people, steroid use seems a way of avoiding the challenges presented by sports rather than overcoming them. This belief does not seem to rest upon claims that the use of steroids is coercive, or that such use is unfair, but seems to arise independently from concerns about the basic ethic of athletic competition. Can such intuitions about the wrongness of performance-enhancing drugs be justified?

If competition in sports is supposed to be a test of the athletic ability of persons, isn't the very heart of competition corrupted if results are affected by performance-enhancing drugs? Presumably, we would not accept a new high-jump record if the winner wore special mechanical aids that added spring to her shoes. Similarly, consider home runs produced by use of a high-tech baseball bat programmed to make square contact with the ball (perhaps through an implanted sensor and computerized control chip) so that it will fly out of the park regardless of the batter's skill. In both of these examples, we are inclined to say that success would not reflect the skill of the athlete but the operation of the special equipment.

Isn't it the same with the use of performance-enhancing drugs? Where such drugs lead to improved play, it is not the person who is responsible for the gains; rather, it is the drug that makes the difference. Isn't this similar to the examples of the mechanical track shoes and the high-tech baseball bat? Isn't the ethic of competition violated, because the skills of the athlete are replaced by technological aids that turn the contest from one of competing persons into one of machines? The logical extension of such a route would be to gradually replace flesh-and-blood athletes by part-human and part-machine cyborgs, or even robots designed to maximize performance in every category. What we would have, if such a nightmare ever became reality, might be enhanced performance, but would it be sport?

Those who believe that the use of performance-enhancing drugs should be permitted may not be convinced by such an argument. They might raise four important objections. First, we do allow new equipment in sports, even if such equipment does enhance performance. Fiberglass poles for vaulting, tennis racquets composed of composites, and the replacement of wooden golf shafts by steel ones are examples of technological innovations that enhance performance.[22] How does the introduction of performance-enhancing drugs differ? Second, changes in diet are widely believed to enhance performance. If runners can "load up" on carbohydrates before a race to improve their times, why can't they take steroids as well? Third, steroids and other performance enhancers are not magic bullets that immediately produce results. They yield improvement only in conjunction with hard training and a demanding work ethic. In fact, they allow muscles to recover faster and therefore permit users to engage in more intense and more frequent workouts than nonusers are able to manage. Finally, why isn't the decision to use steroids just as much a person's decision to make as the decision to use weight training? What reason do we have to say that weight training reflects our status as persons who can make free choices and the use of steroids does not?

Let us consider the point about technological innovations in equipment first. Although it is doubtful whether any one principle explains when an innovation in equipment is acceptable and when it is not, some distinctions can be made. For example, some technological improvements in equipment remedy previous defects. Old wooden shafts in golf clubs twisted to varying degrees under the pressure of the golf swing, producing arbitrary results. The same player could make two equally good swings but get different results because of too much torque in the wooden shaft. Steel golf shafts remedied this defect, providing more consistent results, because they do not twist under the pressure of the stroke. Similarly, improved athletic shoes remove the defects of unnecessary weight and faulty structure. Although both innovations made it easier to perform better, neither changed the character of the game, and both can be regarded as removing handicaps created by faulty equipment that were extraneous to the real challenges set by the sports in question.

Other changes in equipment that have been regarded as permissible cannot so easily be seen as simply removing defects in materials used earlier. In golf, the sand wedge, a club with a specially designed flange, invented by professional Gene Sarazen, made escaping from sand bunkers far easier than before. Many skilled professionals would rather have a missed shot land in the sand than in a difficult lie on grass because the sand wedge has made highly accurate recoveries likely for the advanced player. Similarly, fiberglass poles have made it possible for pole-vaulters to achieve heights previously considered unreachable. In the 2008 Olympics in Beijing, special streamlined full-body swimsuits, designed to enable the athlete to cut through the water with less resistance, were widely believed to contribute to the plethora of records set during the competition. Graphite and other composite materials have contributed to advances in play in golf, tennis, and other sports. In other words, it does not appear true that all technological advances in sports equipment are simply remedies for defects in earlier materials. Why should such advances be allowed and steroids prohibited?

First, it must be acknowledged that sometimes advancements in equipment are prohibited by sports authorities. It simply is not true that all technological advances in equipment are allowable regardless of their effects on the game. Some technological advances are prohibited because they make the game too easy or reduce its challenges in some significant way. Other advancements can make the game more competitive or make its challenges more reasonable. Thus, the use of the sand wedge in golf can be defended on the grounds that without it, bunker shots were simply too difficult. The game was made better by allowing the equipment. Nevertheless, in 2009 the United States Golf Association prohibited the use of wedges and other irons with specially designed grooves in professional and certain other elite competitions (although their use is allowed until 2024 for less elite play). This is because the special grooves allowed top players to get backspin on the ball even after hitting from the rough (an unmowed or less closely mowed area of the course). This allowed elite golfers to control the ball better and hence reduced the penalty for inaccurate drives that missed the fairway. In effect, the special grooves significantly reduced the penalty for lack of skill in a key area of the game and reduced the challenge of the contest to an arguably unacceptable degree. Similarly, the use of polyurethane full-body swimsuits has been banned in major competitions starting in 2010.

Performance-enhancing drugs, it might be argued, also change the nature of those who use the equipment and so undermine the challenge presented by sports. Instead of meeting the challenge of the test, we change the nature of the test takers to minimize the challenge they face. If steroids and other performance-enhancing drugs were permitted, the way athletes were affected by the drug would significantly affect outcomes. But this seems irrelevant to determining which contestant is the better player. Jones should not defeat Smith because Jones's body processes steroids more efficiently than Smith's. We want the winner to be the best athlete, not the individual whose body is best attuned to a performance-enhancing drug! Performance enhancers thus turn sport from a contest among persons into a contest among "designer" bodies that are manufactured through a technological fix.[23] The winners are the individuals whose bodies react best to the available drugs, which hardly seems to be what is meant by sports as a mutual quest of persons for excellence through challenge.

However, a proponent of the use of performance enhancers might ask whether the same thing isn't true of special diets. Thus, "carbohydrate loading," or consuming unusually large amounts of carbohydrates before competition, seems to be a common and accepted practice among long-distance runners, but clearly, some competitors may gain more from the practice than others. Is this an example of outcomes being unfairly affected by athletically irrelevant qualities? Or if it is permissible to adhere to a performance-enhancing diet, why isn't it also acceptable to use performance-enhancing drugs?

Even if this point is ignored, proponents of steroid use might charge that the argument against steroids is inconsistent in another way. Competition in sports has been defended here because it is expressive of our moral status as persons. But by prohibiting athletes from using performance-enhancing drugs, it can be argued that we show disrespect to them as persons. That is, we deny them the control over their own lives that ought to belong to any autonomous, intelligent, and competent individual. In other words, aren't athletes persons? If so, shouldn't their choices, including the choice of using drugs to enhance performance, be respected?[24]

The debate so far raises several key issues. Just when are changes in equipment allowable and when should they be prohibited? Is there a bright, clear line that tells us when changes in equipment or in the persons using it reduce the challenge of the game to an unacceptable extent? Why does steroid use "change the nature of persons," but training, diet, and vitamins do not? And why should our current conception of persons (assuming it is clear enough to be useful) be sacrosanct? It appears that both the proponents and the critics of the use of performance-enhancing drugs in sports have advanced points well worth considering, but that the arguments presented by both sides are still inconclusive. However, as will be argued later, that does not mean they are equal in rational force, only that no one argument taken by itself is decisive.

PERFORMANCE-ENHANCING DRUGS AND THE LEGITIMACY OF RECORDS

One of the complaints that many sports fans, particularly baseball fans, bring against the use of performance-enhancing drugs is that they undermine our ability to make comparisons between achievements of the past and those of "the steroid era." Many fans question whether the home-run records set by Barry Bonds—assuming Bonds was using performance enhancers when the records were set—are truly legitimate. Is it fair to Roger Maris, the holder of the single-season record for home runs for many years, or to career home-run leaders such as Babe Ruth and Hank Aaron, that Bonds be regarded as the home-run king of all time?

A somewhat different but related situation arises in what Sigmund Loland has called "record sports"—sports such as swimming or track and field where the goal of many athletes is to set new records, but the difference between the old performance and the new, record-setting performance is almost infinitesimal, perhaps made possible only by new technology capable of detecting minute differences in times. In such sports athletes may be tempted to use performance enhancers simply to set new records and raise the bar higher. Loland surely is correct when he asks whether such tiny differences in performance are really all that significant.[25]

However, baseball has a long history and a tradition in which fans debate the merits of different players from different eras of the sport. How do the center fielders of today, for example, compare with stars of the 1950s and 1960s, such as contemporaries Duke Snider of the Brooklyn Dodgers, Willie Mays of the New York Giants, and Mickey Mantle of the New York Yankees, three of the great center fielders of all time who graced New York by their play? In baseball, at least before the steroid era, records often lasted for decades, and many knowledgeable observers doubt that Joe DiMaggio's fifty-six-game hitting streak, set in 1941, will ever be surpassed. Should we regard records like those of Aaron, Maris, and Ruth as having been surpassed when it is reasonable to suspect they were broken only with the aid of performance enhancers?

I doubt myself if a decisive answer can be provided to this question, but it will be useful to consider some of the arguments on both sides. Those who argue that indeed the records of the past were broken by today's sluggers, whether or not they used performance enhancers, might make three different points.

First, they might argue that other past changes in baseball also affected performance, but that no one ever argued that records set under these changed conditions were illegitimate. Thus, in 1968, Major League Baseball lowered the height of the pitching mound in order to rejuvenate the offensive side of the game. Bringing the pitcher down to the level of the batter reduced the advantage of the hurler over the hitter. Also, when Ruth set his records, baseball was a racially segregated sport in which white batters never had to compete against all the top pitchers of the time, some of whom were excluded from the Major Leagues because of their race. Were Ruth's records somehow illegitimate because he did not always play against all the best players of his time as a result of the exclusion of minorities from the field of play? In other words, different eras of baseball differ from others in a variety of ways that can affect performance.[26] The steroid era, on this view, is only one more change, and it is not totally dissimilar to those of the past; it does no more to delegitimize present achievement than any other significant change did throughout the history of the sport.

Second, batters have not been the only users of performance-enhancing drugs. Pitchers have been among the alleged users as well. So even if some of the batters improved their performance by using steroids or other performance enhancers, so did some of the pitchers they batted against. This makes their slugging achievements even more impressive, not less so, than if only batters were using steroids, the person arguing for acceptance of records made under the influence of steroids might say.

Third, and finally, performance-enhancing drugs are not magic pills. Bonds, McGwire, and other sluggers, whether their performance was enhanced by drug use or not, demonstrated enormous talent in performing one of the most difficult feats in all of sport—namely, making powerful contact with the kinds of pitches thrown by elite pitchers who also were at the top of their game.

All of these considerations support the view that records set even by users of performance-enhancing drugs are entirely legitimate, even in Major League Baseball. But are they decisive? Let's consider the other side of the case before deciding. What might the person say who is against the inclusion of records made under the influence of performance-enhancing substances?

First of all, the barrage of home-run records that have been set during the steroid era was unprecedented. For the first 122 years of Major League Baseball, only

Ruth, with sixty, and Maris, with sixty-one, hit more than fifty-nine home runs in a season. But from 1995 to 2001, this was done six times by three different players. It is unlikely that all these achievements have been due to a sudden improvement in the athletic abilities of the players without the assistance of performance-enhancing drugs. More important, it is unlikely that these records were set on a level playing field. When the mound was lowered in 1968, reducing the advantage of the pitcher over the hitter, all hitters and all pitchers performed under the same set of conditions. However, many, perhaps a great majority, of Major League players have not used performance-enhancing drugs.

In addition, if the contractual argument presented earlier is plausible, those who did use performance-enhancing drugs were acting in a way they could not reasonably universalize. As we have seen, impartial athletes (deliberating behind the veil of ignorance) would not adopt a rule allowing everyone to use performance-enhancing drugs of the kind at stake. As such, they achieved their records by use of an arguably unethical method and operated egoistically rather than ethically.

Moreover, although baseball did not have an explicit antidrug policy at the time when many of the records were set, there were rules in place that implicitly—and after 1991 explicitly—prohibited the use of performance-enhancing drugs. Thus, as the Mitchell Report points out, "Beginning in 1971 and continuing today, Major League Baseball's drug policy has prohibited the use of any prescription medicine without a valid prescription. By implication, this prohibition applied to steroids even before 1991 when Commissioner Fay Vincent first expressly included steroids in baseball's drug policy."[27]

This point can be pressed even further. If records set with the help of methods that, for one thing, were against the rules, and for another thing, were arguably unethical, were allowed to stand, then less disincentive would be provided to deter future players from trying to achieve success outside the rules and moral framework of the sports involved. Moreover, the records of the players who did conform to proper standards of conduct should stand until they are broken by legitimate (non-drug-enhanced) performances. Why should their achievements be supplanted by performances achieved through illicit methods? Reducing the significance of some of the records which it is reasonable to believe were achieved with the use of performance enhancers would provide a guarantee that those who abide by an appropriate sporting code of conduct will not be disadvantaged by doing so and would help to restore the situation to what it would have been if performance enhancers had not been used. Thus, considerations of deterrence and considerations of fairness both support the claim that certain records achieved in the steroid era of Major League Baseball should not be viewed as legitimate.

How are we to weigh all of these conflicting considerations? As I suggested above, perhaps there is no clearly decisive answer to that question. Perhaps these records should simply be marked by an asterisk, indicating they may have been achieved with the use of performance-enhancing drugs. In this way, the records would not be erased or eliminated; they would be allowed to stand, but with reservations attached to them. Under this reasonable compromise, the record books would indicate to observers of the game that the way in which the achievements were made is open to serious moral question.

A Presumptive Case Against Performance Enhancers

We have provided some reason to believe that the use of performance-enhancing drugs in order to improve performance in sports is unethical. But have we proven our case? Are our reasons good enough to become the basis for action on the part of the sports organizations setting the rules for professional and amateur competitive sports? Why shouldn't the rules be changed to allow the use of such substances, perhaps under medical supervision?

I suggest that, although critics and proponents have advanced important arguments, neither side has won conclusively. However, while it is important to engage in further discussion to advance the argument, it doesn't follow that the debate should leave us paralyzed by analysis and unable to act. While theorists have the luxury to continue debating arguments for and against prohibition of performance-enhancing substances, sports authorities cannot necessarily wait for them to come up with a definitive answer. They must promulgate rules about whether to permit the use of performance-enhancing drugs on the best information they have at present.

Policymakers often have to decide difficult issues over which reasonable persons of good will disagree. If we had to wait for the emergence of decisive arguments on controversial moral issues, we often would be intellectually paralyzed in circumstances demanding some action. In fact, we often have to draw lines between what is permissible and impermissible in areas where reasons for making the distinction do not apply in as sharp a fashion as we would like. For example, the democratic state must distinguish between those who are mature enough to vote and those who are not. Because the maturity of each person cannot be evaluated on the merits of individuals, we attempt to draw a line reasonably. So long as the process by which the line is drawn is itself consistent with democratic values, and the boundary is reasonable, there are good grounds for regarding it as justified. We need to avoid the fallacy of insisting that if we cannot find the perfect place to draw a line, we should draw no line at all. As the French philosopher Voltaire reminded us, "The perfect is the enemy of the good," and so to produce the most defensible policy, we sometimes have to arrive at a reasonable decision even when the grounds for doing so are not airtight.

Thus, we may want to give sports authorities the discretion to prohibit performance enhancers if their best judgment supports such a policy. If sports authorities, such as the NCAA or the IOC, have *reasonable* grounds for making distinctions between impermissible performance-enhancing drugs and permissible diets, equipment changes, and the like, and if they are not acting in an autocratic or dogmatic fashion, then even if no conclusive argument can be given for drawing the line in one place, their decision still has normative force.

Several points emerge from our discussion to support such a conclusion:

1. Athletes who choose to use harmful performance enhancers create a situation in which nonusers must either subject themselves to serious health risks or cease to be competitive. It is far from clear that users have the right to impose this choice on others.
2. It is doubtful whether rational and impartial athletes concerned with regulating competition would support a universal rule allowing the use of potentially harmful performance enhancers.
3. More controversially, the use of harmful performance enhancers moves sport closer to transforming persons into tools for athletic success than do special diets, weight training, or vitamin supplements.
4. The use of harmful performance enhancers by elite athletes is likely to encourage, by example, the use of such harmful substances by aspiring young athletes who are beneath the age of consent, and so may be prohibited in order to prevent or minimize such dangerous consequences.
5. Finally, and perhaps more controversially, in some (perhaps many) sports, such as Major League Baseball, the use of performance-enhancing drugs can cheapen the achievements of the sport (for example, by making home runs too easy to hit), making it difficult or impossible to make a fair comparison of the performance of users and nonusers over time.

Thus, our discussion does suggest that although no conclusive argument or knock-down proof is available, good reasons can be given for prohibiting steroids as performance enhancers, and that official governing bodies in sports can therefore prohibit their use. Unless it can be shown that such decisions are arbitrary, dogmatic, or authoritarian, they are given moral weight because they are promulgated by legitimate governing bodies.[28] Rather than assigning the burden of proof to those who find the use of performance enhancers to be immoral, why not maintain instead that where the sports community is in deep disagreement, the decisions of governing bodies are morally binding as long as they are not unreasonable, undemocratic, or arbitrary?

Moreover, the lines of argument we have considered for prohibiting the use of performance-enhancing drugs, although not determinative, might well be strengthened by extended discussion and debate. Although none of these arguments avoids serious objection, it is far from clear that the objections are decisive enough to justify total rejection of the arguments. Perhaps these arguments are cogent enough to show that the policies of those governing bodies of organized sports that prohibit the use of performance enhancers in their competitions are sufficiently reasonable, at least until the ethical issues involved are more satisfactorily resolved.

Enforcement

If the rules prohibiting the use of performance-enhancing drugs are to be effective, they must be enforced. Enforcement, however, raises a host of ethical issues. For example, drug use often can be detected through urinalysis and other scientific tests, although elite athletes have made attempts at chemically disguising evidence of drug use. But assuming that tests are often effective, should athletes be required to take them? Does this amount to forcing users to incriminate themselves, violating constitutional guarantees against self-incrimination? Do drug tests violate a right to privacy? Do rights to privacy of high-school, intercollegiate, and professional athletes differ in this regard? What about the constitutional prohibition on unreasonable searches? Which methods of enforcement are ethical and which are not?

What are the principal ethical objections to requiring athletes to be tested for performance-enhancing substances? Clearly, they have to do with liberty and privacy. One of the most cherished principles of Anglo-American law, and of the liberal political theories from which it derives, is that the presumption is on the authorities to prove the guilt of an individual

To see why this principle is so important, consider the alternative. Under a presumption of guilt, individuals could be detained, their homes searched, and their lives disrupted simply because prosecutors decided they might find evidence of an infraction if they looked hard enough. Our liberty and our privacy would be minimal at best under such an arrangement. We would have them only to the extent that the authorities permitted us to keep them, which is to say we would not have them in any meaningful sense at all.

Requiring the individual to submit to drug tests seems to those concerned with our liberties to be similar to requiring individuals to open their homes to searches, or to detaining individuals against their will, without evidence that, if it existed, might justify such intrusions. Accordingly, it seems that those of us who are committed to respect for the freedom of the individual must reject the required random testing of athletes for drug use.

But although this argument does have considerable force, it may also admit of exceptions. For example, shouldn't those persons directly responsible for the safety of others be required to show that they are not under the influence of alcohol or other mind-altering drugs? Airline pilots, railroad engineers, surgeons, police officers, and firefighters are among those with special obligations to care for the safety of others. Requiring them to take drug tests seems to be an exception permitted even by Mill's Harm Principle because its purpose is to prevent direct injury to others.

This argument can be gradually extended until it becomes dangerously broad. Thus, although loss of worker efficiency due to drug use is a major national problem, could we justify required testing of all workers in an effort to prevent harm to fellow workers and to consumers? What happens to our civil liberties then?

Although we cannot pursue this important question in depth here, we ought not to be driven down the slippery slope too quickly. Although drug use on the job by some workers may indirectly injure consumers, lines can be drawn. The greater the threat of harm, the more serious the kind of harm at stake, and the more directly it is attendant upon drug use, then the greater the argument for required testing. Usually, either the threat of harm will be sufficiently indirect or weak, or other methods of protection and/or detection will be available. It is therefore doubtful that making exceptions to the general principle of noninterference in instances of direct and serious harm to individuals will undermine civil liberties generally.

Is there another kind of exception that might apply to organized athletics? After all, unlike airline pilots who use drugs, athletes who take steroids do not directly endanger the general public.

Perhaps the idea of a collection of individuals voluntarily taking part in a joint activity requiring the mutual observance of common rules applies here. Thus, in professional baseball, an umpire has the right to require a pitcher to empty his pockets so the umpire can check that the player is not carrying special prohibited substances that, when applied to the baseball, can alter its flight, making it more difficult to hit. Off the field, the umpire would have no right to search the player, but he does have such a right in the special context of the game. This is because the game is fair only if all players observe the same rules. The umpire, with the consent of the competing teams, is charged with enforcing the rules, thereby ensuring a fair contest. As a result, umpires acquire rights in virtue of their role that they do not have as ordinary citizens. The civil rights of the players have in effect been limited in the context of the game because the players accept its rules and enforcement procedures.

A similar argument can be applied to testing for the use of performance-enhancing drugs in organized athletics. Participants consent to playing by publicly acknowledged rules. No one is forced to participate, but once consent is given to participation, players are owed protection from those who would intentionally violate the rules. Without enforcement, no protection would be provided. In particular, if effective means of detection were not used, then athletes would suspect each other of breaking the existing rules. Pressures would exist to use performance-enhancing drugs illegally in attempts to remain competitive.

Because participants voluntarily agree to participate, and because they agree to play under the assumption that the rules will be applied fairly to all, they are owed protection against violators. Drug testing of athletes, in this view, seems not to be a violation of their civil rights but a reasonable protection against being unfairly disadvantaged. To the extent that requiring athletes to submit to drug tests can be defended, it is because each participant is entitled to play under the public conditions specifying the rules of the contest. If umpires in baseball can enforce such an entitlement by requiring pitchers to reveal whether they are carrying illegal substances that can alter the flight of the ball, why wouldn't sports authorities have a similar justification for drug testing to ensure that advantages prohibited by the rules are not obtained through ingestion of illegal substances of a different kind?

That said, room for debate remains about the circumstances or specifics of drug-testing programs. Although professional and elite amateur athletic associations may need to rely on random testing to promote compliance and reassure the public about the fairness of competition, things get trickier when we turn to the level of intercollegiate and scholastic sports. For example, should authorities have to have probable cause to suspect drug use before testing a high-school athlete, or should they be allowed to conduct random testing of all athletes at a school, even if most are not under any suspicion whatsoever? To what extent must privacy be ensured, both during the testing itself and with dissemination of the results? For example, should parents of a high-school athlete be notified if the student is found to be using steroids? What if the student is using drugs, but not those that would enhance athletic performance? Accordingly, even if there is a reasonable case for testing as a mechanism to ensure the fairness of competition, and even if athletes are informed about the possibility of being tested in advance, so they consent to be tested prior to play, there is plenty of room for debate about how tests may be conducted, to whom they may be administered, and what protections (say, for appeal) should be provided to those who are subjected to them.[29]

Summary

Our discussion in this section has explored important lines of argument for and against the view that the use of performance-enhancing drugs in sports is immoral. Although arguments for different positions on these issues need to be defended further, our examination provides provisional, but not conclusive, support for a prohibition on the use of such drugs and supports drug testing as a principal means of detection and enforcement in certain situations. Critics of the use of steroids and other performance enhancers will no doubt wish for an even stronger verdict on their behalf. Perhaps such a verdict will be justified by further critical reflection on the issues we have discussed. As we have seen, however, there are important criticisms of the arguments for prohibiting steroid use, not all of which have yet been answered satisfactorily. In the meantime, while debate continues, rules prohibiting the use of steroids in organized sports can be defended as permissible because they have not been shown to be arbitrary, unreasonable, or illegitimately imposed. To violate those rules covertly solely to gain a competitive advantage seems unjustifiable, whether or not the rules themselves ultimately should be revised.

CREATING "POST-HUMANS"?
THE ETHICS OF GENETIC ENHANCEMENT

Although the use of steroids and other performance-enhancing substances by athletes has attracted widespread attention and generated much controversy, scientific advances in biology and genetics have raised even more profound issues in the ethics of sport. Potential advances in our ability to genetically enhance individuals may in time affect some of the very qualities that we associate with being human. These advances promise many benefits outside the world of sports, especially in the area of medicine, and open up the possibility of curing diseases with genetic origins or prescribing treatments that are precisely designed to fit the specific genetic profile of the patient. However, these advances also open up what many fear is a Pandora's Box of dangers, ranging from the cloning of human beings to the production of genetically engineered super-athletes capable of shattering all existing records in sport.

The specter of the eugenics movement, endorsed by many leading figures in the United States in the early part of the twentieth century and later adapted by the Nazis for their own purposes, often haunts discussions of genetic enhancement. The goal of the eugenics movement was to weed out "defectives"—those regarded as possessing unhealthy or even undesirable traits that could be passed on to offspring—from the population by preventing them from reproducing in order to elevate the genetic fitness of the overall population.

Most reasonable people would agree that the therapeutic use of genetic techniques to cure disease and reduce human suffering is admirable and worthy of our support. But what about using these same techniques to enhance our memories, our attractiveness, our height, and other physical characteristics and abilities in a wide variety of areas perhaps leading to the creation of drastically altered post-humans?[30] As philosopher Michael Sandel has pointed out, "the moral quandary arises when people use such [genetic] therapy not to cure a disease but to reach beyond health, to enhance their physical or cognitive capacities, to lift themselves above the norm."[31] For example, to cite an example discussed by Sandel, what if a genetic therapy used medically to help patients with muscular dystrophy and to reverse muscle loss associated with aging was used by athletes to enhance muscle mass and increase strength well above normal limits? Would such use of a legitimate medical therapy to enhance athletic performance be morally permissible?

Before turning to that issue, we need to distinguish between genetic techniques that affect nonreproductive (somatic) cells, and so are not passed on to offspring, and actual changes in reproductive or germline cells that are passed on through reproduction. The former (techniques affecting nonreproductive cells) would allow two types of cases: first, a competent adult who had a genetic abnormality would be able to choose to have the abnormality corrected, usually to avoid an illness or disorder associated with the abnormality; and second, a competent adult would be permitted to voluntarily agree to genetic enhancement. The latter (techniques affecting reproductive cells) would allow us to design our children to exhibit special abilities or characteristics that would give them advantages in life—say, in athletic competition, musical performance, or other activities where enhanced cognitive and physical skills would enable those who possessed them to excel.

In what follows, the discussion will be largely restricted to enhancement of athletic abilities. However, it is clear that concerns about enhancement apply to many areas of human life. The possibility of making such changes raises the question of what it means to be human and whether we should exercise the power to perhaps bring a new kind of being—the enhanced post-human—into existence. Of course, all of this is beyond our capabilities at present, and many forms of enhancement may not ever be safe enough for humans. Nevertheless, it is still important to engage in debate about genetic enhancement. There are at least two reasons for this in our discussion of ethics in sport: first, it is always helpful to reflect on issues before they arrive right on our doorstep so that we can be prepared for dilemmas that may face us in the not-too-distant future; and second, the discussion will help to sharpen our examination of performance enhancement in sports by enabling us to revisit some issues from a fresh perspective. In particular, in this discussion we will assume that techniques of genetic enhancement will be reasonably safe (thus eliminating those concerns about performance-enhancing drugs that arise from their safety) and medically feasible to perform.

Three Arguments Against Enhancement

Many people regard genetic enhancement as abhorrent on religious grounds. It seems to be "playing God" or tampering with God's design for humanity. However, many other religious people have no such theological objection to enhancement and may regard improving the human species as carrying out God's will. Moreover, theological concerns are not persuasive to atheists or agnostics.

Perhaps more important, in a religiously pluralistic society such as ours, religious concerns need to be supplemented by arguments that appeal to reason if they are to influence policy in a fully legitimate way. Without rational arguments, we run the danger of some religions imposing their theology on those who in good conscience do not share it, and who may have opposing religious beliefs, which shows a lack of respect for the religious concerns of those who dissent.

Another reason for the religious to look for reasoned arguments in this area is the idea that God would prohibit a practice on moral grounds only if it were actually unethical. Thus, we need to have reasons to think a practice is unethical before we can reasonably conclude that God prohibits it. Of course, some theists would want to rely on revelation rather than reason; but, as just noted, in a pluralistic society religions themselves disagree on many fundamental points, so appeals to revelation in areas of moral controversy are not likely to move others from different religious perspectives.

Similarly, arguments that genetic enhancement is "unnatural" are not helpful either. Should genetic therapies that fight disease, and which might save countless lives, be prohibited because they are unnatural? Or, if it is claimed that therapies are "natural," but enhancement is "unnatural," the whole natural-unnatural distinction seems arbitrary. What about medical interventions with antibiotics that cure infections that otherwise would be fatal? Are such interventions "unnatural" because they prevent nature from taking its course? Many people would argue that if we forsake the artificial for the natural, we would have to abandon many, if not all, of the medical and other technological breakthroughs that have saved countless lives since their development. Alternately, one could argue that genetic enhancement is natural because it was achieved by the use of human reason, part of our natural abilities.

One problem is that the idea of the "natural" is just too indeterminate to lead to solutions to moral dilemmas. Are airplanes unnatural because they wouldn't exist in a pretechnological stage of human development, or are they natural because they are possible through application of scientific laws of nature by human reason?

A second problem with arguments based on whether something is "natural" concerns their normative force. Even if something was unnatural, does that automatically make it wrong? If "unnatural" is taken to mean something like "not statistically normal in a pretechnological state," why does statistical abnormality create wrongness? Using electric shocks from a defibrillator to restart the hearts of people suffering cardiac arrest and save them from death may be unnatural in that sense, but it isn't morally wrong.

Accordingly, arguments based on theology or appeals to nature are unlikely to be philosophically or ethically pertinent. What we want to see, where appeal to religion is concerned, are the reasons why a religious perspective might condemn genetic enhancement.

Perhaps a second sort of argument supplies such a reason. We have already seen that liberal political thought attaches great weight to autonomy and freedom of choice by competent adults. Perhaps the problem with manipulation of germline cells in order to design our children—to assign them desirable traits such as height, strength, and speed, so that they might excel as athletes—is that it violates their future autonomy and freedom of choice. By designing children to fulfill certain functions or to excel at certain activities, we ensure that their future is no longer open but is instead fixed by the parents or designers. Isn't this wrong, because, in effect, it makes the children mere means to ends desired by others, without giving them freedom of choice to decide their own futures?

This argument undoubtedly has some force. Many parents of budding young athletes already may push their children too far, sometimes unintentionally causing burnout and discouraging them from participating in sports at all. Wouldn't it be worse if the parents were allowed to design their children to excel in given activities? "Sure you want to play in a band," we can almost hear such a parent exclaiming. "But we created you to play ball. If we wanted a musician, we would have built in those talents, but we didn't!" Indeed, if we pursue this line of reasoning to an extreme, we might imagine parents building into their children the desire to enjoy excelling in areas where they were given genetic abilities, almost like the so-called Gammas, Deltas, and Epsilons in Aldous Huxley's *Brave New World*, who were genetically designed to enjoy repetitive, boring tasks that others were unwilling to perform.

While we should acknowledge that this argument from autonomy has force, it is not decisive. That is because parents can already put pressure on children to excel in areas the parents value more than the child does. Moreover, parents already can engage in forms of genetic selection, ranging from simply picking a mate who seems to have the desired inheritable traits to purchasing eggs or sperm on the market from donors who are likely to have those characteristics.[32] Finally, children who have characteristics likely to make them successful in a given area can still simply stand up to their parents and assert that they want to determine their future for themselves. (I remember one of my children, who had been a successful high-school basketball player, replying as follows to my wife and me when we urged him to try out as a walk-on for his college team: "Mom and Dad, if I play it will be because I want to, not because you want me to!" Why couldn't "designer" children do the same?)

Although these criticisms may diminish the force of the argument from autonomy, so that it is not decisive, they do not diminish its force to the vanishing point. That is because it is plausible to think that the pressure to conform to the desires of parents may be greater for genetically engineered children than for others. That is because such children may feel more indebted to their parents, since they would not even have existed if not for the plans of their designers. So while the autonomy argument is far from decisive, it may have some weight in a comprehensive evaluation of the practice of altering germ cell lines to produce a designer child. Just as the athlete who uses steroids, while not literally coercing opponents, may still pressure others to also use them, parents of designer children may not coerce their offspring or totally eliminate their autonomy, but may more often than not make autonomy more difficult to exercise, which in itself is ethically questionable.

Consider a third argument against genetic enhancement. It is based on equality. If techniques for either making changes in the nonreproductive (somatic) cells of existing athletes (which may be freely chosen by the subjects themselves) or in actual germ lines turn out to be sufficiently expensive, the more affluent will have much more access to them than others. Is this inequality fair or just?

Perhaps it isn't, but proponents of genetic enhancement would have a point if they were to argue that many other inequalities in sports already result from differences in the resources supporting athletes. These include differences in coaching, in training facilities, in access to funds supporting travel, and in the ability to purchase and maintain high-tech equipment. For example, not all runners can afford either to train at high altitude or to work in specially designed oxygen chambers that simulate high-altitude training, both of which raise the carrying capacity of the blood, promoting endurance. Although such inequalities may not be totally fair, they are considered acceptable in sport. Why isn't the same true for genetic enhancement? Alternately, we might stipulate that genetic enhancement of athletes is acceptable only when access to it is equitable and fair.

Since none of the arguments we have considered against genetic enhancement of athletes seem decisive, should we conclude that the practice, were it to become both feasible and safe, is acceptable, and perhaps even desirable? As one of my students wrote, "the promotion of intelligence, long life, attractiveness and athleticism coupled with the reduction of congenital disease or defect, strikes me as indubitably good. To escape the cruelties of nature and recast man as being beholden only to himself could prove to be the most profound (and exhilarating) moment of human existence."[33]

Theorists who welcome the prospects of genetic enhancement in a wide variety of areas, but who also are committed to the values of liberty, autonomy, and respect for persons, have developed a position that some call liberal eugenics. On this view, the benefits of genetic enhancement, not only or even primarily in athletics but in a wide variety of areas, justify the practice, assuming the safety of the subjects is protected. The theory is liberal, however, because it contains certain safeguards associated with liberal political perspectives. For example, only general traits, such as enhanced cognitive or physical skills, may be promoted, so that the autonomy of subjects is protected. We would be prohibited, for example, from producing slaves like those in *Brave New World*, who were genetically designed to love their position in life. In this way, genetic enhancement would expand choice, not limit it, by opening new possibilities of achievement without closing doors to realizing a wide variety of plans of life. Second, access to genetic technology would have to be equitable, so that wealthy elites could not attain a genetically dominant position over everyone else. Third, the government should be neutral with respect to what enhancements should be encouraged. The choice should be up to parents and families, and not be backed by an ideal of human good or perfections promoted by the state.

Is liberal eugenics acceptable? While such a broad question takes us well beyond the realm of sports, we can consider a more limited version restricted to sports and athletics. On this view, genetic enhancement of athletes, including engineering germ cell lines, is morally permissible if it either is freely chosen by the athletes themselves (somatic enhancement) or does not limit the autonomy of genetically enhanced children, does not promote unacceptable inequalities, and does not reflect a conception of the human good supported by the state. Before offering a tentative assessment of such a view, let us consider a recent argument directed against genetic enhancement developed by Michael Sandel in his book *The Case Against Perfection*.

Sandel's Case Against Perfection

Sandel's full argument is too complex to do full justice to here, but we will consider one of his most important suggestions: that debates in ethics need not always revolve around such values as liberty, justice, rights, equality, fairness, or autonomy. Thus, in addition to those sorts of considerations, which focus on ways we may wrong others (such as by treating them unfairly or violating their rights), we might also ask what human goods would be lost if we pursued human perfection through genetic enhancement. For example, if all people did was sit around all day watching the lowest level of mind-numbing TV shows, no one's rights might be violated, but such goods as achievement and the pursuit of excellence would have been relegated to the scrap heap. Similarly, Sandel has argued that important human values would be compromised by an extensive practice of genetic enhancement, even if the principles of liberal eugenics were not violated.

What values does Sandel think would be threatened? Although Sandel's argument is quite complex, perhaps his main supporting point is that the *giftedness* of our genetic heritage, by which he means at least that it arises from the natural genetic lottery, would be undermined. Our nature would be something to be mastered and controlled, not a given that we receive but do not design. But why is that important? After all, we have already seen that the link between the natural and the moral is at best tenuous.

However, Sandel is not relying uncritically on the alleged moral value of the natural. Rather, he thinks that if we ceased to admire our natural talents and abilities, and viewed them as simply products of human design, we would lose humility and solidarity with our fellows. Moreover, the scope of our responsibilities would increase to a dangerous extent. We ourselves (or our parents or designers) would be responsible for our genetic design or innate nature itself. As more and more about our genetic makeup came under our control, the areas in which we could be praised or blamed would expand dramatically. "Today, when a basketball player misses a rebound, his coach can blame him for being out of position," wrote Sandel. "Tomorrow the coach may blame him for being too short."[34]

Because we do not genetically design our children, we, as parents, retain what Sandel called an "openness to the unbidden," or an appreciation of the fact that there are significant contingencies in life beyond our control. If we designed our children, we would come more and more to see ourselves as masters of our world that we might come to view as "a gated community writ large."[35]

As more and more of our characteristics become our own achievement (or our own fault), or that of our designers, solidarity with our fellows is threatened. It would less and less frequently make sense to say of someone less fortunate than ourselves that "but for the luck of the draw, that could be me!" According to Sandel, "perfect genetic control would erode the actual solidarity that arises when men and women reflect on the contingency of their talents and fortunes," resulting in a hardened meritocracy where those who did worse than their fellows in any competitive arena—business as well as sport—would have largely themselves (or their designers) to blame.[36]

Criticism of Sandel's Argument

Although a full evaluation of Sandel's overall case against genetic enhancement would take us too far afield, some major difficulties with it can be noted before we turn to its specific application to sports.

First, Sandel seems to assume a fairly sharp line dividing genetic therapies, which restore health but do not enhance abilities, from enhancement. Sandel approves of the former but not the latter. But surely that line is not always a sharp one. For example, would a genetic change in reproductive cells that leads to having offspring with less need for sleep than normal be a therapy for chronic insomnia, or an enhancement that allows bearers to have more waking hours in which to be productive?

More important, the effects of genetic enhancement may not be as dire as Sandel suggested. For one thing, people might not lose their sense of humility in the face of chance because there would still be all sorts of contingencies that would significantly affect human life. These might range from accidents, disasters, and illnesses to various forms of good fortune, such as experiencing chance encounters with strangers who unexpectedly affect our lives, winning the lottery, or getting a lucky bounce on the golf course.

Finally, and perhaps most important, it is far from clear that solidarity with others would suffer simply because we ceased to regard other people as in part products of the natural genetic lottery. Philosophers influenced by the Kantian idea that we should never be treated as mere means would argue that people are owed respect precisely because they are persons, rational creatures capable of choosing a plan of life and of responding to oral imperatives.[37] Thus, we don't deny medical treatment to a person suffering from a heart attack just because we know that individual was a heavy smoker. The duties we have to others, then, may arise more from their status as autonomous persons who can experience happiness and suffering than with whether they themselves are the result of the genetic lottery or parental design. Accordingly, it is at best unclear whether Sandel's overall case against genetic enhancement is successful. But what about its application to the realm of sport?

To Sandel, one of the great attractions of sport is the value of the talents exhibited in the pursuit of excellence. Although we also appreciate the athlete with less innate talent who plays to his or her capacity because of hard work, it is the athletes who exhibit excellence to the highest degree who are regarded almost with awe. A Tiger Woods, LeBron James, Michael Jordan, or Annika Sorenstam are in a class by themselves because of the excellence of their performance. And while none of these athletes could have succeeded without also working at least as hard as their opponents, natural ability also contributed to their success, or at least that is what Sandel would argue.

But if the physical basis of such excellence can be designed or engineered—if it can, in effect, be purchased on the market—its value is cheapened. Similarly, if everyone could be genetically designed to have an outstanding singing voice, such voices would be common, their value cheapened, and our appreciation for their excellence diminished. Thus, Sandel wrote that "a game in which genetically altered sluggers routinely hit home runs might be amusing for a time, but it would lack the human drama and complexity of baseball, in which the greatest hitters fail more often than they succeed."[38]

However, as readers by now might anticipate, Sandel's argument is open to objection. For one thing, as John Rawls famously argued, the natural genetic differences arising from the natural lottery seem arbitrary from the moral point of view.[39] Is it fair if one person is born with extraordinary hand-eye coordination that others, no matter how hard they work, can never come close to matching? Genetic enhancement would enable us to counteract the arbitrary differences arising from the natural lottery and make the playing field more level, at least in terms of innate ability. Competitive athletics would still be meritocratic, however, because differences in work ethic and in such mental characteristics as ability to stay cool under pressure and to develop superior strategic plans for competition would become crucial.[40]

This objection, however, does not seem as strong as it might at first appear. To begin with, some mental characteristics, such as the capacity to remain calm and control one's nerves under the pressure of competition, may also be subject to some degree of genetic enhancement. More important, I suggest that Sandel is right to think that athletics would lose much of their richness and complexity if we took enhancement to the extreme and reduced athletic competition to a kind of mental chess game between physically similar competitors. Indeed, one of the reasons sports are so fascinating is because they present us with the opportunity to see athletes with very different sets of abilities try to maximize their assets, often in very different ways.

I will say more about this point below, but first, we will look at a second objection presented by sports philosopher William Morgan that cuts to the heart of Sandel's position. Morgan acknowledged that many of us today think of sports the way I suggested above, as exhibiting a mixture of striving to excel and maximizing whatever package of natural assets nature has bestowed upon us. But even if this is the dominant conception, why is it sacrosanct? Morgan is ambivalent about whether the present conception also gives weight to the value of compensating for advantages bestowed arbitrarily by nature. But regardless of whether it does or doesn't, why shouldn't the dominant conception of sports as being dependent in part on natural assets be subject to change? Morgan wrote: "What would be morally amiss in reenvisaging sport, in true meritocratic fashion, as primarily a matter of striving for excellence in which, therefore, simply accepting one's talents as they come because they emanate from the genetic lottery is rejected in favor of genetic engineering?"[41]

After all, as Morgan pointed out, the ethos of sport has changed before, often for the better. To cite his own example, in the Academy Award–winning and cinematically spectacular film *Chariots of Fire* (1981), based on the actual careers of two English Olympic runners in the 1920s, one of the characters, Harold Abraham, is ostracized for using a coach. This was viewed as violating the gentlemanly account of sportsmanship and amateurism prevalent at the time. Are competitive athletics today morally worse because that code, perhaps itself founded on a kind of snobbery of social class, has been modified?

Morgan was suggesting that even if the moral ideal of sport proposed by Sandel is dominant, there may be no reason to regard that ideal as morally superior to an alternative ideal that would allow for enhancement as an acceptable means of striving for excellence. How do we choose between ideals, assuming each is compatible with autonomy and the pertinent rights of all competitors?

There is no widely agreed upon answer to this question, which is why some philosophers endorse the idea that the state should not pick sides but remain neutral in such disputes. However, I suggest that sometimes there can be good reasons for preferring one ideal over another. Although I do not know of a knock-down rebuttal to Morgan's line of argument, and believe it may ultimately turn out to be justified, I think there are reasons for exercising caution before adopting it too quickly.

In particular, there seems to be a major difference between revising a paradigm of good sportsmanship to allow for coaching and revising a paradigm of relying on natural assets to allow for genetic engineering of athletes. The former revision seems true to the educational function of sport, which surely is valuable, through which we learn to honestly face our weaknesses and to strive to overcome them. It also coheres with training in other areas of life. Singers, for example, receive assistance from singing instructors to learn how to use their voices correctly. Indeed, almost every other type of excellence relies on mentoring or instruction to harness natural talents and abilities.

Thus, critics of genetic enhancement can reply to Morgan that coaching helps us to develop and use our abilities to meet the challenge of a sport, but genetic enhancement in effect builds us into creatures for whom the challenge of the sport is weakened, or in extreme cases almost erased. Perhaps this is the point of Sandel's example, cited above, of the sluggers in baseball who cheapen the value of the home run. In effect, they were designed to make home runs relatively easy to hit, so that home runs, when hit by the enhanced batters, are not the achievement they were when hit by the likes of Ruth, Maris, and Aaron. Indeed, if the enhancements became great enough, whole sports could become obsolete because they would have become too easy for enhanced athletes to find interesting and too boring for spectators to pay to watch. Perhaps the sports would be made more difficult so that spectators would still attend. Thus, ballparks would be made larger to make home runs harder to hit. As Sandel warned, sports might simply become mere spectacles, perhaps like slam-dunk contests in professional basketball.

Whether these worries are sufficient to undercut Morgan's important line of argument remains to be seen. After all, some of us already are better equipped by the natural genetic lottery than others to succeed in sports. Is genetic enhancement just continuing a benign process we already find in nature (or, as noted above, does it allow us to correct arbitrary genetic inequalities in athletic ability)? Or would genetic enhancement be, in effect, a game changer, substituting one practice with another? In the new practice, the goal would not be to meet the challenge of the sport by using our abilities to the fullest, but to reduce the challenge itself by building in abilities that render it moot.

Further discussion is needed to settle these issues and indeed many more that can be raised about genetic enhancement. However, we have identified several areas of concern that should lead us to proceed with caution in this area. First, the goal of producing "designer children" who result from engineered changes in germ cell lines may raise questions of autonomy that differ in degree, if not in kind, from those already raised by overdirective parents. Second, although such a result is not inevitable, widespread use of genetic enhancement may, just as Sandel suggested, weaken the ties that bind us by radically expanding the range of things in which bad outcomes are considered our fault. As noted earlier, Sandel warned that the future coach might blame the player for being too short, too slow, or too nervous to function well under the pressure of competition. (True, being too short or too slow already are weaknesses in many sports. But to the extent that they are not under the athlete's control, they are not the athlete's *fault* either.) Finally, genetic enhancement, if taken to the extreme, might cheapen the idea of a quest for excellence through challenge by undermining the strength of the challenge itself.

CONCLUDING COMMENT

When I first started writing about performance-enhancing drugs in the 1980s, my initial intuition was that their use to enhance performance in athletics clearly was wrong, and that such a view could be supported by arguments that were evidently sound. In particular, I was, as it turned out, overly impressed by the argument that athletic contests should not be decided by the (so I thought) athletically irrelevant characteristic of how one's body reacted to a drug. After all, I reasoned, just because your body allows you to metabolize a drug more efficiently than mine does, and so to get more benefit from it, doesn't imply you are a better athlete than I am.

I was roused from what surely was a dogmatic slumber when I presented a paper to that effect at the Olympic Scientific Congress, an academic forum held in Eugene, Oregon, before the 1984 Summer Olympic Games. Much to my shock, I found that a number of my fellow panelists in a session on the ethics of using performance-enhancing drugs were sports libertarians, arguing that mentally competent, adult athletes should be free to choose for themselves whether to become users. Even worse, they did not regard my argument as decisive! Indeed, as we have seen, different athletes can react differently to carbohydrate loading, weight training, and even medicine to relieve a precompetition tension headache, but all of these are permitted and are not regarded as undermining the ethic of good competition in sports.

I still regard the use of performance-enhancing drugs in sport as wrong and, as argued earlier, agree with the conclusion that their use should be prohibited by major sports organizations, such as the International Olympic Committee and Major League Baseball. However, I believe such a conclusion is more open to debate than I at first thought and that the pros and cons are more complex than I realized. I hope the preceding discussion has brought out these complexities while showing that, if we work through them, we can still come to a reasonable conclusion about the issue.

I have been even more tentative about genetic enhancement. Like many writers on the subject, I am thrilled by the exciting developments in our understanding of genetics and biology at the cellular level and welcome the medical advances that I hope and expect will arise from such new understandings. But the use of genetic techniques for purposes of enhancement—which of course assumes there can be a distinction, however blurred, between therapy and enhancement itself—raises complex ethical issues. There are many sports libertarians and others who will welcome the perhaps revolutionary changes in sports brought about by technology and who see no threat to athletics in enhancement. They believe it might simply lead to improved sports where enhanced athletes achieve new levels of excellence. Why not explore how far human or even post-human athletes can go in setting new records and achieving what was at one time thought to be virtually impossible? Why not go where no one has gone before?

My own inclination is to be more cautious. I take Sandel's warning about cheapening the idea of achievement in sport seriously, and I have tried to extend it by considering the effect that enhancement might have on the idea of challenge. Today, athletes work hard to overcome what they consider to be worthy obstacles. But would enhancement produce athletes who found the challenges of sports easy and perhaps boring? Or is this worry groundless, since new challenges would always arise—perhaps even the challenge of playing against opponents who also were enhanced?

Of course, there are other possible problems with genetic enhancement in sports, including possible effects on the autonomy and freedom of athletes, or of the children who have been at least partially genetically designed by others. The conclusions suggested by our very preliminary discussion of genetic enhancement surely are tentative and open to criticism and revision. There are important arguments in favor of permitting genetic enhancement of athletes, so long as they are not forced on anyone and the techniques themselves are safe. And yet, our discussion in this chapter suggests that the burden of proof still rests on proponents.

Perhaps a brave new world of enhanced athletes competing at ever higher levels will be exciting and ethically permissible (even desirable). But serious questions still remain, and it is unclear whether the arguments of proponents will be able to survive criticism in the extended debate that is sure to come.

FIVE

GENDER EQUITY IN SPORT
What Does Justice Require?

In all cases, excepting those of the bear and the leopard, the female is less spirited than the male . . . more shrinking, more difficult to rouse to action, and requires a smaller quantity of nutriment. . . . The fact is, the nature of man is the most rounded off and complete.

ARISTOTLE, *HISTORY OF ANIMALS*, BOOK IX

Games and recreation for all types of girls, by all means, which develop charm and social health, but athletic competition in basketball, track and field sports, and baseball? No!

FREDERICK R. RODGERS, *SCHOOL AND SOCIETY*, 1929

The passages quoted above express attitudes that have probably been dominant in most periods of Western civilization. For example, the belief that women are naturally sedentary was reinforced by the customs of Aristotle's culture, which kept women largely confined to the home. But the view that women are neither fit for nor interested in sport, or that it is somehow not appropriate for women to participate in serious athletic competition, was a dominant one even in our own society well into the late twentieth century, and it still influences policy in many parts of the world.

These attitudes have sometimes been challenged, although the challengers frequently have shared more with proponents of the dominant outlook than they might have acknowledged. For example, a Women's Division of the National Amateur Athletic Federation was formed in 1923 to stress "sports opportunities for all girls, protection from exploitation, enjoyment of sports, female leadership [and] medical examinations."[1] The purpose of this "creed," as it was sometimes called, was to promote greater participation in sports for all women rather than to promote intense competition for highly skilled female athletes. "Soon female competitive athletics began to decrease. . . . In place of competition, play days and sports days were organized. This philosophy of athletics for women and girls continued into the early 1960s."[2]

As a result, women and girls who really did want to participate in competition were usually made to feel strange or unfeminine. Former tennis star Althea Gibson described what it was like to be a female athlete in high school in the South in the 1940s: "The problem I had in Wilmington was the girls in school. . . . 'Look at her throw in that ball just like a man,' they would say, and they looked at me just like I was a freak. . . . I felt as though they ought to see that I didn't do the things they did because I didn't know how to and that I showed off on the football field . . . to show there was something I was good at."[3]

Although the attitudes that troubled Gibson have not been completely eliminated, the role of women in competitive sports has changed drastically. The growth of women's and girls' sports and the intensity and quality of their performances in the 1970s and 1980s were unprecedented. For example, in 1970–1971, 3.7 million boys and only 300,000 girls participated in interscholastic sports. By 1978–1979, after the passage of Title IX, an important law with significant implications for gender equity in athletics,[4] 2 million girls were participating in interscholastic athletics. A similar rate of increase in the participation of women in intercollegiate athletics took place during the same period.

Today, in the United States, women and girls continue to participate in organized athletics in significant numbers. By the late 1990s, over 3.7 million boys and nearly 2.6 million girls participated in high-school sports. The 2006–2007 survey of the National Federation of State High School Associations showed that the number of female participants in high-school sports surpassed the 3 million mark for the first time. Over 4 million males participated as well.[5]

However, controversy continues over just how gender equity in athletics is to be understood and over what principles should be employed in its enforcement. In particular, debate about how Title IX should be interpreted and applied to intercollegiate sports remains intense and reflects, if not different conceptions of gender equity, at least different explanations for and responses to the continuing gap between participation rates of males and females in sports.

SORTING OUT THE ISSUES

Title IX and Gender Equity

The changes described above were not easily achieved. *Sports Illustrated*, in a 1973 article, reported widespread indifference, even among educators, to women's athletics.[6] There is no doubt that before the recent increase in interest in women's athletics and the appearance of broader feminist concerns about gender equality, women's sports were separate and unequal. Only a tiny fraction of athletic funding was devoted to the needs of women students, who were excluded from participation in most varsity and intramural programs.

Such inequalities were sometimes defended on the grounds that relevant differences between men and women justified the differences in treatment. Women were held to be less interested in participating than men, or less aggressive and therefore less in need of the outlet of intense athletic competition. Perhaps more often, inequalities between men and women in sports were not explicitly defended but just taken for granted as part of the then normal cultural and social context.

Although, as we will see, biological differences may be relevant to the form that gender equality takes in sports, they hardly justify the exclusion of women from sports or the relegation of women's sports to second-class status. First, the increased participation of girls and women in organized competitive sports is a most convincing refutation of the claim that they have little interest in taking part. (However, as we will see, whether the interest in participation is substantially the same for men and women as groups is still debated.) Second, the claim that women are naturally less aggressive than men, even if it were true, is irrelevant to the right to participate and compete. After all, males who have less need to discharge aggression against other males are not excluded from participation.

Most important, as was argued in Chapters 2 and 3, claims about the value of athletic competition, as well as the explanation of much of the fascination people have with sport, lie much more in the idea of challenge and the pursuit of excellence than in any alleged discharge of aggression. Opponents respond to each other as persons within the rules of the sports contest. Males and females have an equal claim to participation because members of both sexes may seek the challenges presented by competitive sports. Whether or not sports fulfill other social functions, such as allowing for the harmless discharge of aggressive impulses, their value does not lie primarily in such consequences.

What are the requirements of gender equity in athletic programs at the intercollegiate and interscholastic levels? Does equity simply require lack of discrimination? Should the coaches pick the best players, regardless of sex? Does sex equality require separate teams for women? If so, are such teams required in all sports, or just those in which women are allegedly physiologically disadvantaged with respect to men? Are separate teams for physiologically disadvantaged men also required? Does equality require greater emphasis on competition in sports, such as gymnastics, where women may have physical advantages, or the introduction of new sports in which the sexes can compete equally?

We will begin our examination of these and related questions by considering the most important federal legislation addressing gender equality in sports. Title IX of the Education Amendments of 1972 prohibits sex discrimination in federally assisted education programs. The section of Title IX dealing with athletics states that "no person shall, on the basis of sex, be excluded from participation in, be denied the benefits of, be treated differently from another person or otherwise be discriminated against in any interscholastic, intercollegiate, club, or intramural athletic program offered by a recipient" (Section 86:41a). One interpretation of this section requires that athletic programs not make distinctions on the basis of sex. As long as no discrimination takes place, men and women have been treated by the same standards and so have no grounds to complain of inequity. In this view, sex equality in sports requires that we pay no attention to the sex of participants.

The problem with this is that, if it were applied, far fewer women than at present would be competing in interscholastic or intercollegiate varsity contests in such sports as basketball, soccer, lacrosse, track and field, tennis, and golf. Although many women athletes in such sports have more ability than most men, it does appear that males have important physiological advantages, for example, in size and upper-body strength, that make a crucial difference at top levels of competition in many sports.

To avoid the virtual exclusion of women from varsity competition in such sports, particularly the so-called contact sports, Title IX departs from simple nondiscrimination by allowing institutions to sponsor separate teams for men and women. Title IX does not require that there be separate teams for each sex in each sport an institution offers, but it does stipulate that through an appropriate combination of mixed and single-sex teams, the opportunities for each sex be equivalent.

So far, our discussion suggests a distinction between two approaches to equality between the sexes in sport. According to the first, sex equality is equated with blindness to sex. Thus, a coeducational college that pays no attention to the sex of applicants in deciding whom to admit has adopted the first approach. A second approach is to acknowledge sex differences in an attempt to ensure that members of each sex receive equivalent benefits.

The two approaches are, at best, not easily reconciled and, at worst, plainly inconsistent. The first requires that we ignore sex and assign no special significance to it; the second requires that we recognize sex differences when they are relevant to our practices. Title IX allows separate sports programs for each sex and so sometimes requires viewing sex as a relevant ground for making distinctions, but the requirement of being sex blind, that requires no one be treated differently with regard to sex for some purposes, seems sometimes to also be compelling—for example, with respect to voting rights.

Before turning to current controversies over the meaning and application of Title IX, let us examine the two approaches to equality between the sexes, sex blindness and sex pluralism, to find the degree to which each approach is defensible, before applying these concepts to sports and athletics.

However, before we move on, I would like to introduce a terminological distinction that might help to clarify the discussion that follows. To many scholars, "sex" refers to the biological components of our identities, and "gender" deals with socially constructed differences between males and females within a cultural context. This dichotomy, although sometimes useful, may be too simplistic. Biological differences arguably influence cultural contexts in various ways, as when the prevalence of a specific disease causes people to be more conscious of preventive behaviors, and culture can influence biology, as when changes in diet can prevent a genetic disorder from developing. Accordingly, the line between what is biological and what is social may be difficult to draw. In the rest of this chapter, "gender equity" and "gender equality" will be used most often to refer to specific legal and moral issues raised in our own cultural context by Title IX, whereas "sex equality" will be used primarily to refer to broader philosophical issues of equality and justice between the sexes.

Ideals of Sex Equality

Like virtue, honesty, and truth, sex equality has few contemporary opponents, at least in public. However, shallow agreement on the surface may disguise deeper divisions over the nature of sex equality. Just as equal opportunity can be understood in a variety of ways—as requiring simple nondiscrimination, as requiring conditions of background fairness, as requiring equal life chances for representative persons from all major social groups—so, too, there are diverse and competing conceptions of sex equality. Thus, abstract support for a general ideal of sex equality from a variety of perspectives can obscure deep divisions on just how sex equality is to be understood, what it implies in concrete contexts, and how it might best be achieved.

To those who identify sex equality with assimilation, a society has achieved sex equality when, as one writer put it, no more significance is attached to the sex of persons than is attached to eye color.[7] In this view, sex equality is equated with almost total blindness to sex. In the assimilationist society, at least in its most uncompromising form, one's sex would play no role in the distribution of civil rights or economic benefits and, at most, would play a minimal role in personal and social relations. This assimilationist model of sex equality strongly resembles the integrationist ideal of racial equality. In particular, it implies that "separate but equal" is as unacceptable in sex equality as it is in race. The implication for sports is that having separate athletic programs for men and women actually violates what equity and justice require.

Perhaps the principal argument for the assimilationist ideal is that it is required by the value of personal autonomy. Although "autonomy" is far from the clearest notion employed by moral philosophers, it refers to our capacity to choose our actions and determine the course of our own lives. It has to do with self-determination rather than determination by others.

Defenders of the assimilationist ideal argue that it is justified by the moral requirement of respect for the autonomy of women because autonomy requires the withering away of sex roles. As Richard Wasserstrom, a distinguished advocate of the assimilationist ideal, argued, "sex roles, and all that accompany them, necessarily impose limits—restrictions on what one can do or become. As such, they are . . . at least prima facie wrong."[8] Perhaps what Wasserstrom had in mind is that roles set up proper norms of behavior for those who fill them. Deviation from the norm exposes one to criticism from others. Conformity is enforced by social pressure. The effects of sex roles in sports was seen in a 1975 study, which reported that 90 percent of the respondents, selected from the general population, believed that participation in track and field would detract from a female's femininity, whereas only 2 percent thought participation in swimming, a more traditional sport for girls and women, would have the same effect.[9]

No society can exist without roles of any kind. But according to proponents of the assimilationist model of sex equality, sex roles are especially objectionable. Whether they arise from biological differences between men and women or from socialization and learning, they are imposed rather than chosen. As Wasserstrom maintained, "involuntarily imposed restraints have been imposed on some of the most central factors concerning the way one will shape and live one's life."[10]

The sex-blind conception of equality favored by the assimilationist does seem particularly appropriate to many significant areas of life in our society. For example, in basic civil rights and liberties, justice and equity surely are sex blind. Freedom of assembly, religion, or speech are rights of all persons equally regardless of their sex. Similarly, in employment or the distribution of important social benefits, the making of distinctions by sex is arbitrary and unfair.[11]

But should sex equality be identified across the board with blindness to sex, as the assimilationist model requires? Should it apply only to the public realm, or should it apply to the personal lives of individuals as well? What, for example, are we to say of sexual attraction? If sex equality requires blindness to the sex of others, does it follow that people with relatively fixed sexual preferences, whether for members of the opposite sex or their own, are engaged in the social counterpart of invidious sex discrimination?[12] Might there not be other areas, including some in the public realm, such as athletic competition, where the assimilationist model also breaks down? Accordingly, we might want to consider ideals of sex equality other than assimilationism, for the identification of sex equality with sex blindness may not always capture our sense of what is just or reasonable.

In particular, as we have seen earlier, equal treatment in the sense of identical treatment is not always a requirement of justice or fairness. Sometimes, equality is to be understood as requiring equal respect and concern, which in turn requires us to acknowledge the significance of relevant differences among persons.

A second ideal of sex equality, which recognizes the significance of difference, might be called the pluralistic model. As Wasserstrom pointed out, the pluralistic conception of equality is best illustrated by the tradition of religious tolerance in the United States. According to this tradition, religious equality does not require that we accord to religious differences only the significance presently attached to eye color. Rather, a defensible conception of religious equality stipulates that no religion be placed in a position of dominance over others.[13]

Unlike assimilationism, pluralism does not reject the ideal of "separate but equal" out of hand if separation is not coercively imposed by the dominant group and is justified by equal respect for all. Thus, it might allow separate but equal athletic programs for women. Although pluralists reject rigid sex roles, they concur that important sex differences may exist and should be taken into account in an equitable manner in public policy.

Can the pluralist respond satisfactorily to the charge of the assimilationist that any tolerance of sex roles violates personal autonomy by forcing women (and men) into the straightjacket of fixed social expectations? Is pluralism or assimilationism the more defensible model of sex equality? Which approach has the most acceptable implications for sex equality in sports? We will consider these questions in the next section.

GENDER EQUITY IN ATHLETIC COMPETITION

Pluralism and Sports

Much of the controversy over sex equality in sports concerns whether men's and women's athletic programs are being treated equally in our schools, colleges, and universities. Is the women's program receiving its fair share of the budget? Does the women's basketball team enjoy the same kind of publicity as the men's team? Are there equivalent opportunities for men and women to play intramural sports? What does it mean for opportunities to be equivalent?

Such questions presuppose that separate sports programs for men and women are requirements of equity in sport, or are at least permissible ways of achieving it. But there are different and competing conceptions of sex equality, not all of which would endorse separate athletic programs for men and women. Which of the ideals we have considered, assimilationism or pluralism, is more defensible in sports?

The problem with assimilationism in sports is that sex blindness requires us to ignore what seem to be relevant sex-related differences in the average athletic ability of men and women. Generally, women are not as big, as strong, or as fast as men, although there is some evidence that, over long distances, females may show as much or more stamina than males. It does appear that in the popular contact sports, such as football, lacrosse, and basketball, as well as in baseball, soccer, tennis, and golf, the greater size, speed, and strength of men give them a significant physiological advantage over women. In short, if athletic competition were completely sex-blind, women might be virtually absent from sports competition at the highest levels.

Is it true that in most popular sports, men have physiological advantages over women that are sufficient in degree to justify separate athletic programs for each gender? Some might argue that existing differences are largely the result of the past exclusion of women from many sports and that the differences would diminish or even vanish if boys and girls received equal encouragement and training in their athletic endeavors from an early age. That is, on this view, sex differences in athletics are largely the result of cultural practices that have unfairly excluded women from sport.[14]

Although it is true that the gaps in performance between men and women in many elite sports are shrinking, and although elite women athletes outperform almost all men, women athletes have yet to show they can compete successfully against males at the same competitive level of performance in many sports. Thus, as talented as the top-ranked women's college basketball teams at Connecticut or Tennessee have been, size, strength, and speed differences alone make it difficult to see how they could compete successfully against the men's teams from their own institutions.

Granted, this picture may be changing somewhat as women's and men's times edge closer together in some track-and-field events. Annika Sorenstam, perhaps the best female golfer ever, and Suzy Whaley, a club professional from Connecticut, competed in single events on the (male) PGA Tour in the summer of 2003, and young phenomenon Michelle Wie has played in several events on the PGA Tour. None, however, have made the cutoff that qualifies the top part of the field to complete the tournament (although Wie has come close and did very well in the Men's Public Links National Championship, a major amateur event with a strong field that includes many of the nation's top intercollegiate male golfers). Although Wie has decided as of 2009 that she will compete on the LPGA Tour, which is for women only, the highly talented and very powerful young player has not renounced her goal of someday competing successfully against male professionals and qualifying for the prestigious Masters Tournament held annually in Augusta, Georgia.

Be that as it may, it seems difficult to deny that men have physiological advantages over women in most major sports. Separate competitions for each gender seem the best way in at least the immediate future of ensuring that women participate in athletics at elite levels of competition in those sports where males are physiologically advantaged. However, even if this argument does justify separate teams for males and females in intercollegiate or interscholastic competition, it may not do so in a less intense recreational league or intramural program. Moreover, in sports where one sex does not have significant physiological advantages over the other, sex-blind competition may well be desirable or even required. (Mixed competitions, such as mixed doubles in tennis, are another possibility that needs to be considered.)

Finally, if particular women athletes wish to compete against men and are qualified to do so, they should not be prohibited from doing so based simply on generalizations that most women would not be competitive in such situations. A reasonable understanding of equal opportunity minimally would provide persons on an individual basis the chance to compete if qualified to do so, and not prohibit them from doing so on grounds (such as sex) not related to their athletic qualifications.

Determining which sports the argument about physiological differences applies to may be largely an empirical matter. But is the pluralist argument acceptable even in sports played at high levels of competition and in which there are significant physiological differences between the sexes? We will consider two objections to the defense of pluralism based on physiological sex differences. The first is based on appeal to assimilationism. The second maintains that separate sports programs provide women with the illusion of equality rather than the reality.

Evaluating Pluralism in Sports

To an advocate of the assimilationist ideal, sexual pluralism in sports may seem morally pernicious, as pluralism may only express and reinforce the traditional system of sex roles. In other words, "separate but equal" only masks a system that reinforces the inequality of women, just as racial segregation reinforced inequality between whites and blacks in the era of Jim Crow.

Such a rejoinder is implausible for a variety of reasons. For one thing, the point of having separate athletic programs for women is to expand the options available to them. A proponent of pluralism in athletics can argue that separate athletic programs for men and women in sports where performance is affected by physiological sex differences only increase opportunities for women, rather than limiting them in the way that opportunities for blacks were limited with racial segregation. In addition, the participation of women at elite levels in previously male-dominated sports, such as basketball, surely breaks down stereotypes about what sports are appropriate for women.

A proponent of assimilationism might respond that if the ideal of sex blindness was adopted throughout society, it would not matter that few, if any, women played at the higher levels of athletic competition. This is because in the assimilationist society, when an individual's sex would be regarded as no more important than eye color is regarded in our society, it would not be important that nearly all the top athletes were male. At least, it would not be regarded as any more important than the widely acknowledged fact that virtually no individuals under five feet ten inches in height have a chance to play professional basketball.

This rejoinder, in turn, is open to two strong objections. The first is that, because we are not yet in the assimilationist society, it would be unfair to apply the assimilationist ideal only to sports, an area where it would particularly disadvantage women. It is one thing to say pluralism in sports is unnecessary in the assimilationist society but quite another to say it is unnecessary in ours.

This distinction between the ideal and the actual raises a fundamental point. Sometimes, theorists believe they have succeeded when they present a defensible ideal conception of justice, equality, or liberty, and that practical choices will attain the ideal. But this ignores the issue of whether and of how it is morally permissible to reach the ideal.[15] For example, suppose a defensible ideal of equal opportunity required that we abolish the family on the grounds that some families provide advantages to offspring that other families do not. It doesn't follow that individuals presently part of families can just ignore their duties to other family members on the grounds that in an ideal society the family might not exist. Indeed, if there were no way to adopt the ideal without seriously violating duties to members of presently existing families, that ideal may be morally impermissible for us to act upon.

A similar point may apply to the assimilationist ideal of sexual equality. Even if assimilationism is superior to pluralism as an ideal, it seems morally impermissible to introduce assimilationism in sport, where it would disadvantage women, before it is implemented elsewhere in society.

But even leaving aside implementation, it is far from clear that assimilationism is fair, just, and equitable in all contexts. In particular, competitive sports stand as a counterexample to the thesis that recognition of sex differences always involves coercive sex roles. On the contrary, the recognition of sex differences in sports frees women from traditional restrictions and makes it possible for them to engage in highly competitive forms of athletics in a variety of major, traditionally male, sports. In sports, it seems to be assimilationism rather than pluralism that limits opportunities for women.

Similarly, if there are other significant physiological or psychological sex differences between men and women, equality might involve equal respect for such differences rather than denial of their importance. Socializing men and women to ignore such differences or to inhibit gender-linked forms of behavior may be just as subversive of autonomy as the socializing of women to conform to traditional sex roles. Although a conception of sex equality required by justice surely rules out a rigid system of sex roles, it is doubtful that sex equality requires us to forget about one another's sex.[16]

Unfair to Females?

Does pluralism in sports really work to the advantage of women? A critic might respond that if men really are better in certain sports, the women's teams in those sports necessarily will be thought of as inferior. Rather than liberate women, such teams will stigmatize women. As philosopher Betsy Postow has argued, "The number and prestige of sports in which men are naturally superior help perpetuate an image of general female inferiority which we have moral reason to undermine."[17] This perception of inferiority might be thought to account for the generally lower attendance at contests between women's teams as well as generally lower public recognition of the achievements of top women athletes than of top male athletes.

However, as we have already pointed out, if competitive sports were organized according to the assimilationist model, females would be almost absent at the top levels of competition. Is that preferable to pluralism? Is it fairer?

More important, we need to scrutinize the perception that women's sports are inferior versions of male sports. Perhaps, in spite of achievements of such female stars as Candace Parker, Annika Sorenstam, Sue Bird, Michelle Wie, and Venus and Serena Williams, much of the public still perceives such sports as inferior. But is that perception justified?

The claim that in the traditional major sports women's competition is inferior to that of men at similar levels could mean one or more of the following:

1. Women's programs receive less financial and coaching support than men's programs.
2. Contests between women or between women's teams are less interesting and less exciting than contests between men or between men's teams are.
3. Men's teams will always beat women's teams in a particular sport if both play at roughly the same level of competition (e.g., intercollegiate athletics).

What are the implications of these different interpretations for our discussion of sex equality? If claim number one above is true, and women's programs receive less financial and coaching support than men's programs, this only shows that pluralism has not been fully implemented, not that it should be abandoned. The obvious remedy is to provide equivalent support for the women's programs.

Claim number three, however, is likely to be true. It is hardly likely that even a top women's intercollegiate basketball team will be able to beat an average male intercollegiate team. In fact, if claim number three were not true, there would be no need for separate women's sports teams in the first place. What does claim number three imply about pluralism in sports?

Many would argue that claim number three justifies claim number two. It is precisely because men's teams can beat women's teams at similar levels of competition that women's sports allegedly are inferior and uninteresting. Although much of the sporting public may accept such an inference, it is fallacious. Even if the men's team would usually beat the women's team, it doesn't follow that the men's contest would always be more exciting, more interesting, or of greater competitive intensity than the women's contest. It would be just as fallacious to argue that simply because the worst men's professional basketball team would always be able to beat the best boy's high-school team, a contest between two mediocre professional teams would always be more exciting, more interesting, and more competitively intense than a championship game between two top high-school teams.

If what is of major interest in a competitive sports contest is the challenge each competitor or team poses to the other, and the skill, intensity, and character with which the participants meet the challenge, there is no reason why women's contests should be less exciting or less interesting than men's contests. This has long been known in Iowa, where girls' high-school basketball is a state mania, and at the University of Connecticut and the University of Tennessee, where the championship women's teams have huge followings. It surely is accepted by tennis fans that top women stars such as the Williams sisters get as much attention as their male counterparts.

Indeed, in sports such as tennis and golf, as well as in some team sports, such as basketball, one can plausibly argue that the women's game differs from the men's in ways that make it at least as good as a spectator sport. In tennis, the power of male players' serves limits the extent of volleying, but the women's game is characterized more by clever use of ground strokes. In fact, fan interest in women's professional tennis is at least as high as in the men's game. Similarly, in golf, women must have superb timing and coordination to compensate for their relative lack of strength in comparison to males. (In fact, top female players, such as Michelle Wie, hit drives nearly as long as most top male professionals. Some female professional golfers who are small in stature hit drives of 230–260 yards or more, which may indicate that their swings are more efficient than those of a six-foot, two-inch, male who drives 280 yards.) Why shouldn't it be just as exciting and interesting to watch the timing and tempo of a top female player, such as Annika Sorenstam, as it is to watch the force applied by a male player?

In women's basketball, the dunk or jam is virtually absent, and one-on-one moves may be somewhat less spectacular than in the men's game. However, the intelligent use of screens to get open shots, movement without the ball, and brilliant individual play are all there. It is simply a matter of appreciating different aspects of the game as well as the competitive intensity and character of the women playing it.

If women's sports can be as exciting and interesting as men's sports, in part because they are equally competitive and in part because subtly different qualities are being tested, it is hard to see why pluralism in sports necessarily stigmatizes women. Full appreciation of these sports may require better education of the general public, but it is hard to see why women should be denied the opportunity to compete simply because many fans are fascinated, perhaps unjustifiably so, by the power game played by males. Although spectators may in the long run favor aspects of the men's game over the women's game, there is no reason why this *must* happen, and much reason to believe that, in some sports, the women's and men's games, as is presently the case with professional tennis, may turn out to be equally appealing. If such a suggestion has force, it is not that women's sports are inferior, but rather that more of us need to make the effort to appreciate the diverse qualities that are exhibited in athletic competition.

A Pluralist Proposal

Such considerations may have some appeal even to those feminists who have been suspicious of "separate but equal" as a model of sex equality. However, some analysts may take this defense of a pluralist approach a step further. Why not place more emphasis on sports in which "female" abilities or qualities are especially advantageous? The suggestion here is that we redefine our catalog of major sports. The intuitive idea is that equal opportunity, even on the pluralist model, requires more than equal recognition of or appreciation for women's athletics. It also requires equal emphasis on sports in which women can be the top athletes, and not merely the top "women athletes."

Thus, Postow has recommended that we "increase the number and prestige of sports in which women have a natural statistical superiority to men or at least are not naturally inferior."[18] Jane English has given a concrete example of what Postow may have had in mind: "Perhaps the most extreme example of a sport favoring women's natural skills is the balance beam. Here, small size and flexibility and low center of gravity combine to give women the kind of natural hegemony that men enjoy in football."[19] In other words, our traditional catalog of major sports has a built-in bias toward athletic activities favoring men. The way to remedy this bias is not simply to introduce athletic programs that institutionalize female inferiority; rather, we should radically revise our conception of which sports are most worthy of support and attention.

The suggestion that we should learn to appreciate and develop sports that reward the physiological assets of women, just as we now tend to appreciate those that reward the physiological assets of men, does have merit. Properly understood, it does not require the abolition of women's programs in basketball, volleyball, soccer, tennis, and other traditional sports, but the addition and increased support of other sports, such as gymnastics, in which women are physiologically advantaged (or at least physiologically equal).

This suggestion is supported by considerations of fairness and equity, but two competing considerations have to be kept in mind. First, individuals may continue to prefer traditional or currently more popular sports even after they are introduced to alternatives. The general public may continue to prefer watching and playing basketball and football to watching or participating in gymnastics and high diving. This may be as true for the majority of female athletes as much as anybody else, especially since traditional sports seem open to a wider variety of age groups and body types than gymnastics.

Moreover, to require or compel individuals to attend or participate in certain kinds of sports and prohibit them from playing others would be a serious violation of individual liberty. It is one thing, for example, to require that schools introduce students in physical education classes to a wide variety of sports and athletic activities, many of which are not biased in favor of male physiology, but it is quite another to require that female athletes compete in such activities, even if they are more interested in playing basketball, soccer, lacrosse, tennis, or golf. It is possible that a broad program of public education could change individual preferences; however, such a program, if morally permissible, must appeal to people as autonomous moral agents and not dictate in advance which sports people are required to find more interesting or of greater worth.

Finally, it is important to remember that women's sports can be just as interesting and competitive as the men's version. If so, the claim that pluralism in athletics promotes a stereotype of female inferiority is, at best, highly questionable.

Does Sex Equality Require Forgetting Sex?

The conception of sex equality as blindness to sex is most plausible in the realm of civil and political rights and in the economic marketplace. On this view, the right to vote, the right to freedom of speech, and the right to be free of discrimination in the marketplace should not be dependent upon one's sex.

But whereas assimilationism, or blindness to sex and gender differences, may be the favored conception of sex equality in many areas, such as civil rights, it is doubtful if it is acceptable across the board in all areas of human concern. As our discussion of sports suggests, the assignment of significance to sex is not always a form of sexism.

We have not been shown, then, that separate athletic programs for men and women in those sports where one sex is at a physiological disadvantage are morally suspect or illegitimate. Unlike the doctrine of "separate but equal" in the context of racial segregation, separate athletic programs do not stigmatize one group or the other, are not imposed against the will of either sex, and actually enhance the freedom and opportunity of the previously disadvantaged group. Sports seem to provide a model of a defensible pluralistic approach to sex equality. In sports and perhaps in other areas as well, sex equality does not require blindness to sex.

LEGISLATING EQUALITY: TITLE IX AND ITS CRITICS

What are the implications of the preceding discussion for policy? Much discussion focuses on Title IX of the Educational Amendments of 1972, the federal legislation that applies to gender equity in athletics in educational programs. Let us examine, first, the history of Title IX, and then issues arising from the interpretation of Title IX advanced by the Office of Civil Rights in 1996 to see why this legislation, which has done so much to promote greater equality in athletics, is also the center of a controversy over how best to achieve gender equity in athletics.

The Development of Title IX

As we already have noted, women's participation in competitive athletics was significantly limited before the civil rights movement, the rise of feminism, and the passage of Title IX itself. In the early 1970s, more than 4 million boys participated in high-school athletics compared to approximately 300,000 girls. Gross disparities in participation and expenditures on males and females also were the rule in intercollegiate athletics. James Michener, writing about the period before promulgation of Title IX, reported that "one day I saw the budget of . . . a state institution (a university), supported by tax funds, with a student body divided fifty-fifty between men and women. The athletic department had $3,900,000 to spend, and of this, women received exactly $31,000, a little less than eight-tenths of one percent. On the face of it, this was outrageous."[20]

The passage of Title IX, along with other concurrent social trends, including the emphasis of the early feminist movement on equality for women, resulted in almost immediate jumps in participation by females in athletics and increases in expenditures by educational institutions on athletic programs for women and girls. By 1979, 2 million girls were participating in high-school athletics, compared to about 300,000 before 1972.

However, Title IX was never uncontroversial. In testimony before Congress even in the 1970s, critics charged that it would lead to quotas for female athletes and argued that, at the very least, revenue-producing sports such as football should be exempted from its requirements. Proponents of the legislation responded that the new legislation was not designed as a quota system but as a way to level the playing field by providing women with opportunities in intercollegiate athletics equal to those enjoyed by men.[21] These same controversies, as we shall see, continue today.

Perhaps part of the reason for the continuing controversy can be found in the history of Title IX. Although passed by Congress in 1972, it was only in the late 1990s that a consistent and relatively clear interpretation of the legislation emerged and began to be been applied by the courts, although this interpretation has been the subject of bitter controversy.

Two court cases explain the delay and much of the confusion about implementation. In *Grove City v. Bell*, decided in 1984, the Supreme Court ruled that Title IX applied only to programs directly receiving federal funds.[22] On this interpretation, if College X's physics department received a federal grant, Title IX would apply only to the physics department, and not to the college's athletics program. Since few, if any, athletic programs at high schools or colleges and universities receive federal grants, the Grove City case exempted them from legislative review under Title IX. This led Congress to pass the Civil Rights Restoration Act, which responded to the decision in *Grove City*, in 1988. This act made Title IX apply to an entire institution that received either direct or indirect federal aid. In the second case, *Franklin v. Gwinnett County Public Schools*, decided in 1992, a unanimous Supreme Court ruled that plaintiffs filing Title IX lawsuits were entitled to punitive damages if it had been found that the institution being sued intentionally took steps to avoid compliance with Title IX.[23] In effect, this decision put real teeth into the legislation—namely, the threat of having to pay damages for certain sorts of failures to comply.

Thus, disagreements about the scope and enforcement of Title IX help to explain delays in implementation. Even assuming goodwill on the part of educational institutions, it was unclear how to apply the legislation and what the remedy for failure to comply might be in different kinds of cases.

In 1990, the Office of Civil Rights (OCR) issued a manual for interpreting Title IX that, along with clarifications made in 1996, has become authoritative. The OCR interpretation included what has been called the "three-part test" that has become the center of controversy. Let us consider what Title IX, as it has evolved and as it has been interpreted by the Office of Civil Rights, actually requires.

What Does Title IX Require?

The OCR identifies three major areas of compliance with Title IX: athletic scholarships, accommodation of athletic interests and abilities, and other athletic benefits and awards. The first applies only to those institutions in Divisions I and II of the National Collegiate Athletic Association (NCAA) that award athletic scholarships. It requires roughly that male and female athletes receive proportional shares of available scholarships. The third requires that educational institutions treat male and female athletes equitably in the distribution of fields for practice, equipment, access to trainers, expense allowances, and the like. We will be concerned in our discussion primarily with the second area, accommodation of athletic abilities and interests, since it clearly is most fundamental.

Before turning to that, it will be useful to consider the general understanding of equity that seems to underlie Title IX. It might be natural to assume that Title IX requires identical treatment for men's and women's intercollegiate sports in the sense, say, of requiring identical expenditures on each. However, Title IX is better understood as requiring equivalent treatment rather than identical treatment. Consider an example from another area. Suppose that half the students in a particular school want to develop their musical abilities and half want to learn computer science. The school buys musical instruments adequate for instruction and provides for sufficient computers and faculty to allow the formation of a computer science program. But because computers cost more than musical instruments, the school spends several times the money it spends on the musicians on the students in the computer program. Even so, the opportunities are equal for both groups in the sense of being equivalent. All the students have an equal chance to pursue their interests. Another way of putting it, following the legal philosopher Ronald Dworkin, is to say that both groups of students have been treated with equal respect and concern.[24]

This example suggests that "equal expenditures" and "equal opportunities" are two distinct notions. The examples have clear analogies in the world of sports. For example, suppose equipment for men's teams in a particular sport is more expensive than equipment for the parallel women's team, or that referees for one gender's games are paid on a higher scale than referees for the games of the other gender. Such differences are allowable. Thus, the set of principles underlying Title IX seems to require equal respect and concern for each gender, understood as provision of equivalent opportunities, rather than identical treatment.

Keeping the distinction between identical and equivalent opportunities in mind, let us turn to the OCR's three-part test for compliance. In particular, the OCR proposes that institutions can comply with Title IX in accommodating athletic abilities and interests by meeting any one requirement of the following three:

1. By providing opportunities for participation in the intercollegiate athletics program for students of each sex that are substantially proportionate to their respective enrollments in the student body as a whole.
2. If not, the institution can comply by showing a history and continuing practice of expansion of the intercollegiate athletics program responsive to developing interests and abilities of members of the underrepresented sex.
3. If not, the institution still can comply by showing that the interests and abilities of the underrepresented sex are "fully and effectively accommodated" by the existing program.

Legal compliance is established by satisfying any one of the three tests. An intercollegiate athletic program that fails one prong of the three-part test might still be in compliance with Title IX by satisfying another. The first is regarded as a "safe harbor" in the sense that a finding of proportionality will at the very least establish a strong and virtually overwhelming presumption of compliance. However, failure to show proportionality (it is doubtful whether many institutions of higher education in the country now satisfy this requirement as strictly construed) is not sufficient to establish noncompliance if the other criteria are satisfied.

The three-part OCR test has some important similarities to what might be called a presumptive approach to gender equity. It presumes that both genders will be treated equally, but acknowledges the possibility of there being allowable reasons for inequality. Representation of gender in proportion to its share of the overall student body will normally be taken as virtually conclusive evidence of equal treatment. If proportionality cannot be satisfied, inequality can be justified by showing compliance with one of the other two prongs of the test. Moreover, in assessing whether the interests of the underrepresented gender have been "fully and effectively accommodated," the assumption is that each gender will be treated equally in the absence of justifying reasons for inequality. But justifying reasons are possible. For example, sometimes where there is interest in developing a new women's sport at an institution that does not satisfy the first two prongs, it is reasonable for the institution to expect that interest to continue for a sustained period of time and for sufficient ability to be demonstrated by the prospective participants before taking steps to support the new sports team.

What counts as a justifiable reason for inequality often will be controversial. Does the past success of the men's basketball team at a Division I institution justify their playing a more nationally prominent schedule than the less successful women's team? What if the athletic director promises to upgrade the women's schedule as soon as the team develops sufficiently to compete successfully at that level? Should a 98-pound female gymnast receive the same daily meal allowance as a 275-pound male lineman on the football team when the teams are on the road? Is it an inequity if the lineman is given a greater allowance because he needs more food?

Rather than pursuing the numerous questions that could be raised about what counts as justifiable reasons for inequality, which cannot all be explored here, we shall focus on the more useful task of examining fundamental issues raised by the OCR three-pronged test, particularly those concerning proportionality and the effective accommodation of interests. Because these areas are fundamental, exploring them may help shed some light on other important issues of gender equity that are likely to arise.

Proportionality

The idea that men and women should be represented in an educational institution's athletic program in proportion to their representation in the student body initially sounds plausible. After all, if participation in athletics provides significant benefits and opportunities, and if there is no reason to favor one gender in the distribution of these benefits and opportunities, then one would expect them to be made available to both genders equally. So if 60 percent of the student body is male and 40 percent female, in the absence of discrimination one would expect to find that about 60 percent of the institution's athletes were male and about 40 percent female.

But there are problems with this initial expectation. For one thing, there is about a 3 to 2 ratio of male to female participants in high-school (interscholastic) athletics.[25] Given that there remains a disproportion in the representation of each gender in sports at the precollege level, is it reasonable to expect the proportion of women participating at the college level, which is significantly more demanding than at the high-school level, to suddenly jump?[26] If not, say the critics of the proportionality requirement, then it is unreasonable to place so much emphasis on proportional representation in the first place. Where will the additional female athletes needed to achieve proportionality come from?

This difficulty leads critics to raise a major objection to the proportionality requirement—namely, that regardless of the intentions of its proponents, proportionality functions to decrease opportunities for male athletes rather than increasing them for female athletes. That is because there are two ways to remedy the perceived underrepresentation of women. The first is to raise the proportion of women participating; the second is to reduce the proportion of men participating.

Suppose an institution is 60 percent male and 40 percent female. Suppose further that 70 percent of its 1,000 intercollegiate athletes are male and only 30 percent of its intercollegiate athletes are female. The school could try to raise the percentage of female athletes to around 40 percent, but it may find it very difficult to do so, perhaps largely because of the expense involved and also because of the difficulty of finding interested female athletes. Instead, it can cut male teams and reduce the percentage of men playing to, say, under 60 percent of all athletes. That is, by cutting sports involving 300 male athletes, the school would be left with 700 athletes, 400 of whom would be male and 300 female. Males would now only constitute 57 percent of all athletes and women would constitute 43 percent. In other words, by cutting men's sports, the institution could achieve proportionality and a "safe harbor" from further legal action without adding an additional opportunity for even one female athlete to participate.

Although this hypothetical is undoubtedly an extreme example, the provision that proportionality is a safe harbor from legal action can act as an incentive to trim men's programs and appear to provide equal access to underrepresented women athletes without increasing opportunities for women. In fact, critics of the proportionality requirement charge that numerous less-visible men's sports teams seem to have been cut at various institutions, quite possibly in part to achieve a more respectable-looking ratio of female to male athletes, including well over 150 wrestling programs and many men's tennis, gymnastics, swimming, and golf teams.[27] Accordingly, the requirement of proportionality may have the unintended consequence in American colleges and universities of decreasing the number of slots on athletic teams, possibly without significantly increasing opportunities to participate for women, but mainly through decreasing them for men.

There are two important responses to this kind of criticism. The first is that Title IX does not require satisfaction of the proportionality requirement. Institutions can comply by satisfying one of the other two prongs of the OCR three-part test. The second is that Title IX does not require institutions to eliminate less-visible men's programs, but does allow them to shift resources from high-visibility and arguably bloated men's sports, particularly college football, to women's sports programs.

Critics of proportionality might reply that, although these responses may blunt some of the force of the objection that proportionality reduces opportunities for men without raising them for women, each response also faces difficulties. The first response is that colleges and universities need not achieve proportionality but can satisfy one of the other two requirements laid down by OCR. This point is correct, but in assessing its significance, practical difficulties also need to be considered. Thus, an institution could continue to expand its athletic program for the underrepresented gender (although at some point of expansion it would achieve proportionality and both requirements would be satisfied).

This approach surely is acceptable and is perhaps the fairest method of compliance, but it also raises some difficult questions. In particular, it is important to remember that questions of distributive justice in intercollegiate athletics arise at least at two levels: distribution of resources within the athletic program and distribution within the university generally. Thus, should colleges and universities be required to increase expenditure on athletics at a time when many academic needs are unmet because of lack of funding? Is it more important to add a women's team than to support faculty, provide financial aid to needy students, or make computer facilities more accessible to everyone in the institution? Expansion, then, may be an ideal solution in some contexts but may not be affordable or educationally warranted in others.

Proponents of the proportionality requirement, arguably with good reason, are unlikely to regard such a retort as fair or reasonable. After all, they can point out, men's athletic programs often are extremely costly. Why not reduce funds allocated to them in order to add women's teams rather than blaming women's sports for taking funds from academics and financial aid?

This reply, however, leads to another difficulty. Although it might be possible for some resources to be shifted from football, and perhaps from other high-budget men's sports, to women's programs, particularly at the large Division I football powers, this may not be the case for smaller colleges. Indeed, the implications would be quite different at nonscholarship schools or those competing at the Division III level. In Division III, transferring support to football from other sports might result in smaller rosters, which would mean that those young men at the bottom of the team's ability level could lose the opportunity to play. Since such athletes are playing primarily for love of the game, it is, at best, unfortunate that they would bear the brunt of compliance (although it is true that some funds might be freed up that could be diverted to the women's program).

If this point has force, the move to achieve proportionality by shifting resources from football, while justifiable in many contexts, does not entirely avoid the difficulty of imposition of costs to men. Major college football teams could continue to play at an elite level after, say, a 5 to 10 percent cut in the athletic scholarships they offer, with consequent increased participation by walk-on football players who compete for love of the game. Indeed, under present rules, elite Division I institutions often have a greater number of scholarship players on their football roster than the number of players on the roster of a typical NFL team, so it is hard to believe some cuts in roster size would significantly reduce the quality of play in intercollegiate football. Nevertheless, the slogan "Cut big football budgets" is not necessarily an across-the-board solution to the problems raised by proportionality, particularly at the schools that play football but do not offer athletic scholarships and do not have bloated budgets. At these schools, cuts in rosters would affect walk-on players without necessarily adding opportunities for females.

What of the point that women may not be as interested as men in participating in intercollegiate athletics? In other words, the argument that each gender should be proportionately represented in the university's intercollegiate athletic program presupposes that the members of each gender have an equal interest in participating. It is that very presupposition that critics of proportionality call into question.

In particular, proponents of proportionality reply that females in America have traditionally been discouraged from participating in athletics and are only now beginning to overcome the socialization that has inhibited participation. Therefore, rates of participation are not adequate indicators of true interest. If colleges and universities provide additional women's sports, the participants will eventually come.

But are colleges and universities required to respond to purely hypothetical interests that some women would have had or might have had if they had been socialized differently? Many observers would say yes. After all, if participation in athletics has important educational, personal, and recreational benefits, why shouldn't women be especially encouraged to participate? Similarly, shouldn't the university also take it as part of its mission to expose students to great literature even though they have no interest in it (or even desire to avoid it!)?

Proponents of proportionality add that many more women than those who try out for teams may have an interest in athletics but do not express it for lack of encouragement. Indeed, what counts as an expression of interest in athletics? At the very least, there is an obligation to go beyond crude measures, such as how many women try out for teams, before we conclude that women have less interest in athletics than men. For example, would more women try out if they were encouraged to do so, if a different range of sports was offered, or if the university recruited in a wider range of geographic areas?

What should we conclude about this debate? First, both sides have points of some intellectual merit. The proponents of proportionality argue with plausibility that expressed preferences cannot simply be taken for granted when such preferences have been formed in a social climate that may reflect negative stereotypes about women in sports. Critics of proportionality have a point when they argue that however well intentioned the proponents may be, proportionality in practice is likely to result in further cuts in men's sports, possibly without the compensatory addition of sports for women. It is also far from certain that women's interest in participation is exactly the same as men's. Some scholars have argued that women and men differ in the moral reasoning they typically employ and in the way they socialize.[28] Although such scholarship must be assessed critically, it does suggest that not all gender differences are superficial. Could sex and gender differences also affect preferences for recreation?

In view of these conflicting arguments, it is natural to wonder whether compromise is possible. Although I doubt that any compromise will be fully satisfactory, the following suggestions may help carry the debate between proponents and critics of proportionality closer to a common ground.

First, more emphasis should be placed on fully accommodating the interests of the underrepresented gender, usually women, as required by one of the prongs of the three-part test, and less on proportionality. The usual objection to this is that simply continuing to add varsity sports for women is too expensive, diverting scarce resources from more basic educational purposes. But this rejoinder is not necessarily decisive. First, as suggested above, funds sometimes, and perhaps quite often at the Division I level, could be diverted from expensive men's programs without necessarily cutting sports or even slots on team rosters. For example, many teams could schedule more games locally and cut back on regional and national travel. Similarly, recruiting restrictions could be tightened by cutting back the often large budgets devoted to attracting student-athletes to the institution, most often for high-profile men's sports. (This might require the adoption of common guidelines by all institutions in a conference so that no one institution would be placed at a competitive disadvantage.)

Second, expansion of opportunities for women need not always mean the addition of varsity sports. In fact, in view of the nationwide disproportion of males to females in interscholastic varsity sports in the United States, the addition of developmental programs for women might promote the lifetime involvement of women in athletics without necessarily leading to the addition of full-fledged varsities. Perhaps what would be more appropriate than the addition of varsity sports, in some circumstances, would be the addition of more lower-level recreational programs designed to involve large numbers of women in sports. The addition of a varsity team or two hardly fulfills such a role and surely is better justified for individuals who are already strongly interested in participating. Varsity sports demand commitment and competitive intensity and seem most appropriate for those who are already interested in athletic competition.

This does not mean that institutions should be able to satisfy Title IX "on the cheap," say, by adding disorganized and underfunded intramural leagues. The suggestion is that genuine developmental opportunities, including expert coaching and opportunities to develop skills through training, be made available to significant numbers of women. Although significant expense would be required, it should be less than the continual addition of varsity sports and may eventually increase the overall interest of women in athletics.

Third, compliance with the proportionality requirement should be regarded as a last resort when it is achieved only by cutting men's sports. Institutions that attempt to comply by such means should have the burden of proof on them to show that less drastic means of compliance could not reasonably have been expected to work. Could travel schedules for men's teams have been reduced, recruiting budgets cut, or even slots trimmed from some rosters, rather than actually eliminating a whole sport? Simply cutting men's sports does not result in increasing opportunities for women and should be an acceptable form of compliance only when it is a last resort to satisfy the law.

Finally, in the competition for scarce resources, it should not be forgotten that athletics help participants in meeting challenges, in developing dedication and commitment, in finding self-esteem, and in working for a common goal with people from different cultural, religious, and socioeconomic backgrounds, benefits that should be as available to women as to men. In short, athletics can have a significant educational component for all participants. We will explore this point more fully in later chapters, but it is important to ensure that sports are not assigned too low a priority when the allocation of resources is considered. Although fundamental academic needs normally should take priority over athletic needs, it is not so clear that less fundamental concerns also should always come first. For example, is the addition of significant athletic opportunities for women always less important than the addition of administrative positions or renovation projects?

Our discussion, while raising questions about proportionality, has not called for its elimination but instead has attempted to find some common ground between the critics and the proponents of proportionality. Our proposals for compromise are simply a first attempt to reach a common ground between sides on the proportionality debate. Perhaps they suggest, however, that turning gender equity in sport into a zero-sum contest between men and women is far from the best strategy to pursue. Although transfer of resources from men's to women's athletics may well be called for, particularly in large Division I institutions when budgets for high-profile men's sports are out of line and when all three prongs of the test are unsatisfied, the cutting of less visible men's sports without the addition of new opportunities for women should be a last resort for achieving gender equity in intercollegiate sports.

Equivalent Opportunity

Although the public debate about proportionality has made Title IX seem more about the quantitative aspect of compliance, when seen as a whole, the legislation is best understood as requiring *equivalent* rather than identical opportunities for each gender. Thus, Title IX does not require that total expenditures on men's and women's sports be identical, and even allows for different expenditures in parallel sports if differences arise from such allowable factors as differences in costs of equipment for each group. Moreover, as argued below, the notion of equivalent treatment seems more appropriate a standard for a broad theory of gender equity in athletics than does, say, an identical distribution of resources to each gender.

But what makes opportunities equivalent? There is no easy answer to this question. Once the shift is made away from quantitative criteria that can be measured in dollars and cents, greater weight must be put on qualitative judgments, which, although they may not be "subjective," may well involve controversial and complex value judgments. A full examination of the issues that arise in evaluating whether opportunities are equivalent is not possible here. Factors that would clearly be relevant include the availability and quality of coaching, the availability of practice facilities, equal good-faith efforts in encouraging participation by members of each sex, and promoting women's sports as well as major men's sports.

Thus, educational institutions committed to equality should provide equal media coverage for all teams. However, the games that fans choose to attend, or the publicity the external media decide to devote to particular teams and sports, will often be beyond the control of the school or university. Moreover, it is appropriate that teams that are in contention for regional or national championships receive more attention than teams that are not, but colleges and universities normally should provide similar support for similarly successful teams regardless of gender.

Indeed, superior performance and a supportive institution can generate large, enthusiastic crowds and frequent appearances on national television for women's Division I teams, as demonstrated by the recent successes of the women's basketball teams at the University of Connecticut, Stanford, and the University of Tennessee. The players on the University of Connecticut women's team have attracted wide attention throughout the nation as well as in New England and have been excellent role models both academically and athletically. Star players in the college games, such as Sue Bird and Maya Moore of Connecticut, and Candace Parker, who starred at Tennessee, not only have demonstrated excellence on the court but also have attracted fans to the women's game from all around the United States. Yet, in spite of the presence of such prominent women players, the National Basketball Association (NBA), the professional league for men, still attracts far more national attention and fan support than the Women's National Basketball Association (WNBA), the professional league for women.

Are there instances where the support provided for men's and women's programs should not be equivalent? One kind of case might involve nationally recognized men's intercollegiate teams in such major sports as basketball and football. These sports are alleged to generate huge amounts of revenues and support for their home universities—income that supposedly helps to support not only non-revenue-producing men's teams but also women's teams. Thus, national television networks pay over $1 billion for multiyear rights to televise the NCAA Men's Basketball Championship, and these revenues are distributed among NCAA member institutions to support such activities as participation in national championships by teams in lower-profile or lower-division sports. When men's teams can generate significant income and support, is it legitimate to provide them with such extras as national scheduling, a greater number of coaches, advantageous practice times, and extensive support in the area of public relations?

In considering this issue, it should be noted that men's football and basketball often not only fail to produce a profit but frequently operate deep in the red. Although figuring out just what revenues intercollegiate sports bring in can be complicated, the idea of a revenue-producing sport is more often myth than reality. Thus, "in 1997, fewer than half of the Division I programs (43 percent) reported 'profits' and that the average 'deficit' reported at the other programs was $2.8 million."[29] Although the major men's teams of several major colleges and universities do bring in enormous income, the argument for the special treatment of men's programs in major sports, based on their capacity to generate income, applies to fewer institutions than is often thought. The most recent data supplied by the NCAA show that only eighteen athletic programs, all in the elite Football Bowl section of Division I, generated a profit for the period covered in the report, 2004–2008.[30]

What about institutions where the men's programs in high-visibility sports do generate large amounts of revenue? Even though the argument for special treatment may have some force in such contexts, such a program should be implemented only when certain other conditions are also satisfied. These conditions should be based upon justifiable requirements designed to ensure that the assignment of special status to men's teams in major sports does not block the emergence of women's athletics or deny them the chance to achieve "showcase" status of their own. If we do not accept such conditions of equity, we allow the utility produced by major sports to override the claims of each person to equal respect and equal consideration. The result of such a view is that the individual is reduced to a mere resource for use by others. If we want to respect individuals and their rights, we cannot allow a concern for efficiency alone to override concern for persons and their entitlements.

What moral limitations might apply to institutions where large revenue-producing sports warrant special consideration? It is difficult to formulate an exhaustive list, but perhaps these guidelines can serve as a basis for discussion:

1. The revenues generated, over and above those covering expenses, either must go into the general university budget for the benefit of the entire university community or must be distributed within the athletic program, so that the women's sports program (or perhaps lower-profile men's and women's sports) receives the greatest benefit.
2. The university must be making significant efforts to ensure that some equivalent number of women's sports have a reasonable opportunity to achieve the status of the showcase men's sports.

These criteria ensure that broad segments of the university community can benefit from the revenues generated by the men's program, *with* emphasis on providing greater funding of the lesser-funded sports programs (or to support general academic concerns, such as providing financial aid for needy students), so arguably they could be accepted by all members of the university from a position of impartial choice. That is, following the suggestion made in John Rawls's monumental work *A Theory of Justice*, inequalities can be just when they operate to improve the situation of the less advantaged.[31] Impartial members of the university community—for example, those who reason as if they did not know their position in the athletic program—would have every reason to favor a solution that would work to their benefit whether they participated on a high-profile men's sport or in the women's program.[32] The same principles should also apply to high-profile women's programs, such as the Connecticut women's basketball team, when they generate significant revenues.

So far, we have been considering what the standard of equivalent treatment for men's and women's athletics implies for funding; however, problems with equivalency arise in other areas as well. Are the coaches in the men's and women's program similarly qualified? Are practice times allotted equitably? Are facilities shared? Are women's teams relegated to inferior fields or gyms?

As there is no precise or exhaustive formula for determining what counts as equivalent support, the trick is to strike a balance between blind adherence to a frequently inequitable status quo and too rigid a commitment to inflexible requirements of absolutely identical treatment. For better or worse, the attainment of equity is likely to rest far more on the sound judgment of men and women of good will than on quantitative formulas or rigid principles applied in ignorance of the particular context. Accordingly, even though the formula of equivalent support and respect is vague and raises problems that cannot be dealt with here, it seems far more acceptable than requiring rigid identity of outcomes regardless of differences between the men's and women's athletic programs in specific contexts.

CONCLUSIONS

This chapter has argued for two main conclusions. First, it has maintained that sex equality is not always to be equated with blindness to sex. In particular, the ideal of sex equality as sexual assimilation (sex blindness) seems inappropriate as an ideal to apply across the board to the realm of sports, at least at present. Second, it has been argued that the general emphasis of Title IX on equivalent opportunities for each sex in sports is more justifiable than strict requirements of identical treatment. The operative principle should be equal concern and respect for all participants, and this may sometimes justify differences in actual treatment, sometimes including differences in expenditures between men's and women's athletic programs.

In addition, we have seen that the proportionality requirement has been criticized as too rigid a tool for achieving equity, since it can be satisfied by eliminating opportunities for men without increasing them for women. However, we have argued not that the proportionality requirement should be eliminated but rather that it should be used judiciously and, in particular, only as a last resort when it leads to the elimination of sports for men without increasing opportunities for women.

Our discussion also has raised broader concerns about the nature of sex equality and the evaluation of the assimilationist and pluralist models that go well beyond sports and athletics. Insofar as issues that arise in sports contribute to this broader discussion, they suggest that assimilationist ideals do not easily fit all areas of human life. Thus, one implication of the examination of questions of gender equity and sex equality in sport is that sex equality does not always require forgetting sex but sometimes demands showing equal respect for difference.

SIX

SPORTS ON CAMPUS
Intercollegiate Sports and Their Critics

On the surface and to the casual observer, intercollegiate athletics may appear to be a healthy segment of the American sporting scene. The NCAA men's basketball Division I championship is one of the most popular sporting events in the United States and attracts attention throughout the world. Big-time college football has long held the national limelight, and programs such as those at Notre Dame, Florida, and Penn State have national as well as regional followings. In the 2002–2003 season, the popular University of Connecticut women's basketball team set a record for consecutive wins by a women's team. The team has contributed significantly to the growing attention received by women's college basketball in subsequent years, setting a new record for consecutive wins in 2009–2010.

College athletics have provided sports fans with many thrilling moments over the years. These moments include Michael Jordan's shot that gave North Carolina the NCAA basketball championship over Georgetown in 1982, when Jordan was still relatively unknown, and the last-minute win by Ohio State over Miami in the 2003 Fiesta Bowl in a game that decided the national championship. Even more recently, the success in 2007 of the previously unheralded University of Hawaii's football team thrilled fans of college sports across the country.

But are exciting contests and superb athletes the whole story about college sports? Is there an ethically questionable side to intercollegiate athletics? What about the scandals that continually seem to surface in college sports? Do intercollegiate athletics actually harm the academic and educational functions of the university?

Public criticism of intercollegiate athletics in the United States goes back at least to 1905, when President Theodore Roosevelt summoned the presidents and football coaches of Harvard, Yale, and Princeton to the White House in an attempt to reduce the extreme level of violence then prevalent in the game. In our own day, criticism has focused on the scandal-plagued programs of the large Division I institutions, which offer athletic scholarships and tend to dominate intercollegiate sports. Such scandals have involved academic fraud, the alleged coddling of athletes who have behaved outrageously, and cheating in the effort to recruit the most talented high-school athletic stars. In contrast, intercollegiate athletics at the level of the Ivy League, the highly selective liberal arts colleges, such as those that are members of the New England Small Colleges Athletic Conference (NESCAC), of which my own institution is a member, and the University Athletic Association (UAA), as well as at academically highly respected but also athletically elite Division I universities such as Duke and Stanford, are still thought of as relatively pure examples of what college sports at their best should be. But, as we will see, even that view has come under fire.

Thus, only a few months after North Carolina's victory over Georgetown in 1982, the game that brought Michael Jordan to national attention, another national basketball power, the University of San Francisco (USF), which in the past had been represented by such great players as Bill Russell and K. C. Jones, announced that it had dropped intercollegiate basketball to preserve its "integrity and reputation." According to the Reverend John Lo Shiavo, then president of USF, people at the university (presumably in the athletic program) felt that they had to break NCAA rules in an attempt to remain competitive in big-time intercollegiate athletics.[1]

For example, in one of the most serious of recent abuses involving academics, an NCAA investigation of the University of Minnesota men's basketball program found that from 1994 to 1998, a secretary in the athletics academic counseling office, who was also employed as a tutor for the team, was involved in preparing about four hundred pieces of course work, including providing substantive material for papers, for student athletes in the program. The head coach of the basketball team, Clem Haskins, was found to be "knowledgeable about and complicit in the academic fraud" involved. According to the NCAA investigation, "the violations were significant, widespread, and intentional. More than that, their nature—academic fraud—undermined the bedrock foundation of a university and . . . damaged the academic integrity of the institution."[2] Unfortunately, such cases of academic fraud involving athletes are not just onetime events. In 2007, for example, more than twenty Florida State University football players had to miss the Gaylord Hotels Music City Bowl game against the University of Kentucky because of their alleged involvement in academic fraud involving an Internet course in which they were enrolled. In 2009, allegations of academic fraud as well as serious violations of NCAA regulations at Binghamton University in upstate New York led to the resignation of the men's basketball coach and the director of athletics.

Other problems have plagued college athletics as well. These range from low graduation rates for male athletes in major sports at many Division I institutions to the kind of not only embarrassing but also dangerous misbehavior and sometimes criminal activity of academically marginal athletes in some big-time intercollegiate programs. Although there are many fine athletes and coaches in major college sports, a concern for winning, and the status and income that go with it, too often has taken priority over the academic mission of the university. Thus, the 2002 NCAA Men's

Championship basketball game featured a win by the University of Maryland over the University of Oklahoma. But according to NCAA statistics, fewer than one in five of the scholarship athletes at both programs were able to meet graduation requirements. Out of the seven classes at the University of Oklahoma reported on by the NCAA, arriving as freshmen from 1989 to 1995, not even one player graduated.[3]

In his announcement in 1982 of the termination of USF's basketball program (since reinstated at a lower level of competition), Rev. Shiavo surely raised a fundamental ethical question about college sports when he asked, "How can we contribute to the building of a decent law-abiding society in this country if educational institutions are willing to suffer their principles to be prostituted and involve young people in that prostitution for any purpose and much less for the purpose of winning some games and developing an ill-gotten recognition and income?"[4]

It would be a mistake to think, however, that the problems with intercollegiate athletics are limited to isolated instances of outrageous behavior by athletes, recruiting violations, and academic fraud. Many critics believe the problem lies deeper. The moral questions that can be raised about intercollegiate athletics go well beyond an examination of violations of NCAA rules. We can ask questions about the rules themselves. For example, should colleges and universities be allowed to give athletic scholarships at all? Does the NCAA permit teams to play too many games to the academic detriment of the athletes? For example, how can athletes benefit from classes or pursue a rigorous and demanding major if they participate on a baseball or softball team that plays more than fifty games a season, or requires athletes to spend extended periods of time off campus playing a basketball schedule against ranked teams all across the country?

At an even more fundamental level, we can question whether intercollegiate sports even belong on campus in the first place. After all, shouldn't colleges be educational institutions rather than minor leagues for professional sports? Is the academic mission of the university compatible with a commitment to intercollegiate athletics? Is commitment to excellence in athletics in conflict with commitment to academic excellence?

These questions suggest what might be called the "Incompatibility Thesis." This thesis states that intercollegiate sports are incompatible with the academic functions of colleges and universities. The strong version of this thesis asserts that the incompatibility is between academic values and *any* serious form of intercollegiate athletics. A weaker version holds that the incompatibility lies only between academic values and elite Division I athletic programs, those that offer athletic scholarships and whose teams, particularly in high-profile sports, regularly compete for national rankings.

This chapter is an examination of the Incompatibility Thesis, and more broadly, of the value, if any, of intercollegiate athletics. Its central question is what place an athletic program should have on a college or university campus. We shall be concerned not only with the proper role of athletics on campus but with the very nature and mission of the university.

THE ROLE OF SPORTS IN THE UNIVERSITY— THE CASE FOR INCOMPATIBILITY

Why should a university support an intercollegiate athletic program? After all, some distinguished institutions, including the University of Chicago, Emory University, and the California Institute of Technology, have well-deserved reputations for academic excellence yet at various times in their history have not supported a full intercollegiate athletic program, or, in some cases, have not had any such program at all.

In evaluating the role of intercollegiate athletics in the academy, it will be useful to distinguish three separate questions:

1. Is it wrong for colleges and universities to have an intercollegiate athletic program? Are any athletic programs morally impermissible?
2. Is it desirable for colleges and universities to have an intercollegiate athletic program?
3. If colleges and universities should have an intercollegiate athletic program, what kind of program is most justifiable?

It may be, for example, that it is not wrong in the sense of being morally prohibited for colleges and universities to support intercollegiate athletics programs, but that such programs are undesirable because the money spent on them could be better spent elsewhere. Perhaps all sorts of intercollegiate athletic programs are not equally desirable. For example, intercollegiate athletic programs may be desirable if run along the lines of Ivy League or Division III programs but not if run more expansively.

Is there any reason for thinking that intercollegiate athletics programs are wrong? Should intercollegiate sports be prohibited? The question here is a broad one for many sorts of programs, ranging from those of Division III schools (such institutions do not offer athletic scholarships, they compete regionally for the most part rather than nationally, and they emphasize athletics less than schools in Divisions I and II) right up to the athletic giants such as Michigan, Oklahoma, Texas, and Notre Dame. One argument for the view that it is wrong for universities to support serious intercollegiate athletic programs rests on the Incompatibility Thesis. The wrongness arises from the corruption of academic values by athletic values.

Perhaps it is best to begin by considering an idealized but important model of what the university should be in our attempt to ascertain just what academic values ought to be regarded as fundamental. By assessing this model and seeing its relationship to various forms that intercollegiate athletics can take, we may be able to offer a judicious assessment of the proper role, if any, of intercollegiate athletics.

THE UNIVERSITY AS A REFUGE OF SCHOLARSHIP

Why have the college or university at all? What would be lacking in an educational system that devoted the elementary and high-school years to imparting basic skills in reading, writing, and mathematics? After high school, students would either seek employment or go on to specialized professional training. Does a college education serve a function that such a system would fail to satisfy?

Traditionally, the role of education in the liberal arts has been thought to fill an important gap that is ignored by merely professional training and that is not fully approachable by those still mastering basic skills. Education in the liberal arts exposes students to "the best that has been thought and said" in their own and other cultures. By reflecting critically and analytically on the significant works, including artistic achievements, that the best minds have produced throughout human history, students should become better able to acquire a broad perspective on the human situation, learn to analyze difficult problems critically, and appreciate excellence in the arts, humanities, and sciences. And although there is often controversy about what works should be studied and what counts as "best," debates over that issue can themselves have enormous educational value.

Similar rhetoric can be found in the catalogs of most colleges and universities, for behind the language lies an institution that, though evolving, traces its heritage from ancient Greece, through the medieval universities of Europe, to the modern colleges and universities of our own time. The most important function of these institutions, it can be argued, is to transmit the best of human intellectual achievement, to subject different viewpoints to critical analysis, and to add to human knowledge through research.

Although today's huge "multi-universities" have many functions, including provision of professional training in medicine, business, education, nursing, and law, it can be argued that the most important function of the university still is to transmit, examine, and extend the realm of human knowledge. This function often places the university, or at least some of its members, in an adversarial relationship with the rest of society, because the university's function commits it to the often critical examination of popular ideas of a given time and culture. If that function were not performed, many bad ideas would not be subjected to criticism, and even good ideas would be less appreciated or understood because their advocates would never have to modify or defend them in the face of objection.[5]

Critical inquiry, then, is a major function of colleges and universities; it is fundamental to a democratic society because it gives citizens the information and skills they need to function as citizens. And by exposing ideas to critical scrutiny, it allows for the kind of correction of errors and checks on power that are lacking in tyrannies and dictatorships.

Accordingly, let us consider critical inquiry as a normative claim about what the principal function of the university should be. Can a case be made for the inclusion of an intercollegiate sports program in the university conceived not as a business or as a training ground for tomorrow's professionals but as a center of scholarship, critical thought, and training for citizenship in the democratic state? Are intercollegiate athletics at least compatible with the major educational mission of the university? Can athletics actually contribute to or enhance that mission?

A DEFENSE OF THE INCOMPATIBILITY THESIS

Why are athletic programs thought to be incompatible with academic values, particularly the kind of education involved in critical inquiry in the arts, sciences, social sciences, and humanities? Some of the points already touched on support the Incompatibility Thesis, especially when applied to elite Division I athletics.

First, the enormous pressures to win, often generated by the need to keep jobs, produce revenues, and promote the visibility of the institution, all too often generate cheating. The academic fraud we have seen at Minnesota, Florida State, and other institutions testifies to the strength of these pressures and to the values associated with victory at all costs.[6]

Second, even if we ignore the abuses in some major intercollegiate athletic programs, there seems to be a basic contradiction between the aims of education and the aims of athletics; thus, the time students spend on the athletic fields is time spent away from their studies. Likewise, athletes either uninterested in academic work or unprepared to do it undermine the academic mission of many institutions.

Finally, many of the values associated with athletics, such as obedience to the orders of coaches, seem at odds with the kind of inquiring and questioning minds professors attempt to develop in the classroom; indeed, some critics see athletics as a mindless activity in which only physical skills are developed. Thus, to many college and university faculty, athletics are at best a necessary evil, perhaps useful in allowing students to let off steam, but in basic conflict with educational values.

The Corruption of Intercollegiate Sports

In many of the athletically prominent colleges and universities of our land, sports have become big business. Television revenues and the visibility and support accompanying success in the major "visibility sports," such as men's football and basketball, seem to many to undermine the educational ideal of sports. To gain visibility, and the revenues and support that go with it, a program must be successful.

But "success" in this context means "winning," and so the temptation is to do what is necessary to win. For example, coaches who teach their athletes effectively and who recruit only academically qualified players may not be as valuable to an institution interested in athletic success as a coach who wins, who can handle the media, and whose scruples about recruiting are less strict. Corners get cut. Other schools feel they, too, must cut even more corners, just to be competitive, and soon serious abuses become far too common.

Violations of NCAA rules and the misbehavior of athletes who are only marginally qualified as students get much of the publicity. However, perhaps the most significant form of abuse goes deeper: If the purpose of participation becomes winning for the sake of external goods, such as visibility and financial support, won't players come to be viewed as mere means to that end rather than as students to be educated? Indeed, to keep players eligible, athletic programs could view education as an obstacle that must be overcome; many players could be inadequately educated and perhaps never graduate. Former star Minnesota Viking lineman Alan Page has described a meeting of eight defensive linemen to go over the team's playbook:

> We had each spent four years in colleges with decent reputations . . . and I remember that two of us could read the playbook, two others had some trouble with it but managed, and four of my teammates couldn't read it at all. . . . The problem seems to be that these athletes—and there are many more like them, blacks and whites—were never expected to learn to read and write. They floated through up to this point because they were talented athletes.[7]

Various reforms made by the NCAA over the past twenty-five years, especially under the leadership of Myles Brand, who served as president of the NCAA from 2003 to 2009, may have contributed to some improvement since Page was a player. The overall graduation rate for student-athletes at NCAA institutions is higher than for students at large. Graduation rates for African American athletes also are higher than for African American students who are not athletes. However, serious problems remain, particularly in the high-visibility sports of men's football and basketball. Although highly regarded institutions such as Penn State and Duke report high graduation rates even in those sports, some other programs remain seriously deficient.

For example, for students entering college in 1995–1996, the overall graduation rate was 58 percent. The graduation rate for all athletes was 60 percent and for all male athletes 54 percent. However, male basketball players graduated only at a 43 percent rate and African American basketball players fared even more poorly, graduating at a 35 percent rate (although that rate was comparable to the overall graduation rate for black male students). Some individual institutions did far worse: The

University of Oklahoma and the University of Nevada at Las Vegas graduated no male basketball players, and Florida State and the University of Cincinnati graduated no male African American basketball players. In fact, forty-two institutions failed to graduate *any* black male basketball players between 1991–1992 and 1994–1995.[8]

Thus, perhaps the morally most damaging charge brought against major intercollegiate athletics is that it exploits the participating athlete. Such athletes are ostensibly offered scholarships to play their sport in return for an education, but too often, critics claim, the athlete is expected to give everything on the field, sometimes to the huge financial benefit of the university, and little or no time or effort is taken to ensure success in the classroom.

For example, football at major universities, and often at smaller schools as well, is virtually a year-round sport. Practice starts in late summer. The season can extend into December, and even further if postseason competition in the major bowls is involved. The season itself may be followed by an off-season "informal" weight-training program; this goes through winter and may, in turn, be followed by spring practice. Not only does the time devoted to practice leave athletes little time for the nonathletic aspects of university life, but it also affects academic achievement and, as we discussed earlier, may well encourage academic fraud.

Finally, it is often argued that in Division I, highly visible men's football and basketball programs generate revenue for the university that may support non-revenue-producing sports, including women's teams, and that even generate excess funds that can be used for educational purposes. But while many of these programs do produce revenue through gate receipts, television exposure, and licensing fees on logos, they also have enormous expenditures. Think of the costs of offering more than fifty football scholarships, recruiting the players, and building facilities—such as adding "skyboxes" to football stadiums to the tune of millions of dollars—to say nothing of travel expenses and highly paid coaches—and it becomes clear why only a handful of athletic programs, even in Division I, actually turn a profit. Even highly successful football programs that make money one year may go deeply into debt shortly afterward.[9]

The Problems of the Black Athlete

The problems discussed above, especially those involving the alleged exploitation of athletes, may apply particularly to the black athlete. Although blacks constitute about 12 percent of the population of the United States, they make up well over a third of college football and basketball players, about 40 percent of professional football players, and about two-thirds of professional basketball players. Disproportionate representation is even greater in the major intercollegiate programs and at the very top levels of major professional sports, where all-star teams often are dominated by black players.

One plausible explanation for the high representation of black athletes in many sports is discrimination and lack of opportunity in inner-city areas. If African Americans, for example, perceive many doors as closed to them because of discrimination, sports may seem the best escape route from poverty and the ghetto. The effects of discrimination and the focus of the mass media on athletes may also lead to there being a dearth of nonathletic role models in the black community, a gap filled by successful black athletes. Or such alternate role models may exist but may be less appreciated than is warranted because of the attention focused on such black athletic superstars as Michael Jordan, Shaquille O'Neal, and Kobe Bryant. As a result, success in athletics may come to be more highly valued in the black community than in the white community. Thus, blacks become disproportionately involved in athletics, especially such sports as basketball, track, football, and baseball, which normally do not require large investments in equipment and for which inexpensive facilities are widely available in urban areas. Although some may suspect that genetic differences contribute to the disproportionate representation of black athletes in some sports, the kinds of environmental factors pointed to above surely are especially influential. Which natural talents are expressed in action depends in great part on the environmental stimuli to which agents are exposed and the choices they make within that context.[10]

If it is true that sports are more often viewed as the path of choice to upward mobility in the black community than the white community, we might worry whether black athletes are more vulnerable to the dangers of big-time college athletics, particularly the failure to get a rigorous education, than whites. For example, many black youngsters might tend to see sports as the major and perhaps only avenue to success open to them and may therefore be more likely than white students to neglect their studies. The hope of obtaining an athletic scholarship and playing professional sports may prevent them from developing the educational tools that make for success in other areas. Once in college, black athletes in football and basketball may overestimate their chances of making the professional leagues, or not even be concerned about graduation because they hope or expect to be drafted early by a professional team.

Although athletic scholarships are available for many athletes, including underprivileged blacks and whites, the odds of obtaining them are not high. Unfortunately, there is some evidence that African American youngsters have a greater tendency than whites to overestimate their chances of playing college and professional sports and so may assign a higher priority to athletic than academic success.[11] Some writers even argue that athletics in the United States, often considered in popular thought as a road to equal opportunity for African Americans, have been harmful to them.[12] Although such a thesis may be overstated, for many of those who neglect educational opportunities, athletic talent may be far more likely to lead down a dead-end street than to the pot of gold at the end of the rainbow seemingly provided by professional sports.

A Summary: The Case Against Major Intercollegiate Athletics

To review, the criticisms of "big-time" intercollegiate athletics arise from the change of emphasis from athletics as an educationally valuable activity supplementing the normal academic curriculum to athletics as a source of revenue, support, and high visibility. These benefits—revenue, support, and visibility—depend upon winning, which in turn depends largely on recruiting the best athletes. The pressure to win can become so intense that coaches and athletes as well as university administrations (often under pressure from influential alumni boosters) make decisions that reflect athletic rather than educational priorities. At their worst, the pressures lead to recruiting violations, to misbehavior, and even to crime and other abuses, all of which have too often dominated the sports pages of our daily newspapers. Moreover, athletes may be given the opportunity to get an education but lose the opportunity because of their own lack of educational commitment.

The kind of disrespect for the educational mission of the university, along with violations of NCAA rules and misbehavior by athletes themselves, undermines overall respect for the university. If the ideal of the university is that of an institution concerned for the discovery and preservation of truth and the recognition of human excellence, isn't that ideal compromised by sacrificing the education of athletes for athletic victories, and even more so by outright cheating? Even though it is true that the modern university has become what has been called a social service station, fulfilling a variety of social needs, its most important function is still to formulate, test, teach, and evaluate achievement in the arts, sciences, humanities, and professions. How can the university claim to represent such fundamental values when it subverts them in its own practice?

Reasonable people may doubt, then, whether intercollegiate sports should be played at the level of national competition and intensity found in the major football and basketball conferences of our nation. Many would argue that the only reputable intercollegiate athletic programs are those resembling the Division III or Ivy League levels where no athletic scholarships are given, athletes are expected to be students, and competition is normally regional rather than national. Perhaps this level of intercollegiate competition is the only kind compatible with respect for the athlete as a person, with respect for the educational value of athletic competition, and with respect for the integrity of the university.

DEFENSES OF COLLEGE ATHLETICS

Perhaps, however, the above critique is overstated. After all, even if there are major problems in some high-profile programs at athletically elite universities, the majority of programs, even in Division I, are not highly visible. Many high-profile programs at major universities, such as Duke, Stanford, and North Carolina at Chapel Hill, are not prone to scandal, and athletes in those programs have high graduation rates. Moreover, the vast majority of college athletes play with no desire to become professionals, and the majority of athletic programs compete at the Division II and Division III levels of the NCAA. So, proponents argue, in many cases athletic programs at colleges and universities not only do not undermine the academic mission of the university but sometimes may actually reinforce it. Let us consider the case for such a view in more detail.

College Athletics and Entertainment

Millions of sports fans enjoy high-profile college contests such as those that occur in football bowl games, the men's NCAA Division I basketball championship, and, increasingly, the women's championship. In effect, proponents of big-time college sports argue that even if few intercollegiate athletic programs make an overall profit, they still produce enormous amounts of benefits—what utilitarian philosophers call "utility"—for society.

Proponents of such a view might argue that the critics of high-profile intercollegiate athletics conceive of the mission of the university too narrowly. If the mission of the university is instead conceived broadly, to encompass more than purely academic and intellectual concerns, why couldn't it plausibly be extended to cover the provision of various public services, including the provision of entertainment to the student body and the wider community that intercollegiate athletics can provide? According to proponents of this view, it is clear that the university already in fact does provide entertainment for the community in a variety of areas including theater, music, and other performing arts, such as dance, as well as through programming on college-sponsored radio and television stations. Intercollegiate athletics are simply another way in which academic institutions can and do provide this good to their students and staff and to the population at large.

Thus, Peter French, who, as we will see is critical of other sorts of defenses of intercollegiate athletics, pointed out in his 2004 book *Ethics and College Sports: Ethics, Sports, and the University* that the mission statements of many universities, especially large state institutions, include explicit mention of service to the community, often including reference to serving the economic and cultural needs of the population. Similarly, some mission statements of athletic departments, sanctioned by their universities, specifically include entertainment among the functions of their programs. Developing this line of thought, French maintained that

the honest and potentially successful defense of intercollegiate athletics, especially including the elite sports, is that they are the way, or at least one way and probably the most visible and successful way the university responds to its public service obligations in the area of public entertainment. In fact, they likely touch the lives of more members of the public in a positive and effective way than any other service the university may extend in that direction.[13]

Accordingly, once we abandon the assumption that the mission of the university should be purely academic, encompassing only teaching and scholarship in recognized academic disciplines to the exclusion of anything else, the inclusion of athletics can be seen in a new light. The sponsorship of intercollegiate athletics can then be defended as fulfilling other legitimate functions of the university. As French put it, "the tension in the university, particularly within the faculty, that sets the academic and athletic side of the campus at odds is caused by the general failure to appreciate the multiple missions of a contemporary university and on the part of the academic faculty typically to think that only their function is the 'real' mission of the university."[14]

How should such a position be evaluated? First, even if correct, this position applies with the most force to highly visible sports, such as men's football and basketball and perhaps women's basketball, at large, athletically elite universities, particularly state institutions. So even if French's argument does have force, that force is greatest when applied to high-profile sports at athletically elite levels of the NCAA and loses strength (although probably not to the vanishing point) when applied to different sorts of institutions or to lower-profile sports.

A second criticism is that even if the university does have an obligation to provide entertainment, the kind of entertainment provided by athletics differs in kind from the other kinds of entertainment that the university legitimately provides, such as concerts and art exhibits. Programs in the arts, as French recognizes, arguably have a much more direct link to the academic mission of colleges and universities than do intercollegiate athletics. These can be defended as extensions of academics, whereas, at least according to the critics, athletics cannot.

Is this second criticism decisive? I think not, for two reasons. First, as we have seen, the issue of what activities of the university are fundamental is itself an ethically contested issue. To assume that only entertainment closely linked to academic programs is legitimate is to beg the question about what functions universities should fulfill. More important, however, the objection begs the question in a more basic way. If the presumed divide between athletics and academics is nowhere near as deep as the critics assume, and if there is or can be a significant degree of coherence and mutual support between the two, at least at some kinds of institutions, then intercollegiate athletics do not differ from university-sponsored entertainment in other areas, such as the arts, to the degree the critics assume. I will explore this point more fully in later sections of this chapter.

That leads to the third criticism of the entertainment defense, namely, that athletic programs involve abuses of academic ethics that other activities of the university, including artistic performances, normally do not involve. Given the scandals, including cases of academic fraud, that have plagued high-profile athletic programs at elite Division I schools, this criticism clearly is true. The low graduation rates, particularly of minority athletes, at some institutions clearly are unacceptable. Moreover, if the admissions standards for athletes differ so drastically from those for other students that a significant number of athletes are unprepared for college-level work and if, as a result, their academic course load is so diluted as to be educationally vacuous, then the charge of abuse is also warranted.

However, such abuses occur mainly in high-profile sports at some institutions and are not reason enough to regard all forms of intercollegiate athletics, even at the Division I level, as involving abuses of academic values. Moreover, the NCAA has taken some meaningful steps to raise graduation rates and ensure that athletes are taking a core of serious academic courses. For example, Division I athletic programs with poor graduation rates will have the number of athletic scholarships they can offer reduced. Presumably, this will provide an incentive to coaches to make sure athletes graduate, and the coaches will then encourage athletes to study and help them develop strategies that will lead to success. Even if incentives also exist to circumvent such rules, perhaps by diluting the academic content of the courses that athletes take, the stricter rules should help by setting the bar higher than it is at present. In addition, penalties might deter violations.

A broader concern applies even to elite athletic programs that do encourage athletes to pursue their education and graduate. The intensity of competition, the missed class time involved in playing a national schedule, the extended length of seasons, and off-season training schedules may demand such a heavy time commitment that the pursuit of educational goals is severely compromised. Thus, revenue is generated when high-profile teams earn national ranking, but that requires playing a national schedule, and the scheduling of games is then influenced more by gaining attractive time slots on television and traveling to games in distant locations than by the requirements of class attendance. These factors raise a plethora of questions for those who would defend elite, high-profile intercollegiate sports as presently constituted.

French's defense of elite, high-profile intercollegiate sports as forms of entertainment legitimately provided by universities does, however, have some force. It is at least arguable, as he suggested, that provision of entertainment is one of the legitimate functions of colleges and universities, particularly large public institutions. However, such activity is legitimate only if it does not undermine the chances for the athletes to receive an education, does not subvert academic norms (as would be the case with academic fraud), and, more broadly, does not involve a kind of disdain for the academic mission of the university, which might come to be regarded as an obstacle to athletic participation rather than as essential to the student-athlete's intellectual and personal development.

The entertainment argument also suggests, however, that both sides in this debate may have erred by relying on a dubious common assumption. That assumption is that athletics and academics are two sharply distinct kinds of activities. As we will see in the next two sections, that assumption itself is open to serious challenge.

Can Athletics Enhance Academics?

At most, the argument so far shows that athletics at the level of major intercollegiate sports, given appropriate and effective regulation, can provide benefits such as a sense of community, fun, visibility, and perhaps revenue for some highly successful, high-profile programs. Skeptics may question whether regulations can be effective, given the many incentives to win, and claim that the argument shows athletics to be a necessary evil, at best, but that response may well be too bleak. Most athletes in elite Division I programs graduate, often at higher rates than other students. Female athletes do particularly well, but many athletes, even in high-visibility men's programs, also graduate at high rates at institutions whose athletic programs have achieved national prominence.[15] Although graduation rates are not always an indication of the rigor of the programs in which athletes are enrolled, greater faculty control would surely enhance the quality of education received by athletes at high-profile institutions.

But even if this limited defense of elite Division I athletics has force, an even stronger kind of argument should also be considered. This argument claims not merely that, under suitable conditions, big-time athletics and academics can be minimally compatible, and so should be accepted for their utilitarian benefits, but that intercollegiate athletics in the right circumstances can enhance or contribute to the academic mission of colleges and universities.

Athletics and the Performing Arts

An argument supporting such a view was advanced by philosopher Myles Brand, former president of Indiana University and, as noted earlier, president of the NCAA from 2003 until his death in 2009. Brand, like French, believed that the critics of intercollegiate athletics took too narrow a view of what colleges and universities should be about. But where French has argued for a pluralistic view of the mission of the university, including purposes beyond the purely academic, Brand argued for a broader notion of what counts as academic in the first place.

Brand started from what he called a "seemingly small point," namely, that "when the educational experience of student-athletes is compared with those studying the performing arts such as music, dance, and theater as well as the studio arts, it is difficult to find substantive differences."[16] Thus, like student-athletes, student musicians practice for many hours, often more than are required of them, and perform in events that are often college sponsored and where audience members may be charged an admission fee. Performance and practices often are intense. In addition, there is competition for places in the performing groups, just as there is for becoming a player on a sports team. Some preference may be given in the university admissions process to talented students in the arts, and some of these students may have aspirations for professional careers, although, as is the case with student-athletes in the NCAA, almost all go on to careers in other areas of endeavor. According to Brand, "these similarities point to a convergence of educational experiences between student-athletes and others . . . but the activities of the student-athletes alone are not considered to be academic, or to be in conflict with academics."[17] Is there any plausible justification for this distinction?

Brand's reply was that there is no such justification. The distinction is arbitrary, perhaps expressing a prejudice held by many academics against the body and against physical rather than intellectual activity. Brand concluded, then, that intercollegiate athletics fall within the domain of the academic, at least if performances in the arts do so as well.

Brand's position raises serious questions, not least of which is the question of how sharp the line between the academic and the nonacademic really is. Pondering this question, some critics might maintain that the goal of elite intercollegiate athletics seems to be to win and to generate the revenue produced by winning, not to express artistic or intellectual values, as is the case with performances in music, dance, and theater. Thus, these critics would say that the line between academic and nonacademic is quite sharp, and that athletics is clearly nonacademic, whereas theater and music are clearly academic activities.

However, although this criticism does not completely lack force, it does seem overdrawn. First of all, the overwhelming majority of intercollegiate athletic contests do not involve high-profile sports and are not intended to be revenue producing. Second, although artists normally may not aim at "winning," they do aim at excellence in performance. Similarly, although the cult of winning may have gotten out of hand in many areas of sports, intercollegiate athletes often can be seen as aiming at excellence as well, with winning the natural by-product of top performance, just as acclaim or awards can be the by-product of outstanding achievement by an artist or actor. So there might be a difference, as Brand's critics argue, between performance in athletics and performance in the arts, but perhaps it is not as sharp a distinction as the critics suggest.

Brand's critics also might argue that music and dance are embedded in a long tradition of intellectual achievement. Performance in these areas takes place in a context of artistic thought and often expresses or illustrates important themes of human existence or basic human values. Moreover, as one of my own students, a very talented musician, pointed out, an artistic performance may involve mastering a work; the performer needs to, for example, learn a musical composition, analyze different interpretations of it, understand its underlying logic or theme, and study its history and that of the tradition to which it belongs.[18]

However, athletics also can be studied as taking place within a tradition and a history. Moreover, athletic competition can express or illustrate important values, such as dedication, excellence, and perseverance in the face of adversity. Brand's case would be stronger, however, if intercollegiate athletes not only participated in sports but also studied their history, their social significance, and the ethical dilemmas that arise within them, just as artists may not only perform but also are students of art as well. In other words, Brand's argument would apply most fully when intercollegiate athletes not only participate in sports but also study them within an academic framework, just as students in the arts often take courses in, say, the history of music, art, or theater.

In addition, Brand's argument raises the question of just which skills should be regarded as within the proper domain of a university or college education. If we include not only dance recitals and musical performances but also basketball and soccer games, what about skillful performance in activities ranging from poker to cooking, or from gardening to playing Monopoly? Must we become so inclusive that no exercise of skill can be excluded from the realm of the academic? Moreover, should we view those exercises of skill that do seem to be closely related to the academic enterprise, *possibly* including athletics, to be offered for academic credit, or should they be viewed as adjuncts that reinforce a more traditional academic education but, as Elaine of *Seinfeld* might express it, are not "credit worthy?"

Brand's argument, then, though controversial, does raise issues worthy of further consideration. In particular, is it arbitrary to include musical and dance performances within the realm of the academic but then exclude athletic performance? Perhaps the university should recognize in its academic program, either through credit or through cocurricular recognition, contributions to the community that exhibit a variety of mental and physical skills, including those exhibited in dance, music, photography, and athletics. Rather than pursuing this issue in greater depth, however, let us consider another approach that maintains that athletics and academics are or can be compatible, perhaps even mutually reinforcing, precisely because of the cognitive skills employed in each enterprise.

Athletics, Education, and Cognitive Skills

Consider again the model of athletic competition as a mutual quest for excellence through challenge as developed in Chapters 2 and 3. Arguably, such competition has several features that make it a desirable supplement to a broad liberal arts education. On this model, athletic competition can be thought of as a test through which competitors commit their minds and bodies to the pursuit of excellence. To meet such a test, they must learn to analyze and overcome weakness, to work hard to improve, to understand their own strengths and weaknesses, and to react intelligently and skillfully to situations that arise in the contest. In the sports contest, they must use judgment, make decisions that are open to reflective criticism (often known as second-guessing), apply standards of assessment, critically analyze play, and exhibit perseverance and coolness under pressure. During a season, athletes can learn and grow by understanding their physical and psychological weaknesses and by trying to improve.

Many of these same traits are also required for successful study in the humanities and sciences. An important part of education is learning to know and understand oneself, and that kind of self-knowledge is one of the most valuable kinds of knowledge that can emerge from participation in sports. In addition, athletes must learn to think critically about their own performance and that of teammates and opponents, to learn from the criticism of others, to focus on the task before them in the contest and avoid distraction, and to appreciate standards of excellence even when the standards are met better by opponents than by themselves. These skills are similar and arguably may reinforce similar critical skills and the ability to appreciate achievement in the classroom.

If this point is valid, then academics and intercollegiate athletics, when properly conducted, can be and often are mutually reinforcing. This mutual reinforcement can occur in at least three ways. First, the acquisition by athletes of the kinds of skills specified above can help to promote the acquisition of parallel skills in the classroom. Athletes who learn to accept and integrate criticism of their athletic performance may be primed to accept and apply criticism of their writing or logical analysis as well. Second, the exhibition of skills by athletes to spectators may illustrate the value of such skills to a wider audience. Thus, a team that overcomes ideological differences to perform well can illustrate the value of teamwork, whereas a team dominated by selfish individuals who care mainly about their own statistics can illustrate what happens when egoism predominates. Third, the values implicit in sport can serve as grounds for criticism in academic performance as well. Thus, a professor might chastise an athlete for not working as hard on drills in a language course as the athlete does on the field; or an athlete can point out to a professor that he should not be stereotyped as an unintellectual "jock" because participation in sports has taught him to think outside the box about strategies and, by extension, other topics, increasing his problem-solving skills. These three aspects of mutual reinforcement can be thought of as causal, illustrative, and justificatory.[19]

In calling for the best that is within each participant, a good athletic program can provide educational experiences that are unusually intense and unusually valuable and that reinforce and help develop many of the same traits that promote learning elsewhere. But even leaving aside such consequences, the good sports contest is a crucible in which important learning takes place and involves the discipline, understanding, and analysis that are related to learning in other parts of the curriculum.

Critics might object that even if these points are correct, they do not show that intercollegiate athletics is a necessary or unique part of an educational curriculum.[20] After all, if the same values are directly promoted, taught, and exemplified in the classroom, the additional indirect reinforcement provided by athletics is at best marginal and at worst distracts students from more academic pursuits where the most important aspects of education are dealt with. At most, critics might argue, intramural programs may well be warranted, but not the kind of intense activity found in varsity intercollegiate athletics.[21]

This sort of critical rejoinder is not decisive. Although the critics surely are right to argue that athletics do not play a unique educational role, sports may still be in a relationship of significant mutual reinforcement with academics. As philosopher Paul Weiss pointed out, students, particularly undergraduates, are novices in the academic disciplines they study. At best, the more advanced undergraduates may become apprentices by assisting professors in research, but they rarely have the chance to be at the cutting edge of achievement in a discipline until later in their careers. Athletics, along with the performing arts, are perhaps the only areas in most colleges and universities where students can achieve and demonstrate excellence—and not just as apprentice learners but in performances that rank among the best at a high level of comparative judgment.[22]

Perhaps more important, appreciation of achievement in athletics is widespread, far more so than understanding of achievement in mathematics, physics, philosophy, or other specialized disciplines. Because of this, athletics can and should serve as a kind of common denominator that allows people from vastly different backgrounds, cultures, social classes, and academic interests to experience together the lessons of striving to meet challenges. These experiences not only can be educationally valuable to the participants but also can inspire, teach, and inform other members of the wider university community who also enjoy the competition. Moreover, because athletic contests are accessible to and attract the interest of wide segments of the population, they can be a unifying force in an intellectual community that is often split along ideological, ethnic, religious, socioeconomic, and disciplinary lines. Although this function is perhaps distinct from the primary educational functions of universities, it makes intercollegiate athletics an important aspect of academic communities. Sports, in short, help to create bonds that allow communication to persist when it might otherwise break down because of differences within the university.

Moreover, as noted above, sports can illustrate important values and express critical standards that apply elsewhere. Social scientist Michael Putnam, author of the widely discussed study *Bowling Alone*, has provided data indicating that the greater the ethnic and racial diversity within a neighborhood, the more trust among residents tends to be diminished. However, further work by such writers as James Q. Wilson suggests that sports teams counter this general rule because in sports, participants from diverse ethnic, racial, ideological, and socioeconomic backgrounds work together for a common cause. As a result, team members form bonds despite their differences. Athletic teams may be ahead of much of the rest of society in this respect, setting a standard for the rest of society to emulate.[23]

Accordingly, because of the intensity and high level of the competition, intercollegiate athletics can serve as a common medium through which large and diverse segments of the academic community can demonstrate and appreciate excellent performance and the struggle to meet challenge. Michael Oriad, a professor of English at Oregon State University, captured the effects of his institution's basketball program and its then coach, Ralph Miller, when he wrote:

> My colleagues and I recognize the most important functions of the university to be teaching, research, and service. . . . But on Friday or Saturday night from December through March, we cannot conceive of a finer place to be than in Gill Coliseum watching what the locals have termed the Orange Express. . . . Most of us never appreciated the art of passing until we saw how O.S.U. executes it. . . . It is a particular kind of excellence that our basketball team exhibits and that most appeals to us. Ralph Miller speaks the truth when he calls himself not a coach but a teacher, and we teachers in other disciplines appreciate what his pupils have learned to do.[24]

Our discussion suggests, then, that even if, contrary to Brand's suggestion, intercollegiate athletics are not strictly part of an education in the way the classroom experience is, they add a desirable educational component to the university and can even reinforce central academic values. Of course, our account has been highly intellectual and is not meant to deny that intercollegiate athletics can provide other benefits to the academic community as well. These benefits include opportunities for relaxation, to make new friends and meet different kinds of people, to promote a sense of community on campus, and, as Peter French has argued, to entertain local, regional, and sometimes national audiences.

In all fairness, this model of athletics does not easily fit the major intercollegiate athletic programs found at the athletic pinnacle of Division I. The institutions that come closest to meeting it most probably are schools like those in the Ivy League, perhaps other major universities that award athletic scholarships but have strong academic reputations—such as Duke, Notre Dame, North Carolina, and Stanford—and many of the institutions in Division III (the largest division within the NCAA), where athletic scholarships are not awarded, where athletes take the same courses as other students, and where athletics is regarded as an adjunct to the educational program.

Our discussion suggests, then, that an important case can be made for the thesis that where athletes have a legitimate chance to get a good education, and where academic values are honored, intercollegiate athletics can reinforce those values in a variety of ways. Athletics and academics need not be incompatible; instead, they can and should be mutually reinforcing. Where athletically elite Division I institutions fail to meet proper standards and to promote coherence of academic and athletic goals, the values implicit in mutual coherence provide grounds for criticism of their policies.

However, although it may be comforting to think of intercollegiate athletics at such schools (such as members of the Ivy League and Division III of the NCAA) as pure and pristine, at least compared to the kind of problems that have plagued big-time intercollegiate athletics, some recent criticism has called even that assumption into question. This criticism goes directly to the heart of the claim that athletics can enhance academics and have a significant educational role to play at many institutions of higher education.

Do Intercollegiate Athletics Fail the Game of Life?

In their book *The Game of Life*, James L. Shulman and William G. Bowen, officers of the prestigious Mellon Foundation (Bowen is also a former president of Princeton University), use material from an extensive database comparing the academic performance of athletes and nonathletes as well as their careers after college and conclude that intercollegiate athletics is even more harmful at the Ivy League universities and highly selective liberal arts colleges than at large universities with high-profile athletic programs.[25]

Critics point out that at smaller, more academically selective schools, athletes constitute a high percentage of the student body, as much as 30 to 40 percent. In the late 1950s, athletes at the schools studied by Shulman and Bowen performed well academically, often better than their peers. This, the authors maintain, is no longer so. Furthermore, they suggest that if athletes are given too great an admissions advantage, and perform much worse academically than their classmates, they can drag down the academic atmosphere of the whole institution. Shulman and Bowen propose that a "culture of athletics," a kind of "jock culture," exacerbates this problem. This culture, they point out, apart from its consequences, may be inherently in conflict with academic values.

Although the highly selective schools in the book's database may not be typical of the majority of institutions of higher education, these schools have an importance larger than their numbers would indicate. Not only are they widely regarded as academic standard-bearers, but they also appear to have resisted the temptations inherent in major intercollegiate sports. Many observers will conclude that if intercollegiate sports are harmful even in such a context, nowhere in higher education can they be a positive educational and ethical influence.

Much of the argument of *The Game of Life* rests on statistical comparisons between athletes and nonathletes in terms of academic performance while in school and achievements after graduation. Because the argument is based on an exhaustive analysis of a major database, it cannot fully be analyzed here; however, we can look at some of the questions about methodology that go well beyond one particular study.[26]

Although it may seem methodologically sound to compare the academic performance of athletes to those of nonathletes at colleges and universities, we need to be careful about the conclusions we draw from such a comparison. Suppose the athletes do worse than the nonathletes. Does this mean that the academic stature of the student body could be raised if we stopped giving preference in admissions to talented athletes who applied?

Not necessarily. Much depends on how much preference is given and on who would have been accepted if athletic talent was not taken into positive consideration in the admissions process. If schools are comparing academically less-qualified athletes not to potential academic superstars but to applicants who are academically weaker, then the applicants who would have replaced the athletes might not have done all that well either.[27] In other words, how strong academically were the candidates who would have been accepted had some degree of preference not been extended to athletes in the admissions process?

To assess the effect of athletics on the academic stature of the student body, we also would need to consider another issue (one not given significant attention in *The Game of Life*), namely, the extent to which a competitive athletic program might attract athletes (as well as nonathletes who are fans of intercollegiate athletics) who are outstanding students and who want to participate in intercollegiate athletics at a respectable level of competition. This was brought home to me in the spring of 2001 when an excellent student in my seminar, who was also a top player on our women's basketball and softball teams, remarked, after I had summarized *The Game of Life* for the class, that "I would never have come here if I hadn't been a recruited athlete." Thus, in evaluating the effect of athletics on academics, one must consider not only weaker students who would not have been admitted if they had not been athletes but also top students who would have attended other institutions if they had not been attracted by the opportunities to participate in athletics, or to be a spectator at athletic competitions, at the school where they matriculated.

Finally, it is important to remember that the academic performance of many, perhaps most, athletes does not differ significantly from the performance of other students, as suggested by data in *The Game of Life* itself. In fact, Shulman and Bowen's data suggest that female athletes do as well academically as other students, on average, and that—again, on average—the academic performance of male athletes in many sports other than men's football and basketball does not differ much from that of other students. The widest divergence from the performance of the overall student body probably is in male high-profile sports, where the population of student-athletes is also more socioeconomically diverse than the student body as a whole.

This raises the issue of whether the recruitment of athletes might contribute to the diversity of an institution's student body. We have already seen, for example, that African Americans are disproportionately represented on the major sports teams of athletically elite Division I schools. In their analysis in *The Game of Life*, Shulman and Bowen find a much more modest contribution at the schools in their sample, presumably because less weight is given to athletics in recruiting at those schools than in big-time college athletics and because the majority of student-athletes at such schools play lower-profile sports, such as golf, lacrosse, tennis, and crew, that historically have not always attracted or been open to minority participation.

However, by considering diversity among all athletes, the study may have under-emphasized how high-profile men's sports can contribute to diversity. In particular, male student-athletes in high-profile sports such as football do disproportionately tend to come from socioeconomic backgrounds that gave them fewer advantages in life than other students enjoyed.[28] As we have seen, the high-profile men's sports are the very ones in which the academic performance of the student-athletes is least satisfactory. But if athletes in high-profile sports tend to do less well than others academically, this may be due to a complex combination of factors, including their somewhat different educational backgrounds, their cultural attitudes, and the amount of time required by serious commitment to intercollegiate athletics.

Our discussion suggests that measuring the effect of athletic recruitment at academically selective schools is a complex matter. Because some of these complexities may not have been given adequate attention by Shulman and Bowen, the quantitative analysis underlying *The Game of Life*, while raising issues of concern, arguably is not always compelling. But rather than focusing simply on quantitative analysis, important as it is, let us turn to more philosophical criticisms of the claim that athletics and academics can be mutually reinforcing.

The "Culture of Athletics" and Academics

At a large state university, athletes may constitute a small percentage of students simply because the institution is so large. As we have seen, that may not be true at smaller Division III schools, such as liberal arts colleges, or even at Ivy League undergraduate colleges. If athletes' values and attitudes are different from the values and attitudes of other students, and inimical to the educational mission of the institution, then a critical mass of athletes can negatively affect the educational atmosphere of an institution apart from their academic performance as individuals. In other words, "jock culture" and academic culture may be in conflict.

Thus, Shulman and Bowen identified a cluster of traits characterizing a culture of athletics. Although they did not precisely define this culture, they noted that athletes have a tendency to socialize mainly with other athletes, to pursue different majors from those pursued by the rest of the student population, and, for male athletes especially, to focus more on financial success after college than other students. This culture of athletics has been fostered by youngsters' early specialization into particular sports, by recruiting policies that reward such specialization (the search for a well-rounded class rather than well-rounded individuals), and by the consequent estrangement of athletes from the academic missions of their institutions.

Although the idea that a culture of athletics adversely affects athletes' academic performance may be plausible as a partial explanation, it is questionable whether it is the whole story, or even the most significant part of the story. This kind of explanation suggests that athletes, even at highly selective and academically demanding institutions, lack a true commitment to academic success. But surely the picture may be more complex than this conclusion implies.

Institutional factors built into selective colleges and universities may also play a significant role, as might cultural factors having little to do with athletics. For example, athletes whose parents did not go to college or who attended different sorts of institutions may be unaccustomed to interaction with faculty, particularly during their freshman year. These are the very students who might be most in need of academic support from professors, but they may not know how to go about getting it.[29] Even worse, if too many faculty members exhibit outright disdain for intercollegiate athletics, or, more likely, are indifferent to athletes, players may sense this and be more reluctant than other students to seek help from those faculty members. Again, because review sessions or outside lectures may be scheduled during practice or game times, athletes may be more likely than others to miss them. Moreover, the amount of time and energy that goes into athletic training may be more demanding than many other kinds of extracurricular commitments. It is unclear, then, just how much "jock culture," assuming it exists, affects academic performance and whether it has a greater or lesser effect than other explanatory factors.

Should the culture of athletics be viewed primarily negatively, as in *The Game of Life*, or is a more positive assessment plausible? Is there an ideal distribution of students across concentrations, let alone of values or career goals, that institutions should seek to foster? If not, why should we regard the culture of athletics as negatively as the critics suggest?

The Game of Life suggests that athletes, both male and female, increasingly tend to have more conservative values than their peers. But surely the different values attributed to some athletes can be a contribution to diversity on campus, at least if "diversity" is not understood in a narrow and partisan way. If so, athletic recruiting not only can contribute a degree of socioeconomic diversity to a campus, as suggested above, but can contribute to a potentially intellectually fruitful mix of values within the academic community as well.

Athletics and Educational Values

Let us return more directly to what might be called the academic defense against the Incompatibility Thesis. According to this defense, athletics, properly structured, are not only compatible with academic values but may enhance and reinforce them. This point was defended earlier when it was argued that an athletic contest, conceived of as a mutual quest for excellence through challenge, is educational or has educational components closely related to academic virtues. Let us return to this point from another direction.

Surely, a major part of intellectual inquiry is a willingness to question what often is taken for granted, including one's own cherished beliefs. I find that my own students, at least when they are new to philosophy, are quite good at articulating their own views but less than satisfactory at anticipating serious objections to their own positions and meeting the challenges that would be presented by a thoughtful critic. Similar behavior on the athletic field can lead to the serious underestimation of an opponent or overestimation of one's own ability, misjudgments that are often made all too visible to participants and spectators alike through exposure in competitive contests.

That is, the kind of intellectual honesty and respect for truth so crucial for intellectual inquiry are closely related to similar virtues necessary for athletic success and personal improvement in sport. Participation in competitive athletics can require intellectual honesty and a concern for truth, including accuracy about one's own values and talents, in ways parallel to academic inquiry.

Thus, participation in competitive athletics conducted within a defensible educational and ethical set of requirements can be educational in its own right. And although there need not always be a causal relationship between the development of these virtues in one context (say in athletics) and in the other (say academics), there also is no reason why these qualities should not be mutually reinforcing, given the proper emphasis by coaches and professors. Even where the connection is not causal, as noted earlier, athletics, when properly conducted, may illustrate and exhibit the importance of such values as intellectual honesty and the importance of critical reflection on performance and provide standards for criticizing those who might reject such values.

Perhaps if both coaches and academic faculty made a greater attempt to emphasize the common values central to both academics and athletics, athletics and academics might in the right circumstances be mutually reinforcing rather than antithetical to each other.

Our discussion so far may have assumed that we are all in agreement about just what the academic mission of undergraduate education in the liberal arts and sciences—which are central to the ideal of critical inquiry—should be. Our discussion has associated that mission with the promotion of critical inquiry, which involves understanding major achievements in different fields, mastery of critical tools needed to assess them, and the ability to apply those tools in evaluating and assessing major positions in a variety of fields and disciplines.

This does not mean, however, that colleges and universities should have as their primary role the replication of more and more professors. It is important and even essential that students develop enthusiasm for some intellectual pursuit or activity, but it does not follow that the goal of undergraduate education is simply to produce scholars.

Surely one additional major goal is to train people to function as intelligent citizens in a democracy. If so, many of the skills learned in sport and developed through competition (and expressed to spectators through scheduled contests) can contribute to that objective. These would include learning teamwork skills, including how to cooperate with those very different from oneself in pursuit of a common enterprise; learning to appreciate achievement (including that of opponents); and learning to view opponents as persons who contribute to one's own development. Our democracy might be much healthier if many of the attitudes the ethical athlete would have toward a worthy opponent, as outlined in Chapters 2 and 3, were also applied toward those who engage in reasonable debate within the democratic process.

Finally, let me suggest, however tentatively, a contribution that competitive athletics make to liberal arts colleges that in my view is too often ignored. The contribution I have in mind is *ethical*. Competitive sport is by its very nature a value-laden activity. If carried out properly, such sports involve fair play, respect for opponents, and understanding and appreciation of (even reverence for) the traditions, practices, and values central to one's sport. Sport at its best is an unalienated activity participants engage in for its own sake, as well as for whatever external rewards participation may promote. As many scholars of sport have argued, concern for external rewards crowds out the love of the game, and its internal values often corrupt sport and lead to many of the excesses of commercialized big-time sport in the United States.

However, the kinds of institutions that are best equipped to promote harmony between athletics and academics, such as many of the institutions studied in *The Game of Life*, are just the ones where the participants play primarily for love of the game and where commercialization is minimal. Although it remains controversial whether participation in athletics at these institutions actually makes the participants more ethical than otherwise (whether in sport or in unrelated activities), competitive sport arguably can express or illustrate these values to a wider community. Thus, competitive sport at such institutions exemplifies the pursuit of an activity for its own sake and illustrates the attempt to meet challenges simply for the sake of testing oneself and learning from the test. As such, it stands in contrast to a crude sort of utilitarianism approach that asks what everything is good for in terms of immediate payoffs, or to a view that rejects achievement and standards of excellence as arbitrary or mere matters of opinion. Of course, other activities, especially in the arts, also do the same. The suggestion here is not that athletics are unique in the way suggested but only that their role in illustrating, expressing, and possibly reinforcing important values is significant and should not be ignored. The French philosopher Albert Camus was making an important point of general educational importance when he remarked that the only context in which he really learned ethics was sport.[30]

CONCLUDING COMMENT

The principal thesis of this chapter has been that although academic values and intercollegiate athletics may often be in conflict, especially at the athletically elite colleges and universities that pursue national recognition at the top of Division I, this conflict is far from inevitable. Athletics can too often be the tail that wags the academic dog, as was indicated by one university president who, when seeking funds before a state legislature, was said to have stated, "We need to build a university our football team can be proud of." But athletics, properly integrated into the academic community, can also fill important and valuable functions. In the proper context, intercollegiate athletics can even enhance and reinforce the academic mission of the institution.

This academic defense is probably best realized within the framework of institutions that do not offer athletic scholarships and that tend to integrate athletics into the overall academic community. This does not mean that athletic programs, even at colleges and universities that most exemplify the model of the mutual quest for excellence—let alone those of many Division I athletic powerhouses—are fine just as they are. However, our discussion suggests that harsh criticism of intercollegiate athletics, while justifiable in some specific instances, may be far too bleak when applied across the board and regardless of context. The role of athletics in academia can and should continue to be subject to critical scrutiny, but at the same time we should not ignore the positive contribution of athletics to many college and university communities.

THE COMMERCIALIZATION
OF SPORT

Marketing and Corruption in
Competitive Athletics

A t its very best, competitive sport can express a quest for human excellence, exhibit beauty, and create excitement and drama that fascinate millions of people throughout the world. But is its popularity its Achilles' heel? High-profile sporting events, top athletes, and dramatic athletic contests, at least in popular sports, are in demand. People want to see such events, sometimes identify with sports stars, and show tremendous loyalty to the teams or individuals with whom they identify. But because elite sports are in demand, they become something people will pay to see. In other words, sports have become more than a mutual quest for excellence: Market forces have transformed them into a commodity. Good sports often sell!

Top professional athletes and coaches in popular sports make many millions of dollars in a season, often many, many times more than teachers, college presidents, oncologists, to say nothing of the president of the United States. Professional sports franchises can be worth hundreds of millions of dollars or more. Even at the level of college sports in the United States, high-profile Division I football and basketball are referred to, if sometimes inaccurately, as "revenue-producing" sports. High-profile athletes provide entertainment and, like other entertainers, can have a huge impact on younger fans. Sports dominate the mass media, and television rights to major events, such as the NCAA Men's Basketball Championships, sell for billions. Sport, then, is not only engaged in by athletes at various levels of play; elite sports, including major professional sports, also have become commercial institutions with governing bodies and business other than sporting interests.

Has this commercialization of sport been for good or ill? What sort of ethical problems does it raise? Has sport, as many critics have charged, been corrupted by its role in the world of commerce and markets? Has it become just another commodity, something to be bought and sold, and has this commercialization not only robbed it of its purity but also damaged the values central to what makes sport a significant area of achievement and endeavor?

In this chapter, we will examine selected issues arising from the commercialization of sport. In particular, we will explore claims that the commercialization of sport has led to its corruption, then look at specific issues raised by attempts to "market" sports to a mass audience.

THE CORRUPTION THESIS: THE CORRUPTION OF SPORT BY COMMERCE

A persistent theme in the writings of many critics of modern sport is that sport today has been corrupted by the marketplace.[1] What does this claim mean? The term "corruption" refers to decay, a falling off from an original and perhaps noble purpose. We can understand corruption to mean that the values central to sport, such as those of fair competition, sportsmanship, and perhaps the mutual quest for excellence, are being or already have been undermined by the growing commercialization of sport.

One area of concern is the relationship between the mass marketing of sports and participation by masses of people. Critics have argued that the emphasis on elite athletes and the marketing of elite sports contests, along with coverage by mass media, have had a harmful effect on participation in sports by the ordinary person. For example, in his provocative and readable book *Sports in America*, James Michener warned that "we place an undue emphasis on the gifted athletes fifteen to twenty-two, a preposterous emphasis on a few professionals aged twenty-three to thirty-five, and never enough on the mass of our population aged twenty-three to seventy-five."[2] Since Michener's book was published in 1976, we have seen a drastic reduction in the physical education classes given in public schools in the United States and an epidemic of obesity among American youth that exposes millions of children to premature hypertension and type 2 diabetes, diseases previously thought to afflict only the middle-aged and elderly.

Perhaps the greatest concern is that the commercialization of sport actually corrupts the sport itself. For example, rule changes can be introduced that make the game more entertaining for the mass of fans who do not understand the nuances of the game. These changes can make the game more marketable but also can take away from the subtlety of the game or the skill needed to play it. For example, the introduction of the designated hitter into Major League Baseball may have made the game more exciting to fans who wanted more action and more frequent home runs; but, arguably, it minimized subtle strategic decisions, such as whether to have someone pinch-hit for a pitcher or have the pitcher sacrifice through a bunt, and it may also have contributed to the cheapening of the home run. Perhaps an even better example is the kind of loose officiating that observers claim has become commonplace in the National Basketball Association. Critics charge that NBA officiating allows stars to score more points but also allows them to get away with what ordinarily would be rule violations—such as traveling with the ball—thus minimizing skills but maximizing sales.

Commercialization can affect sporting contests in other ways. For example, "TV time-outs," designed to stop play to allow the showing of commercials on televised broadcasts, disrupt the flow of many games, particularly in professional and college basketball, and can even affect outcomes by allowing less well-conditioned teams to recover during the many additional breaks in the action. Television also seems to dictate the scheduling of many high-visibility college sports events, often without regard to either the academic obligations of the participating athletes or whether the timing of the game will allow for peak performance.

The role of money in sport can cut even deeper, especially in professional sports, because the wealthiest teams often find it easier to win. As some critics of sport have concluded, "commodification is pathological when it leads to the violation of the . . . meanings of the central culture of the game."[3] Isn't the entire ethic of competition undermined when the richest teams can buy the best players and in effect field a vastly superior team before the game has even begun? Although the success of the New York Yankees over decades has led to the phenomenon of Yankee hating, especially virulent in Boston and dramatized in the 1950s hit musical *Damn Yankees,* it seems more understandable in recent years when the Yankees, as one of the wealthiest franchises in Major League Baseball, can simply outbid other teams for the best players.

Similarly, the desire for profits can lead to longer and longer seasons; this, in turn, can create incentives for athletes not to play every game to the limit, thereby saving their bodies for the long haul and season-ending playoffs when championships are decided. Thus, the value of a regular season game is cheapened as athletes "pace themselves" (that is, not play their hardest for the whole game), and the regular season is seen simply as a preliminary for postseason play. At the same time, fans are often asked to pay more and more to attend the devalued regular season games, and many are priced out of the market altogether. Some writers have argued that the playoff system is not the ideal method of identifying the best team, and that the lengthier regular season is more representative of what the teams can do.[4]

The influence of money can also change the relationship between fans and players. As professional sports become more and more commercially oriented, players can be viewed as commodities to be bought, sold, and traded from team to team. As a result, they may be seen less as persons and more as products and viewed as defective if they do not produce high performance on the field. As the income available to sports stars surpasses that of the average fans many times over, fans may become alienated from players, who may be viewed (sometimes, but far from always, with justification) as spoiled, inaccessible, and remote. Since professional teams aim at making a profit, tickets may be priced beyond the means of traditional fan bases, thereby creating even more alienation.

As sports become more entertaining but perhaps less nuanced, they may draw new fans to the game who lack knowledge and respect for its traditions and ethos. These less-educated fans may contribute to a steamroller effect in which their sport is changed more and more frequently to become ever more entertaining, but at the price of important principles that make the game challenging and traditions that have been part of its history. Thus, baseball authorities may have been reluctant to enact strict rules for testing players for performance-enhancing drugs because such drug use may lead to stronger players and more home runs. Home runs are exciting, and so more home runs may be thought to attract more fans; but, as we discussed earlier, in the long run drug use may cheapen the value of the home run, lessen the challenge of the game, and make comparisons to the performances of stars of the past impossible.

These remarks suggest what might be called the "Corruption Thesis." This thesis states that the commercialization of sport, the transformation of elite sport into a product that can be bought and sold, corrupts sport. This is because the kinds of values that broad internalists (see Chapter 3) would regard as central to sport can conflict with the market value of sport. As William J. Morgan has argued, commercialization installs market values, such as the pursuit of money and fame, "as the proper ends of sporting practices thereby depriving their practitioners of any reason, let alone a compelling one, to value or engage the particular competitive challenges they present, the select athletic skills they call upon, and the human qualities and virtues they excite."[5]

Athletic excellence, according to Morgan and other proponents of the Corruption Thesis, thus becomes only an instrument to achieving external goods of sport such as fame, power, and wealth. The importance of internal goods, those skills and excellences created by the practice that are intelligible only by references to its rules and the challenges they present, is diminished or regarded as only instrumental to more important extrinsic rewards. What is entertaining is what sells, but it might not necessarily be good sport.

Morgan illustrated this point in his 2006 book, *Why Sports Morally Matter*, by describing a change in attitudes he has observed in his students over the years in a class he teaches on ethics and sport. In the past, his students were able to relate to ideas of sportsmanship and respect for the internal values of sports, such as respect for the challenge of the game, its traditions, and values. Today, however, more students seem to regard sports as simply means to external ends, and the rules as something to be manipulated for one's own advantage.[6]

In an attempt to combat the more recent cynicism toward the internal values of sport, Morgan told his class about the famous 1967 international championship tennis match between Hungarian Istvan Gulyas and the Czech star Jan Kukal. At a key point in the match, Kukal collapsed on the court with severe cramps. Although Gulyas was entitled to the win if Kukal could not resume play within a required time period, Gulyas persuaded the officials to give Kukal the extra time he needed for recovery. Kukal not only recovered but eventually won the match!

Morgan expected his students to admire Gulyas's unselfishness and sportsmanship. (Remember the quotation cited in Chapter 3 when David Duval stated that if he was playing Tiger Woods for a major golf championship, he would want Tiger to be playing his best so that a victory over him would be truly significant.) Morgan was shocked to find out, however, that his students not only did not endorse Gulyas's generous action but actually condemned it. On his view, this was because the students had not internalized the basic values of competition in sports (or, in terms of this book, the idea of sports as a mutual quest for excellence), but instead viewed sport through an egoistic lens.

"Because the students' only apparent vocabulary for evaluating actions in sports was in terms of their positive (benefits) or negative (costs) effects on the aims and desires of the individuals who play them," Morgan wrote, "Gulyas's strategic misuse of the rules was mistakenly branded as a moral failure."[7] While I have not noticed such a dramatic change in my own students' moral attitudes toward sport, perhaps because I teach at an institution that competes in Division III of the NCAA rather than at an athletically elite Division I sports power, there is little doubt that many participants and fans alike have adopted the purely instrumental attitude toward sports that concerns Morgan.

According to the Corruption Thesis, the change in student attitudes and many of the effects of the commercialization of sport cited above, such as the disruption of the flow of televised basketball games by TV time-outs, are simply symptoms of an underlying corruption of sport. According to this general account, because of the undue influence of the economic market on sports, they have been reduced or are in danger of being reduced to a commodity, a means for satisfying our other desires, such as the desire for fame and fortune, rather than remaining valuable activities in their own right with their own ethic of a mutually acceptable challenge and pursuit of excellence through competition.

Is the Corruption Thesis defensible? Has commercialization spoiled sport, as the remarks above suggest, or is there another side to the story? For example, has the mass marketing of sports broadened their appeal and made elite sport accessible to millions of spectators through greater coverage in the media? Let us consider the commercialization-of-sport critique in more detail.

EXAMINING THE CORRUPTION THESIS

Participation and Elite Sport

Let us begin with the line of criticism suggested by Michener that we are a nation of spectators rather than participants. Critics of American sports point out that millions of us spend our weekends glued to the television screen, watching football, baseball, basketball, and golf, rather than playing a sport ourselves. Moreover, most of us watch sports in relative isolation, as networks such as ESPN bring more and more major games into our homes, rather than, say, in the communal setting of a local high-school game. The time devoted to observing sports rather than participating in them is seen by critics as unfortunate, not only because of ill effects on the health of those who only sit and watch, but also because spectators miss out on the other basic benefits of participation. According to this view, the true result of the "star" system is to drive people from participation on the playing field to the grandstand, or more often, the living room couch, instead.

There is no doubt that many Americans do need to adopt a healthier lifestyle that includes a sound diet and exercise. But does emphasis on elite athletes and major sports competitions actually lower participation in sports? After all, there can be many other reasons why people don't exercise, ranging from lack of time to lack of inclination.

In fact, the thesis that emphasis on top athletes reduces participation by the many rests on at least two hidden assumptions, neither of which is clearly correct. First, it is assumed that watching sports tends to preclude participation: Spectators tend not to play precisely because they are spectators. But the truth or falsehood of this assumption is hardly obvious. On the contrary, many fans, particularly youngsters, may be motivated to try to emulate the moves of the successful athletes they see on television. What schoolyard basketball player has not tried to copy the moves of Michael Jordan or LeBron James? Spectators may promote participation rather than lower it because they often observe the techniques of top players and apply them to their own games. As social critic Christopher Lasch has noted, "it is by watching those who have mastered a sport . . . that we derive standards against which to measure ourselves."[8]

What about the fan who is a spectator only? Here we must be careful not to jump to the conclusion that such individuals are not participants simply because they are fans. Perhaps they wouldn't be participants even if they weren't fans. Maybe they enjoy watching skilled performers but would not be motivated to play themselves even if there were no top athletes to watch. Or perhaps there are inadequate facilities for participation in their area, as is true for many golfers in metropolitan areas. Accordingly, the simple assumption that emphasis on big-time sports and on the skills of an athletic elite reduces mass participation is open to serious question. Thus, the growth in women's participation in athletics since the passage of Title IX indicates that increasing the presentation of elite events in the mass media does not necessarily reduce participation.

Moreover, participation in some outdoor recreational activities is increasing, and this supports the same conclusion. For example, one major survey indicated that the number of people participating in walking as a form of recreation grew from about 93 million in 1982 to over 133 million in 1994–1995. There was a 14 percent increase in those running or jogging and a 16 percent increase in those swimming during the same period. According to a 2009 study, over 170 million Americans were participants in physical recreational activities, although some were only occasionally involved.[9] Although the population also grew during this period, and perhaps even more people would have participated if they had not been glued to the couch watching games on television, data suggest that the effect of elite sport on participation may be much more complex than critics have postulated. Thus, it is true that millions of Americans do not exercise at all, which, as we already noted, contributes to serious conditions, such as type 2 diabetes, which is increasingly afflicting even younger members of our society.

A second assumption about the relationship between participation in sports and watching them is open to even more serious question. According to a moderate version of this second assumption, being a participant in sports is of greater value than being a spectator. Playing is better than watching. In its most extreme form, this assumption characterizes watching sporting events as a passive, almost slothful activity that requires minimal intellectual and emotional capacities. The stereotype of the beer-drinking, overweight football fan who spends the whole weekend in front of the television set watching games expresses the disdain in which mere fans are sometimes held.

In rebuttal, one might point out that none of us can participate in everything. Most of us are spectators of some practice or other; theater, music, and dance come immediately to mind. After all, we don't sneer at spectators, commonly known as audiences, at the ballet or a play, even though few members of the audience are also dancers, actors, or musicians.

Moreover, spectators of sports, like audiences in other areas, are often called upon to exercise critical judgment and apply standards of excellence. As Lasch has pointed out, "Far from destroying the value of sports, the attendance of spectators makes them complete. Indeed, one of the virtues of contemporary sports lies in their resistance to the erosion of standards and their capacity to appeal to a knowledgeable audience."[10]

Consider, for example, a fine double play executed at a crucial point in a pressure-packed baseball game. An observer unacquainted with baseball might appreciate the grace and fluidity of the players' movements; however, such a spectator could not see the movements as examples of excellence at baseball. To such an uninformed spectator, a botched double play would be indistinguishable from a well-executed one, since the failure of the fielder to, say, pivot properly while throwing from second base to first base would be unappreciated.

Thus, it is unclear that watching games is of less value than playing in them, just as it is unclear that appreciating a ballet is less valuable than dancing in it. Indeed, audiences and performers often feed off each other, and superb performers in the arts as well as in sports find their performances enhanced by the reactions of spectators.

Even if there is less value in watching than in participating, it is far from clear that the intelligent observation of sports, or of other human activities in which excellence is demonstrated, is without any sort of value at all. Spectators at sporting events can be rude, ignorant, or passive, but so can audiences of other kinds. And truly appreciating a competitive athletic contest requires intelligence, observation, and the critical application of standards of excellence.

A critic might respond that although such points have force, they are an intellectualized account of what it is to be a sports fan. Spectators don't just appreciate good performances; they also root for their teams to win. Indeed, the atmosphere at an important college basketball game often far more resembles the atmosphere at a revival meeting than that of a seminar on excellence in sports. As the critics of commercialization have argued, mass audiences have become less appreciative of excellence and more interested in partying and being entertained. More and more fans see themselves as consumers out to get their money's worth and have fun, which perhaps explains the increase in their boorish behavior.

Loyalty to our favorite teams and players and expressing emotion in support of them surely play a major role in sports. And why shouldn't they? In many other areas of life, too, we develop special relationships with the people and things we care about. Nevertheless, loyalty and emotion should not get out of hand. The behavior of fans who go on rampages, destroying property and threatening life, should not be tolerated. Even where overt violence is absent, the partisan, hostile character of crowds at many sporting events threatens to intimidate visiting players and referees alike. Thus, it is true that commercialization, along with excessive partisanship, may often attract mass audiences unfamiliar with the nuances of the game and just out for a good time. When combined with the easy availability of alcohol at many contests, the combination may just be a recipe for trouble. Nevertheless, perhaps spectators would act this way even in the absence of mass media and the kind of commercialization that we have today, as they may have done, say, at the gladiatorial games in ancient Rome.

Although the critical perspective toward sports that was attributed to fans is only part of the story, and undoubtedly idealized at that, it serves as a moral and intellectual constraint on the emotionalism generated by excessively provincial fan loyalty, ignorance of the traditions and nuances of the sport, or just plain bad behavior. A moral requirement of good sportsmanship for fans is that they retain their critical perspective. Even though we need not be ashamed of caring about our team's fate and wanting them to win, when we care so much that we become unable to appreciate good play by the opposition, we are not only showing disrespect for the opposing players as persons but also undermining the very justification for athletic competition. If competition in sports should be conceived of as a mutual quest for excellence, then spectators should retain enough detachment to appreciate who best meets the challenge. Otherwise, sports are reduced to a mere means for satisfying our own egos rather than constituting an arena in which spectators and athletes alike can learn and grow by understanding and meeting ever-increasing challenges to their athletic and critical skills. Fans, then, should be what philosopher Nicholas Dixon calls "moderate partisans," combining loyalty to their team with allegiance to the core internal values of the sport, rather than either "total partisans," who care only for their team, or "total purists," who are devoted only to excellence but are without loyalty to or affiliation with others.[11]

Finally, we must not forget the positive side to commercialization. Commercialization and the mass media have made athletic contests available to large audiences all over the world and arguably have made sport more open by making it more accessible to all. The trick is to enjoy this benefit while minimizing the deleterious effects of mass consumption. More will be said about how this might be accomplished later in the chapter.

Our discussion suggests that, first, it is unclear whether emphasis on elite sport in the mass media lowers participation. Second, watching athletic contests may have its own kind of value. Sporting audiences, no less than other audiences, are called upon to appreciate excellence and to apply critical standards of judgment. Emotional bonds to favorite teams and players, when constrained by the norms of respect for persons and appreciation of excellence, can enrich our existence and motivate us to do our best.

The Internal Goods of Sports

We have considered the claim that too much emphasis has been placed on the star athlete and too little on participation by the many. It may remain controversial just how much emphasis is too much, but some important distinctions have emerged from our discussion among the kinds of goods that sport can promote. Michener and others who worry about lack of participation in sport seem focused on what might be regarded as the *basic benefits* of involvement with sport.[12] These benefits involve better health through exercise, the fun of recreation, and the joy of competition. Presumably, they are available to all participants, not just elite players. The basic benefits are to be contrasted with what have been called the "scarce benefits," or goods of sport—namely, fame and wealth. By their very nature, these are available only to elite stars at the highest levels of athletic competition. Those who worry that we have overemphasized the performance of elite athletes fear that the majority of people will lose out on the basic benefits by becoming passive observers of the pursuit of fame and fortune by the elite. Those worried about commercialization fear that emphasis on the scarce benefits will corrupt sport.

Our discussion suggests that emphasis on the basic and the scarce benefits of sport alone sets up far too narrow a framework for discussion. Discussing the distribution of the scarce and basic benefits only immediately suggests tension between the athletic elite and the greater bulk of the population, which includes many individuals who lack adequate opportunity to pursue the basic benefits. But emphasis on opposition between an elite and the rest of us may be misleading. In philosophy, the questions we ask may determine the answers we consider. In restricting ourselves only to questions about scarce and basic benefits, we may have cut ourselves off from considering the relationships that exist between outstanding performances by the few, on the one hand, and the enjoyment and appreciation of the many, on the other.

In particular, scarce and basic benefits are external to sports; that is, each logically can be conceived and obtained apart from sports themselves. They are what we call "external goods." Goods such as health, fun, fame, and wealth can be understood and obtained by those who have no understanding of or relationship to sports.

In addition to such external goods, there are also goods that are *internal* to sports. Goods are internal to a practice or activity when they cannot be understood or enjoyed independently of that practice or activity. For example, the concept of a "home run" is unintelligible apart from the practice and rules of baseball; the elegance of a winning combination in chess cannot be understood or enjoyed without an understanding of the rules and strategy that characterize the game of chess.[13]

The distinction between the internal and external goods of sports is central to our concerns in this chapter because the conformity to standards of excellence implicit in various sports creates shared internal goods available to the whole community. Spectators appreciate and share in the enjoyment of the internal goods created by top performers at all levels of athletic competition. Thus, often ignored by those who fear overemphasis on an athletic elite is that skilled participants in sports are as capable of creating internal goods, shared by large numbers of people, as are skilled participants in, say, dance or theater. As argued in the previous section, audiences who can appreciate these goods are no more passive than those who appreciate the arts and humanities.

Thus, when it comes to an evaluation of the Corruption Thesis and the degree to which sport has become commercialized, we need to look at positive as well as negative aspects of commercialization. Perhaps, as argued above, the alleged conflict between benefits for an elite and benefits for large numbers of others has been overstated, and the role of top athletes in creating internal goods that can be appreciated and enjoyed by unprecedented numbers of observers has not been given the attention it deserves by critics of the current sporting scene.

Does Commercialization Undermine Internal Values?

One of the principal arguments in favor of the Corruption Thesis is that the transformation of elite sport into a commodity is in conflict with the very internal goods that make sport so valuable. This is largely because sport needs to be entertaining if it is to sell. But for it to be entertaining to mass audiences, it needs to enjoy mass appeal. Therefore, sport becomes cruder, perhaps more violent, and certainly less nuanced. Players come to value external goals over internal ones, and thus sport is further corrupted. For example, since many professional basketball players' salaries are based more on scoring averages than on fitting into a team, the offense on a basketball team must ensure that a star player gets his quota of shots. More generally, the players come to see their sport as a business, and personal profit becomes more important than the good of the game. Many young stars are too immature to handle their wealth and celebrity status, and stories of self-destructive and criminal behavior by star athletes have become far too common.

Although even the casual observer of contemporary sport will acknowledge that this critique has much force, it is not the whole story. For one thing, as just noted above, the presentation of major sporting events by the mass media has allowed millions of spectators to observe top athletes at the highest levels of competition, something that might well have never been possible without commercialization. Of equal importance, not all changes in the rules of sport have been for the worse, even when one of the reasons for the change was to make the sport more entertaining.

For example, the introduction of the shot clock and the three-point field goal in basketball did make the game more entertaining, but also arguably made it better and more challenging. The three-point shot helped open the court for fast, fluid play; gave teams more options on both defense and offense, thereby making the game more nuanced; and produced more chances for comebacks and exciting finishes. Similarly, the shot clock made the game more entertaining by limiting the extent to which teams with a lead could stall rather than attempt shots, but it also made it faster by bringing out the tremendous athleticism of top players.

Remember, also, that some advocates of the Corruption Thesis have maintained that the playoff system, primarily supported by sports organizations because it brings in money, is not the ideal method of identifying the best team, and that the lengthier regular season is much more representative of how well the teams can play.[14] But surely there is another side to this argument. Although the regular season often shows which team is best, that may not always (or even usually) be the case. The regular season may end with a league leader collapsing near the end of its schedule but holding onto a big lead that it built up earlier. It clearly was not the best team by the season's end. What about a young team that improved and was playing better than the leaders at the season's end? What about a team whose star players were injured for much of the regular season and as a result did not finish first, but was clearly the best team by the season's end when the stars returned? In such cases, performance under the intense pressure of the playoffs may show which team is best more clearly than the regular season did.

Moreover, as Stephen Finn has pointed out, playoffs may bring about dramatic moments, or what I would call internal goods to be enjoyed by fans and participants alike, that justify some loss of accuracy in determining which team is best.[15] To use Finn's example, perhaps the win by the New York Giants over the previously undefeated New England Patriots in the 2007 Super Bowl created such internal goods even if New England, by some standards, actually was the better team.

If these points have force, playoffs may be both commercially successful and compatible with the central values of sport as a mutual quest for excellence through competition. Indeed, if the goals of sports competition should include creation of internal goods enjoyable by the many and not just the few, commercialization may promote benefits that need to be balanced against its costs.

What about the effects of commercialization on individual athletes? Critics of commercialization argue plausibly that the big money available to top athletes has had a corrupting effect on many young players (although it has also lifted many athletes out of poverty). It also is true that many players have become transients, going from team to team as market forces dictate, through trades and free agency agreements. This may well have had a deleterious effect on fan-player relationships, as professional players are far less likely to be viewed as members of a common community. Rather, they are too often seen as mere products or resources whose function is to provide wins; they quickly lose the support of fans and may even open themselves to abuse when they fail.

An example of this change involves a comparison of fan reaction to Gil Hodges's failure in the 1952 World Series and Bill Buckner's famous error in the 1986 series. Hodges, later to become a World Series winner as manager of the New York Mets, was, in 1952, a star slugger and top fielding first baseman for the National League champions, the Brooklyn Dodgers. The Dodgers had led the way in breaking the color line in Major League Baseball in the late 1940s, and Jackie Robinson, the first African American to play Major League Baseball, was a star of the 1952 team, along with Roy Campanella, Pee Wee Reese, and Duke Snider. The team was beloved in Brooklyn and, indeed, gave Brooklyn much of its identity. The series was against the archenemy, the crosstown New York Yankees, a team with its own stars, including Mickey Mantle, Yogi Berra, and Phil Rizzuto. Feelings ran high in Brooklyn, which had never won a World Series, and which loved its team. (I even remember my parents letting me stay home from school for several days to watch the games on television!)

The Dodgers lost in a thrilling series that ran seven games. Throughout the series, Hodges time after time failed to get a hit. However, as his hitless streak continued, fan support for him became more and more vocal. The fans suffered with him rather than regarding him as a failed product to be treated with derision and disgust. The Dodgers might well have won if Hodges had gotten just a few key hits, but he went hitless throughout the series. Nevertheless, fan support for Hodges by the Dodger faithful throughout the off-season was overwhelming. Hodges responded by having an outstanding season for Brooklyn in 1953, and the Dodgers ran away from the rest of the league to win the pennant once again.

Contrast this with the treatment given to Red Sox player Bill Buckner after his crucial error in game six of the 1986 World Series contributed to Boston's loss of the series to the New York Mets. The Red Sox led in the ninth inning of the sixth game. One more out would have given them a victory in the World Series. A ground ball was hit toward first base that would have ended the game, if fielded cleanly. Although the grounder was not routine, it should not have presented extraordinary difficulty to a Major Leaguer; however, Buckner, first baseman for the Red Sox, failed to field the ball. The batter for the Mets was safe on first base, and the Mets went on to win the game, and the next day, the series.

Although Buckner lived in Boston, he was reviled by fans during the off-season. The harassment became so great that Buckner felt he had to move from the area and leave the Boston team. In effect, Buckner was driven out of Boston by the reaction of the fans to his error. In contrast, Hodges had been supported by his fans in spite of his failure in the 1952 World Series, and he remained a star for many years. What accounts for the difference in treatment?

Although the reasons are complex, some critics of contemporary sport might argue that the growing commercialization of the game since Hodges's time as a player was a contributing factor. True, Red Sox fans were frustrated by a long series of perceived failures by their team, but the Dodgers had never won a World Series before 1952. Dodger fans were also frustrated, but they still treated Hodges with compassion. Indeed, it is plausible that, because fans in 1986 were not as close to players as in 1952, they tended to regard them more as high-priced products than as fellow members of a sports community. They were expected to produce rather than being respected as individuals.

In addition, some would argue that the Buckner example is just one instance of a disturbing trend toward more and more abusive behavior by fans, which in turn is at least partially the result of the increasing commercialization of sport and the consequent split alienating fans not only from players but from the traditions and principles of the game.

Although the force of any explanatory hypothesis is empirical rather than purely philosophical, the claim that commercialization of sport and its marketing as a product have frequently been harmful has the ring of plausibility; but it, too, can be overstated. Commercialization may have had a corrupting effect on many athletes, but it does not seem to have affected others' love of the game. Many great professional and top amateur athletes and coaches retain a tremendous work ethic and are exemplars of respect for their games. Michael Jordan, Lance Armstrong, Annika Sorenstam, Grant Hill, Joe Paterno, Derek Jeter, and Billie Jean King are among the many who come immediately to mind.

And although the behavior of spectators and players alike has deteriorated in many respects in recent years, it is doubtful whether all the blame can be placed on the commercialization of sport. What of the general decline in ethical standards throughout society? These, in turn, may be due to strains on the family, inadequacies in the educational system, declining economic security, alcohol and drug abuse, and a variety of complex factors that go well outside the world of sport. Indeed, it is not in the interest of professional teams, sports organizations, or top athletes to encourage abusive behavior among fans or in society at large.

How, then, are we to assess the Corruption Thesis? First, is it simply a matter of adding up the benefits and harms caused by commercialization in a kind of utilitarian cost-benefit analysis? Do the benefits produced outweigh the bad effects, or does the bad outweigh the good? Or does commercialization violate some fundamental moral principle so that it is wrong, at least if carried too far, regardless of the results of the utilitarian calculus?

Our own discussion suggests that the transformation of elite sport into a commodity does present real dangers to an ethic of sport. We also have argued that there are compensating benefits and that the criticism of commercialization may sometimes be exaggerated, as we found to be the case with criticism of the playoff system. Rather than engage in a purely consequential analysis of the effects of commercialization, it may be more profitable to ask what moral principles should apply to professional and elite sports in our society. In any event, commercialization is so entrenched that it has probably become a permanent feature of the sporting scene, one with positive as well as negative aspects. Let us consider, then, whether there is an ethical framework that would regulate the effects of economic markets in sport so that we could enjoy the benefits of commercialization while also maintaining respect for the internal values of sport. Perhaps we can arrive at such a framework by considering ethical issues that arise in the business of sport.

THE ETHICAL RESPONSIBILITIES OF
BUSINESS AND SPORTS MANAGEMENT

Business and Social Responsibility

What ethical principles should constrain the commercialization of sport? On whom do the responsibilities for applying these principles fall?

The second question is crucial. Part of the process of commercialization has been the transformation of many professional sports franchises into corporations, some with international connections in the recruiting of players and marketing of their products. Equipment companies, such as Nike, are transnational corporations as well and exert enormous influence on the world of sport. We also need to consider the role of sports regulatory organizations, such as the National Football League, the Professional Golfers Association, and Major League Baseball, which, through officials such as the commissioner of baseball, are supposed to serve as a check on corporate interests that might be harmful to the game.

Some might think the answer is relatively easy to determine, at least as far as corporations are concerned. Professional sports franchises, they might say, are the same as other business organizations in fundamental ways. Their role is to make a profit, and to expect them to do otherwise is to ask them to disregard their obligations to stockholders or to, in effect, requisition the money of private owners for public purposes without their consent. As the economist Milton Friedman, winner of the Nobel Prize and defender of the free market, once put it, "there is one and only one social responsibility of business—to use its resources and engage in activities designed to increase its profits as long as it stays within the rules of the game, which is to say, engages in open and free competition, without deception and fraud."[16]

Friedman's view is open to criticism, however; in a way, it is similar to the claim that the only moral responsibility of the athlete is to try to win within the rules. As we have seen, athletes may well have other moral responsibilities, such as respecting the principles presupposed by their sport, showing appropriate respect for their sport, and carrying out both negative and positive obligations to bring about good competitive contests. Can similar points be brought against the thesis that the only social responsibility of business is to make profits?

To begin, consider what arguments might support Friedman's view. A utilitarian might say that the economy simply works best if business aims at profits, for this promotes the most efficient allocation of resources. Second, where corporations are concerned, one might argue that the managers have a moral responsibility to use the stockholders' funds in the way intended by the investors themselves, which surely is to get the best financial return possible. Wouldn't the allocation of funds for other purposes, including the pursuit of moral goals, in effect be taking from the investors without their consent, or, as some Kantians might argue, be treating the investors as mere means or instruments for the achievment of social goods? Wouldn't this be stealing? Rule utilitarians could argue for a similar conclusion by maintaining that the investment would be discouraged and the economy harmed if investors could not be sure that their money would be used for its intended purpose of making the company more profitable. Accordingly, don't professional sports teams, equipment companies, and other sports-related businesses have exactly the duty Friedman specifies—to make as much of a profit as the market allows?

These arguments, although important, are not decisive; even if a totally free market could be achieved and did promote economic efficiency, economic efficiency is not always the only value at stake in morally evaluating social policy. The most efficient system, for example, may not be the most just. Friedman's own analysis conceded this point by acknowledging that profits may be pursued subject to the constraint of other values—namely, nondeception and avoidance of fraud. But why should those be the only values corporations take into account? What about, for example, workers' safety, the safety of products, and concern for the environment?

Such concerns undermine the claim that the only obligation of corporations is to make a profit. However, what of the argument that for managers to appropriate investments to secure ethical goals is to divert money from the purpose stockholders intended when investing, which is to make a profit, and is in effect stealing from them? But this claim assumes the very point at issue—namely, that it is correct to regard making a profit as the only obligation of a business. If businesses have other obligations, such as promoting workers' safety and not committing injustices, and stockholders have good reason to be aware of those obligations, then the balancing of profits against appropriate ethical constraints is an obligation of business, not an improper distraction from its true goals.

Although the issue here is complex, several writers have suggested that the relationship between business, particularly corporations, and society is contractual, or at least based on a kind of reciprocity. The terms on which a corporation can exist, what legally counts as a corporation, and its various privileges and powers are defined by society through the legal system. In short, society grants business a certain sphere of legitimate activity but has a right to expect it to honor certain duties in return. The political scientist Robert A. Dahl expressed this sort of view:

> Today it is absurd to regard the corporation simply as an enterprise established for the sole purpose of allowing profit making. We the citizens give them special rights, powers, and privileges . . . and benefits on the understanding that their activities will fulfill purposes. . . . Every corporation should be thought of as a social enterprise whose existence and decisions can be justified only insofar as they serve public or social purposes.[17]

As Norman E. Bowie commented, "The corporation must not only benefit those who create it, it must benefit those who permit it (namely society as a whole)."[18]

The point here is that large corporations don't operate in a social vacuum. Rather, the legal and political order often lays down the constraints under which corporations can operate. Even more, it provides benefits that enable them to prosper through tax codes and provision of other forms of public support. Thus, sports stadiums in which professional teams play may be funded in part by the public.

Since corporations are not purely private entities, and since they benefit from public support in a variety of ways, reciprocity requires that they also pay appropriate attention to broad values of central concern to the public in the democratic state. As one prominent approach to business ethics put it, corporations have responsibilities to "stakeholders," those whom corporate actions might seriously harm, as well as stockholders.[19]

But doesn't this view itself start from the questionable assumption that society has a right to dictate the terms on which those who have legitimately acquired wealth may invest it? After all, isn't it the stockholder's or owner's money? On what grounds can society regulate what they do with it?

These questions reflect a position in political philosophy often referred to as "libertarianism." Libertarians believe that the fundamental human right is the right not to be interfered with by others, particularly not to be used for the purposes of others. In their view, at least in an extreme form, the appropriation of property without consent is unjust interference with personal freedom. Thus, libertarians would regard any income tax used for redistributive purposes, such as provision of education, health care, or basic welfare benefits for the poor, as a gross violation of our most fundamental right.[20]

However, if it is conceded that society does have a right to regulate the economy to an appropriate extent, as happens in Western democracies, including the United States, the contractual analysis of business responsibilities seems defensible. Regulation can be seen as defensible to the extent that it enhances social welfare and recognizes nonlibertarian basic rights, such as the right to public education, compatible with a reasonable and significant degree of economic freedom.

Although a full exploration of libertarianism and its critics would take us too far afield, further reflection may well support the modern welfare state's rejection of libertarianism and its endorsement of a broader set of economic as well as liberty rights.[21] The same reasons that may lead us to defend the right to the kind of personal liberty that libertarians rightly defend, and to embody versions of it in our basic constitution, may also support broader welfare rights to basic necessities. For example, libertarian rights to personal liberty seem important because we justifiably view persons as centers of autonomy entitled to make their own choices about how they should live. But welfare rights are also important to preserving autonomy and choice. How autonomous can one be without food, shelter, education, or health care? How much control over one's life would one have then? Libertarianism can be reasonably rejected, then, as arbitrarily regarding only liberty rights to freedom from interference as fundamental while rejecting all welfare rights, even though some form of welfare rights seem as necessary to securing our control over our destinies as liberty itself.

We can approach this point from the ideal social contract we considered when assessing the use of performance-enhancing drugs in Chapter 4. Reasonable and impartial people (following John Rawls's idea of choosing the principles of society as if in ignorance of one's position in it as well as of personal characteristics that might contribute to personal success or failure) arguably would reject a society organized entirely around the freedom of market transactions, since they would (being impartial) need to consider the disabled, the poor, the frail elderly, children in need of education and health care, and (especially relevant for our purposes) the commitments of many to social practices regarded as having value over and above their value as commodities, such as the practice of sport.[22]

Accordingly, although libertarians are right to emphasize liberty and the preservation of freedom that protects us from exploitation by society, it is reasonable to think that limitations on the economic market designed to preserve fundamental values and rights are also justifiable. This implies, to return to the social responsibilities of corporations, that business is not entitled to do anything it pleases to increase profits, but that it can be constrained to operate according to reasonable principles designed to protect fundamental rights and values. Stockholders, therefore, have no right to expect that corporations in which they invest may do anything to increase profit, no matter how ethically repugnant, such as disregard the safety of workers or consumers. Rather, business, including corporate entities in businesses connected to sport, such as professional teams, can and should be expected to pursue profits within reasonable ethical constraints.

Moral Responsibilities of Business to Sport

But although we might agree that business has some ethical obligations, such as not deliberately marketing unsafe or defective products, what are the obligations of businesses closely connected with sport? In particular, what moral constraints, if any, apply to major league professional sports teams?

According to one view, sports teams may have the same obligations as other businesses with respect to safety and the environment but have no special obligation to preserve and protect important principles of sport. If making sport more entertaining sells, then, since they are in business, sports teams ought to do it. What sells is what pleases fans; making sport more entertaining and therefore more profitable increases overall utility by making fans happy and also by increasing financial returns for owners and players alike.

But should professional sport be regarded as only a form of entertainment? Focusing only on what sells, and never on the competitiveness or integrity of the game, may not even be in the best financial interests of owners and players. Suppose, for example, that newer football fans wanted to see more and more violence in the game. To sell more tickets, professional football eliminated rules that protected vulnerable players such as quarterbacks and punt returners, moving toward and even beyond the so-called Extreme Football League experiment of the late 1990s.

The result would likely be a rash of injuries to star players, followed by less exciting contests, and then, probably, fewer sales. Pro football might come to be regarded as more like professional wrestling, a form of unsophisticated entertainment rather than a thrilling sport, and fans might turn their attention from it to sports perceived to be truer to the idea of competitive challenge. (In fact, Extreme Football did not sell.) Similarly, if professional basketball players became more and more focused on great individual moves that looked good on televised highlight films, and less and less on fundamentals and team play, fans would likely lose interest in the professional game and turn to college basketball instead.

Thus, it may be to the *mutual advantage* of sports teams in a common league or sport to agree to arrangements that limit their freedom to tamper too much with the integrity of the game. Leagues may create an official bureaucracy, such as the Office of the Commissioner of Baseball or the PGA Tour, that has the explicit function of protecting the good of the sport. Although it is important for such officials to be truly independent of owners and players, each of whom may become too focused on short-term financial gain, such independence may be difficult to achieve. However, the creation of official regulatory institutions, which have as at least part of their mission the preservation of the integrity and competitiveness of the game, is a structural mechanism for preserving some of the values of sport as a mutual quest for excellence even in the professional arena.

This argument from mutual advantage suggests that it is in each team's overall interest to set limits on the pursuit of profits. If all teams engaged in the unlimited pursuit of profit, sport might become so diminished by commercialization that it attracted less and less interest, and so everyone would lose.

Mutual advantage aside, would it be morally wrong on other grounds for the sports industry to turn a sport into merely a form of entertainment, even though that would severely diminish the key principles of skill and competition central to the game? In fact, it is doubtful whether the moral obligations of business can be reduced to considerations of mutual advantage alone. What if one team was so dominant that it was not to its advantage to cooperate in setting limits? Or what if one group—say, traditional sports fans concerned about preserving the integrity of the game—was so weak that it was not in the interest of more powerful companies and firms to negotiate with them? Considerations of mutual advantage, in many areas, seem to conflict with rather than exhaust the demands of fairness and other fundamental moral principles.[23]

Let us apply this idea to concrete examples. Suppose that Major League Baseball introduced a much livelier ball than the one used at present that led to home runs becoming routine. Further, say it became common for teams to score twenty runs in a game, but, for some reason, many fans found this entertaining and bought more tickets. What would have been lost, however, would be the balanced contest between pitcher and hitter that has always been central to the game. Or, even worse, suppose professional basketball games came to have scripted endings, just as professional wrestling matches are now said to have. Games would become less like contests and more and more like dramatic plays that followed exciting and entertaining scripts. Thrilling comebacks, last-minute shots, and comical mistakes might help to fill arenas, but they would all be choreographed in advance, the outcome decided by the writers of the day's "play" rather than by the play of the game.

What, if anything, would be wrong about such scenarios? After all, the owners would profit, as would the players (perhaps better referred to in the last example as "actors"), and masses of fans would enjoy the entertainment provided. The "purists" who objected that true sport no longer existed would be powerless and ignored. Such changes might be to the mutual advantage of many, but would they be justifiable ethically?

It is probably true that if sports were transformed in such a manner, they would not remain interesting to many people. Good sport is entertaining because it demonstrates human skills and virtues in meeting difficult challenges to mind and body alike, rather than mimicking such values by following a script. To the extent that professional wrestling or partially scripted exhibition games, such as those of the talented Harlem Globetrotters, are popular, it is because they are parasitic on genuine competitive sport where the outcome of the game depends on the performances and skills of players and coaches. In other words, it is activity governed by the underlying principles of sport as a mutual quest for excellence that make sport of interest in the first place. (That is why it is to the mutual advantage of members of the sports industry to preserve those values rather than allowing them to diminish or disappear.)

More important, something of great value would be lost if sport were transformed solely to a commercially viable form of entertainment at the cost of losing its basic character—namely, the value of sport as a mutual quest for excellence through challenge. Although professional sports do not exactly fit this model, and in many ways (sometimes justifiably) try to appeal to mass audiences, their appeal has value precisely because it reflects the underlying principles of sport, not entertainment.

Another way of making this point begins by asking who would be harmed if commercialization were allowed to transform sport too radically in the direction of pure commercial entertainment. Surely it would be members of the broader sports community: players, officials, and fans who were devoted to the principles of the sport and who respected the game. If sport, as argued in earlier chapters of this book, embodies and expresses values of enduring significance, such as the importance of dedication in overcoming challenge, or the value of standards of excellence, then the broader community would lose as well.

If it is justifiable to regard corruption in the values of sport as wrong, or, more simply, if it is wrong to corrupt values of such fundamental importance, there is an argument for concluding that the sports industry is more than just a marketer of sport; it can also be regarded as having a fiduciary relationship to sport. This means the industry has some responsibility for preserving both the integrity of sport and respect for its central values. This may not only be in the best interests of the industry, as indicated by the argument from mutual advantage, but may extend beyond self-interest to the protection of what is of deep value as well.

An Example: Technology and the Good of the Game

The growth of technology and its application to sport have raised a host of ethical issues that bear on our discussion. One of them concerns the possibility of conflict between the marketing of technologically advanced equipment and what is good for the game. Advanced technology, if it is available only to some competitors, can tilt the playing field in a way that is arguably suspect. If an individual or team wins a contest because of access to technology unavailable to opponents, has the best team or player really triumphed? Norwegian philosopher Gunnar Breivik has suggested that performance-enhancing technology should be made available to all competitors if it is available to any.[24] Otherwise, the wealthiest teams (or countries, if we are thinking of the Olympics) would have competitive advantages unrelated to athletic ability. Sport would become as much a competition between teams of scientists and engineers as contests between athletes.

If one issue concerning new technology concerns access to it, another concerns threats to the challenge of the game itself. Might new technological breakthroughs in equipment, even if available to all competitors, simply make the sport too easy by significantly reducing the challenges it faces? Let us examine this second issue in more depth by considering an alleged example of making the game too easy through technology.

For some time, the United States Golf Association (USGA), the chief rule-making body for golf in the United States, Mexico, and Canada, has had growing concerns about whether technological advances in golf club design might reduce the challenges of the game, particularly by making existing golf courses too easy because of the greater distance the newer clubs allow golfers to hit the ball. Recently, the organization adopted a standard limiting the "spring-like effect," or the extent to which the clubface of drivers might rebound, in an effort to keep technology under control. However, the Royal and Ancient, the rule-making body in England that has authority over the rest of the golfing world, did not agree, and as a result, for several years (1999–2002), clubs that conformed to the rules for tournament play elsewhere failed to conform in the United States and other countries where USGA rules applied. (Both associations agreed to a common standard in the fall of 2002.)

Although smaller companies had been marketing nonconforming drivers in the United States for some time, and others have been purchased abroad for use here, the stakes went up once industry giant Callaway challenged the USGA by offering a nonconforming driver for sale on the American market. In a spirited defense by its innovative founder, the late Ely Callaway, the company argued that the effect of nonconforming drivers on elite golf was marginal but that they could make the extremely difficult game of golf more fun for recreational golfers by allowing them to hit the ball farther than they could with conforming clubs. After all, it can be argued that no one is hurt if the nonconforming clubs merely help a segment of the golfing-challenged public to hit the ball farther and score better (the two may not even go together, since longer shots may simply go deeper into the woods!). Perhaps, as a kind of compromise, rules for tournament play among professionals and top amateurs could still prohibit the use of the clubs, but the clubs could be allowed for players at other levels to make a game that is often difficult to learn more manageable for them. In this view, since no one is hurt and many are helped, Callaway's action increases the net welfare of the golfing community and so is to be applauded rather than condemned.

But is this argument decisive? This kind of reasoning maintains that the ethical thing to do is what provides the most benefit and the least loss for all affected, and therefore seems utilitarian. But before we accept the results of this kind of moral cost-benefit analysis, at least two questions need to be asked. First, have the costs and benefits been correctly assessed? Second, are consequences the only relevant considerations? Do other sorts of moral considerations, such as fairness or respect for our opponent, also need to be considered?

It may be useful now to consider briefly the kind of argument advanced by the great sixteenth-century British philosopher Thomas Hobbes, who tried to show us why we would have had to invent the state if it had not evolved on its own. Hobbes argued that in the absence of a central authority, we would find ourselves in what he called "the state of nature." With no enforceable common standards left to soften rivalry and restrain our baser impulses, competition would be unbridled and life would end up "nasty, brutish, and short."

Although the consequences in sport are not nearly so dire, critics argue that the kind of argument presented by Callaway threatens to plunge golf as we know it into an analog of the Hobbesian state of nature (and may also have implications for national concerns about the erosion of standards).

If some golfers decided it was permissible to use a club that violated the rule, why couldn't other golfers use a nonconforming ball that could go farther than conforming balls under the same conditions? Why couldn't still other golfers decide that it was all right to carry fifteen clubs instead of the fourteen allowed by the rules? Eventually, each group of golfers would be playing its own version of golf, and none would be playing the standard version. (In fact, isn't it a mystery why anyone would spend many hundreds of dollars on an illegal club when the same results could be obtained for only a few dollars by playing an illegal ball, or, for no money at all, by teeing off a few yards ahead of the marker indicating the beginning of each hole?)

But is this Balkanization of golf so bad? Why shouldn't different groups of golfers play by their own rules? Of course, we need a set of uniform rules for serious competition among elite professional and amateur players, but the vast majority of players are recreational golfers who rarely, if ever, play in highly competitive events. What harm is done if nonconforming clubs are used in recreational but not in competitive play?

This rejoinder has at least two flaws, the second of which may be of social significance that goes well beyond golf. First, it assumes that there is a sharp line between competitive and recreational play, when in fact there are many competitive levels, ranging from a course championship through regional, state, and national amateur competitions, to the professional tours, that are not always clearly distinct.

But let us consider a more fundamental difficulty that applies beyond golf to many other competitive sports. As our discussion in earlier chapters has suggested, what makes sport so fascinating is that its rules create a challenge that, if the sport is well designed, can test our hearts, minds, and physical abilities to the limit. Golf has long been known as particularly challenging: It is a game no one ever fully conquers. If equipment is allowed to make the game too easy, the challenge, if not lost, is significantly reduced, and achievement becomes too easy to obtain.

Consider the golfer who buys a nonconforming club, uses a nonconforming ball, and places the ball in easy positions to hit rather than "playing it as it lies" as the rules require. Suppose this golfer breaks 90, that is, completes the round taking fewer than 90 strokes, for the first time. (For many golfers, breaking 90 on a reasonably difficult golf course is the dividing line between being a true player and a novice, or "hacker.") Well, did the player really break 90 at golf? Arguably, the player was playing another game having some resemblance to golf—let's call it modified golf—and although the player broke 90 in modified golf, it is far from clear that 90 was broken in golf.

That is, the cost of making the game too easy is that achievement is cheapened. Even worse, focus is placed on a result, the score, which in this case is breaking 90—rather than the process of achieving it. In an effort to make ourselves feel good—"Guess what! I broke 90 for the first time today!"—we have eliminated the conditions that give a score of below 90 its significance. (Grade inflation might have the same unintended consequence in higher education.) This is more than—or at least different from—a utilitarian point about which practices tend to satisfy or frustrate people's preferences; it is a point about the value of striving for achievement and challenge in a difficult enterprise and even more about our nature as persons. By reducing standards to make success ever easier, we lose the opportunity to try to meet challenges that force us to stretch the limits of our abilities, a point that applies to a variety of areas, especially education, as well as golf.

But, skeptics might retort, your argument against nonconforming clubs is grossly overstated. Other advances in equipment, ranging from the introduction of the sand wedge to the use of graphite shafts and the introduction of large-headed titanium drivers, and, most especially, the evolution of the golf ball, have already made the game easier for the average player. Similar advances have been made in other sports, where changes in the composition of tennis racquets, cross-country skis, poles for vaulting, swimsuits, and other equipment have resulted in new standards of achievement.

These points have force but do not tell the whole story. Surely some technological changes are welcome and improve the sport. The pertinent issues, however, are where lines are to be drawn—how much improvement alters the nature of the game—and who is to draw the line, the governing bodies of various sports, or equipment companies? In fact, so many swimming records have been broken in so short a time since the introduction of full-body polyurethane swimsuits that use of such suits was prohibited in major competitions beginning in 2010. This decision seems reasonable, since such rapid changes in performance seem largely due to enhancement by the technology rather than to sudden improvements in the skills of the athletes.

But to return to the example from golf, the real price of widespread recreational use of the nonconforming clubs, then, would be a devaluation of the challenge of golf and a weakening of the bonds of solidarity that unite golfers, as golfers would come to be divided into different groups according to which version of a series of games resembling golf they chose to play. Life in the golfing "state of nature" may not be "nasty, brutish, and short," as it would be in the Hobbesian one, but the true significance of one's score would be a mystery, since it would not always be clear which version of modified golf one was playing. Some golf companies might gain financially from the promotion and sale of nonconforming drivers. But their policies arguably would harm the game by reducing its challenge. They would make it easier for golfers to gain self-esteem, but at the cost of losing respect. In the golfing state of nature, good scores might come more easily, but what would they be worth?

An Ethical Compromise

In the debate, points of some merit have been made by both sides. The equipment companies surely are correct to point out that technological advances are part of sport, have often made sport more exciting, and can benefit recreational as well as elite players by bringing the game within the grasp of ordinary participants. But surely governing bodies of sports are also correct to say that equipment companies should not be the judge of when technological advances cease to be good for the game, or even harm it by reducing its challenges, and that a line sometimes may need to be drawn, even if not always in a perfect place.

The challenge of where to draw the line is significant. Preserving the integrity of the challenges of a sport is only one consideration that needs to be taken into account. Safety may be another. Thus, the use of aluminum rather than the traditional wood bats in baseball has raised concerns because the velocity with which the ball rebounds from such bats is so high that the safety of pitchers is threatened. A ball hit sharply right back at the pitcher's mound may come so quickly that the pitcher has no defense against being hit and perhaps suffering a serious injury. Cost is another factor. In golf, courses may simply be lengthened to mitigate the impact of "hot" clubs and balls. But longer courses are more expensive to build and maintain, and extra costs may be passed on to participants. This could make the game less accessible to many players, thereby reducing their numbers and actually hurting the equipment companies in the long run by reducing the size of their market. (Remember the argument from mutual advantage discussed above.)

Although there often will be no perfect place to draw the line about when technologically advanced equipment is and is not permissible, all these factors suggest that it is best to have a line drawn rather than have none at all. Otherwise, we might find ourselves in the sporting analog of Hobbes's state of nature where the unconstrained pursuit of commercial interests is all too likely to undermine the good of the sport.

Hobbes's own solution to the problem of the state of nature was to argue that all power should be conceded to a sovereign who would make the rules for all. But, as proponents of democracy have long argued, such a solution has grave dangers of its own: Sovereigns may rule arbitrarily and need not focus on the best interests of their subjects.

In sports, a more desirable solution would be for governing bodies to have control of where the line on technology is set, but to operate in an open manner that takes into account the interests of the constituents of the sporting community, including fans, equipment companies, sports teams, recreational and elite athletes, and the principles of the game itself. When there are disagreements, different points of view need to be expressed and heard by the governing authorities. Finally, the sports governing bodies, such as the USGA in golf, need to make decisions constrained by concern for the basic values underlying their sport and the more general constraints set by the value and nature of competition in sport.

These authorities will not always make the best possible decisions; however, as in drawing a line with respect to performance-enhancing drugs, decisions must be reasonable and nonarbitrary, must be based on dialogue among different constituencies of the sport, and must give due weight to underlying principles of sport that apply to the situation.

This does not mean that business concerns should always give way to reasonable interpretations of principle. Great increases in the entertainment value of a sport and its interest to a wide audience may sometimes justify modifications in the rules, even those that make the game less nuanced but more accessible to the casual fan. (Perhaps the introduction of the designated-hitter rule in baseball might be such a modification.) How the balance is to be struck when interests or values conflict may depend heavily on contextual factors specific to each sport. Nevertheless, our discussion supports the view that sports organizations properly exercise a fiduciary responsibility to preserve the integrity of competitive sport.

REASSESSING THE CORRUPTION THESIS

We began this chapter by considering the Corruption Thesis. We have taken this thesis to be making an empirical claim about causality—namely, that as sport becomes more and more commercialized, market forces tend to subvert the central principles of an ethic of good competition and replace it by what sells, by what has entertainment but not necessarily sporting value. What does our discussion suggest about the truth of the Corruption Thesis?

First, the growing commercialization of sport does sometimes represent a threat to its integrity. The argument of earlier chapters suggests that sport does have an internal morality of its own that is centered around principles presupposed by a mutual quest for excellence through challenge. Moreover, the internal principles or values of sport can be threatened by commercialization. For example, skills central to a sport can be reduced in significance by rule changes designed to make the sport more entertaining to relatively unsophisticated mass audiences. Or a professional sport can be structured so that the wealthiest teams can dominate competition season after season. The pursuit of wealth can lead teams, as well as individual athletes, to sever their roots with local or regional communities in an attempt to reach larger audiences, but at the price of creating alienation and disaffection in the serious sports community. And, as Morgan has argued, commercialization can change the social meaning of sport, replacing the values of achievement, excellence, and good competition with a focus on the external rewards of winning games and setting records.

Nevertheless, our discussion also suggests that commercialization is not always harmful, and that proper governance of elite, commercially viable sports has the potential to reduce significantly the conflict between commercialization and the integrity of competitive sport.

For one thing, commercialization allows the internal goods created by elite athletes to be available to enormous numbers of people. Elite sport, including professional sports, has the potential to play a positive social role in this regard by exhibiting and expressing standards of excellence, achievement, and commitment. Second, commercialization can lead to improvements in many sports. New equipment that improves play without undermining the central challenges of the game, such as the sand wedge in golf or well-designed running shoes in track, might be introduced, for example, or rule changes, such as the three-point shot in basketball, might be instituted. Such changes might both improve the game and make it more entertaining to mass audiences.

But commercialized sport can play a predominately positive social role only if it operates within ethical boundaries that set parameters for the pursuit of profit. Thus, a second point suggested by our discussion is that the sports industry has a fiduciary moral responsibility toward the practices with which it is involved. This requires that governance of elite sports, especially professional sports, should reflect more than commercial interests concerned with generating wealth from the game. Governance should also give voice to and reflect the concerns of those whose allegiance is to the basic principles of competitive sport. If the argument of this chapter has force, this is not only because sports industries stand to lose if sport is cheapened beyond repair (the argument from mutual advantage), but because impartial reasoning suggests that the values central to good sporting competition are of sufficient weight to set moral limits on the pursuit of private interest.

EIGHT

SPORTS, MORAL EDUCATION, AND SOCIAL RESPONSIBILITY

In previous chapters, we have examined whether and under what conditions competition in sport is ethical as well as ethical issues that arise within competition, such as those involving fair play, cheating, and the use of performance-enhancing drugs. In addition, we have looked at issues involving gender equity, intercollegiate athletics, and the commercialization of sport. We will conclude our examination by briefly considering some of the broader social implications of the ethical values that should apply in sport. In particular, we should ask whether sports can and should play a significant role in broader spheres of moral development, especially in education and in our personal lives.

Because claims for the moral import of sports have often been exaggerated, and because of many abuses within the practice of competitive sports, many people regard sports as a reflection of our moral decline rather than a positive moral influence, and the ethical issues in sports as symptomatic of that decline. But perhaps such a negative view has been overstated. Do sports have an important positive role to play in our moral lives?

MORALITY AND SPORTS

The Reductionist Thesis

How are values in sports related to values in the larger society? According to one influential thesis, which we can call reductionism, values in sports are reflections and perhaps reinforcers of values in the broader society. This view is "reductionist" in that it attempts to explain all values in sports as expressions of dominant social values, thereby reducing the values in sports to those of the wider society. This kind of reductionism implies that if a society is intensely competitive and stresses the advancement of individuals over that of the group, sports will reflect and perhaps reinforce adherence to those values. If, in another society, competition is frowned upon, and loyalty to the group is held to be more important than individual advancement, there will be less emphasis on the importance of winning and more on teamwork than in the first society. Some reductionists might add that the emphasis on such values in sports may reflect back on the prevailing social values and reinforce commitment to them in the broader culture.

Reductionism can be understood as an explanatory theory if its claim is that the nature of values in sports is fully explained by the existence of values in society. It can also be understood as a normative theory if it holds that the worth or justification of values in sports is no different from the worth or justification of more fundamental social values.

For example, writer Paul Hoch, a critic of American sport, sees football as reflecting his pessimistic view of American society as militaristic, capitalistic, and egoistic.[1] In his view, football reflects and reinforces these values, which he regards as prevalent in our society. Some forms of Marxism also tend to be reductionist not only in their view of values in sports but also about values generally; some Marxists tend to view all social institutions as reflections of the values of the economic structure of society. An emphasis on individual moral rights, according to this kind of Marxist analysis, is not part of a universal, objective morality, but characteristic of capitalistic, competitive societies in which individuals compete with one another for success in the market. Individuals "stand on their rights" against others precisely because the free market puts them in cutthroat competition with each other. Thus, claims about equal individual rights might well be unintelligible in a feudal society, where the hierarchical structure emphasizes the morality of one's station and its duties, or in tightly knit communities where the individual, rather than being viewed as an autonomous unit, is in part defined by his or her place in the communal structure.

The reductionist position faces some serious objections if it is extended to cover all ideas and values. If ideas, moral codes, and social practices are mere reflections of underlying and more fundamental economic relations, isn't that true of the reductionist thesis itself? If so, and if reductionism is used to debunk the universalist claims to objectivity and truth, the reductionist thesis cannot claim to be an objective truth applying in all times and places but can itself be dismissed as a parochial belief fostered by a particular economic system.[2]

Of course, reductionism, or even Marxism, need not be based on so crude a form of economic determinism.[3] Moreover, such a criticism does not apply to limited reductionist analyses that apply only to values in sports, because such analyses do not claim that all values are mere reflections of a more fundamental underlying basis. Rather, their claim is only that values in sports are expressions of dominant social values, not all values everywhere.

Perhaps the major objection to reductionist analyses of the values in sports is that sports often seem to express values that go counter to prevailing moral beliefs.

An interesting example is given by Drew Hyland, a former Princeton basketball star and now a philosopher. Hyland has suggested that because of the merits and skills of the basketball players on local playground basketball courts, playground basketball games can help—and in America's past have helped—participants to overcome racial prejudice and suspicions. When the only way to retain one's place on a crowded neighborhood court is to put together a winning team, whether other persons are good players will tend to count far more than their race, religion, or even sex. "In this situation, the preservation of . . . racism has a clear price, the likelihood that you will lose and have to sit."[4] Indeed, as we have seen in Chapter 6, prominent social scientist James Q. Wilson, in his discussion of the work of Michael Putnam, identified sports teams as one of the few American institutions where high levels of trust among diverse groups are actually found.

Our own discussion throughout this book also indicates that some values internal to sports are not necessarily mere reflections of a prevailing social order. For example, if dominant ideologies within a society were to devalue excellence and challenge, the values expressed in good sports contests, conceived of as mutual quests for excellence through challenge, would conflict with rather than reflect dominant social values. If so, sports might be an important source of moral values and even have a significant role to play in moral education, a topic we will explore later in this chapter.

The Inner Morality of Sport

Suppose a person claims to be a serious athlete committed to competitive success but, in spite of having time to practice, virtually never does so. In addition, this person shows no desire to learn about his weaknesses in his sport or to analyze strategies that might be used successfully against opponents. Surely, in the absence of a special explanation, this individual's behavior would undermine his claim to be a dedicated athlete.

This example suggests that certain values, such as discipline and dedication, are central to competitive sports in the sense that an individual or team concerned with competitive success would have strong reason to act upon them. As noted above, in a society in which little emphasis was placed on achievement or hard work, those committed to competitive success in sports would be endorsing and acting upon values that conflicted with the prevailing values of their culture. If such athletes became sufficiently influential, their values might change and even replace the prevailing value system.

Other values also seem closely connected with a desire to compete in sports and athletics. Consider concern for playing by the rules. Although some athletes may be tempted to cheat and may even do so on occasion, no athlete can normally endorse disrespect for the rules as a universal value to be held by all athletes. For if cheating became a universal practice, there would be no athletic competitions in the first place. The very idea of a sports competition is that it is an activity governed by appropriate constitutive rules that, at least partially, define the game.

Concern for excellence and recognition of excellent performance are other values intimately connected to competitive sports. Even if a competitor's main concern is winning rather than achieving excellence, such an athlete must intend to play better than the opposition. This presupposes a conception of better and worse play, and therefore a conception of standards for evaluating performance.

Some values may be so intimately connected with sports that they are internal to it. Goods are internal to a practice or activity when they cannot be understood or enjoyed independently of that practice or activity. For example, the value of being a skilled playmaker cannot even be understood without some understanding of the constitutive rules of basketball and appreciation of its strategies and nuances. In a society where such external goods as fame and wealth were highly valued by the majority, athletes who valued securing the internal goods of sports might exemplify a way of life that conflicted with the norms of the majority, and might undermine or question them.

Although there are different and competing conceptions about which ethical principles should apply to competitive sports, an ethics of competition can stand apart from and even conflict with moral principles widely accepted in other domains. Thus, the notion of competitive sports as a mutual quest for excellence conflicts with the view that competitive values are bad, wrong, or always to be abjured as well as with the view that defeating others should be the only fundamental goal of the competitive athlete.

These illustrations strongly suggest not only that the reductionist thesis is seriously flawed but also that the practice of competitive sports and athletics is value laden in important ways. Some values, such as concern for excellence, discipline, and dedication, are traits that all competitive athletes have strong reason to commend and act upon themselves. Others, such as respect for the rules, are values that all competitive athletes have good reason to maintain; they should be part of the universal set of norms upon which all athletes should act. Still other values, such as the importance of the demonstration of excellence in particular sports, are internal goals that all serious players of the sport normally seek to exemplify and that reflect standards for evaluating one's own play and the play of others. Finally, conceptions concerning the ethic of competition, such as the mutual quest for excellence, constitute moral standards purporting to be morally justified.

These different normative features constitute what might be called the inner morality of sport. They may be more or less in harmony with the ethic of some cultures, or subgroups within cultures, but they can conflict with the moral codes of others and may promote change in existing moralities.[5] Although there may be different interpretations of the inner morality of sport, and perhaps even different and conflicting inner moralities of sport, such a moral code (or codes) seems capable of profoundly influencing social and individual moral development.

This does not mean that an internal morality of sport is unique to the context of sport. For example, achievement in many areas, including medicine, scholarship, and teaching, requires dedication and commitment. An artist may value excellence just as much as an athlete, if not more than an athlete. Moreover, the internal morality of sport may cohere with major philosophical ethical systems, and its fundamental values may even be derivable from such systems. Kantianism, with its emphasis on respect for persons, as well as "perfectionism," which in some forms emphasizes excellence through achievement, are examples of such systems. The antireductionist claim, then, is not that an internal morality of sport is unique or logically independent of major ethical principles that apply elsewhere, but rather, that the values found in sport can conflict with those dominant in the wider society, and so are not mere reflections of prevailing social morality.[6]

If athletes can act upon an inner morality (or moralities) of sport that can be expressed through their actions on the field, we can ask what its broad social role might be. Such a question is too broad to deal with exhaustively here, but one issue is worth our special attention. Sport, as some of our earlier discussions have indicated, has long been thought to influence character development. Accordingly, the role that sports can play in moral education is well worth further consideration.

Sports and Moral Education

Because moral values play a large role in sport, it is not surprising that sports are often thought of as an area where values can and should be taught and transmitted to the next generation. We have seen in Chapter 2 that a traditional defense of athletic competition rests on its allegedly good effects on character. In Chapter 6, it was argued that intercollegiate and interscholastic sports can have educational value when conducted properly.

Many people see a decline in values in our society. Random violence seems to be all too common. Drugs, gangs, and urban decay create risks for youngsters that seem to be higher than those faced by children of the previous generation. With the rise in the divorce rate and the decline of the nuclear family, many children seem to be receiving less attention at home than in previous generations. The schools increasingly are asked to take on extra responsibilities, such as sex education, which used to be left, however wisely or unwisely, to the home, church, or synagogue. It is natural to ask, then, whether the schools should provide moral education and direction. Should sports have a role in moral education? If so, what should that role be?

Should schools be involved in teaching values? If so, whose values should be taught? Should there be formal courses in moral instruction? What, if anything, gives public schools, and through them the state, the right to decide upon an "official" morality to be taught to our children?

These questions suggest two important difficulties with the idea that schools should be responsible for moral education. The first might be called the problem of partisanship and the second the problem of indoctrination.[7] According to the first, the public schools have no business teaching values because there is no one set of values that all agree upon. The schools, and through them the state, have no business deciding on a particular set of values and making them the official ideology of the land. Imagine how you would feel, for example, if you were a political and social conservative (or liberal) and the schools taught liberal (or conservative) values as the correct morality. Second, even if we could agree on the values that should be taught, we would be indoctrinating many of our students. Since many students are not yet sufficiently mature to evaluate complex moral systems rationally, we would be imposing a value system upon them without their autonomous consent.

Because of these difficulties, existing programs of moral education often either attempt to help students clarify their own values or teach procedures of moral reasoning, such as trying to see things through the perspective of others, rather than endorsing substantive moral principles. Such views attempt to avoid the charges of partisanship and indoctrination by restricting themselves to the form rather than the content of moral thought and by encouraging development of autonomy. Even these approaches have been severely criticized on various grounds, including the charge that they express the hidden agenda of an abstract but highly partisan morality. Thus, advocates of such approaches have been accused, in the case of values clarification, of teaching a disguised moral relativism ("It doesn't matter what values you hold as long as you can clearly articulate them and authentically accept them"); or, in the case of concern for the form of moral reasoning, of presupposing a "male-oriented" universalist ethic of impartiality (as opposed, for example, to a communitarian, or "female-oriented," ethic of caring).[8]

Whether or not these criticisms are justified, our discussion of the inner morality of sport suggests that informal moral education is going on in the schools all the time. For example, coaches of athletic teams normally stress dedication, discipline, teamwork, concern for excellence, and respect for the rules. Indeed, it is hard to see how they could avoid teaching such values, since some values are presupposed by the attempt to succeed in competitive sports. Coaches may also teach related values associated with their conception of the ethics of competition, including sportsmanship, fair play, and the principles required by conceiving of sports as a mutual quest for excellence by the participants.

Classroom teachers also are involved in informal moral education. Related to the inner morality of sport, one can argue that there is an inner morality of scholarship, which minimally requires civility in the classroom, respect for evidence, willingness to consider the views of others, and respect for them as fellow participants in critical inquiry. Dedication, discipline, and respect for the rules of evidence apply not just to sports but to intellectual inquiry as well. Thus, elementary-school teachers who insist on civility and nonviolent behavior in the classroom encourage their pupils to discuss their differences rather than simply allow them to beat up opponents.

Not only do teachers and coaches often stress such values, it seems entirely appropriate that they do so. An emphasis in the classroom on concern for evidence and willingness to listen to other points of view clearly is not neutral in the sense of being value free; rather, it seems to be presupposed by the educational process itself. Similarly, an emphasis on the playing field on teamwork, discipline, striving for excellence, and respect for the rules is presupposed by competition in sports and athletics. Accordingly, such values may be neutral in the sense that they would be agreed upon by those concerned for the practices at issue (education and competition in sports). The inner morality of sport (and of scholarship) is neutral rather than partisan in that it concerns values that all committed to the activities in question have good reason to support.

If this last point is justifiable, the inner morality of sport seems to avoid the charge of partisanship directed against the idea of moral education in the public schools. But is it really free of ideological bias? Aren't we trying to have it both ways here? On the one hand, the claim is that there is an inner morality of sport that is independent of and can even conflict with prevailing social values; on the other, it is claimed that such values are nonpartisan and, in some sense, neutral. Are these claims mutually compatible?

Critics of competitive sports agree that there is an ideology of athletics but reject it as overly competitive, egoistic, and conservative. We saw in Chapter 4 that some critics of current practices in competitive athletics identify adherence to the rules with blind subservience to the existing order, regardless of its moral standing. The critics are correct if they are pointing out that sports can be used to transmit messages about values extrinsic to athletic competition. For example, a coach can call for blind loyalty to the team regardless of the behavior of the players and equate that with the sentiment of "my country right or wrong."

Although such values as discipline and respect for the rules might be central to an inner morality of sport, it can be argued that blind loyalty is not. The difference is that the former values, but not the latter, are presupposed by the practice of competitive sports. Discipline, unlike blind loyalty to a team, is a value that anyone interested in competing well in sports has reason to pursue, regardless of ideology. Similarly, respect for the rules cannot be equated with blind loyalty to the status quo; rather, respect for the rules is a way of recognizing the equal moral standing of others by abiding by the public conditions for competition that every competitor is entitled to believe will apply. Respect for the equal moral standing of others is not value free, because it is incompatible with viewing the interests of others as of less moral significance than one's own, but it does seem to be presupposed by the idea of fair and meaningful competition.

Similarly, the classroom teacher who insists that students discuss differences rationally rather than forcing their opinions on others through violence is rejecting some values, such as belief in the use of intimidation as a means of settling disagreements, in favor of others, such as belief in settling agreements rationally and belief in fostering respect for others as participants in the discussion; however, the favored values, in this case, are central to education in a way that the rejected values are not. Thus, we can argue plausibly that in applying the inner morality of sport and the inner morality of scholarship, the schools are not imposing an "official" or partisan ideology upon pupils but instead teaching values that are presupposed by activities properly included in the educational curriculum.

What about the charge of indoctrination? Many coaches and teachers do not explicitly discuss the core moralities they are acting upon but simply impose them on students, many of whom are themselves too young or immature to make competent and autonomous decisions about morality. Teachers who insist that the bigger children in their elementary-school classes do not beat up smaller ones are not offering a philosophical defense of civility but simply commanding their pupils to be civil. Similarly, by disciplining young athletes who loaf in practice, coaches are not engaging in Socratic dialogue about the value of commitment and dedication but rather insisting that their players show discipline and commitment. If this isn't indoctrination, what is? In particular, what gives athletic coaches the right to impose such values on players?

In assessing this point, we need to ask if what is going on is indoctrination in a pejorative sense of that term. In particular, as some writers have suggested, perhaps not all values can be autonomously adopted; rather, some may be presupposed by the practice of autonomous reflection.[9] For example, before one can autonomously evaluate the justifiability of conflicting points of view, one must acquire the disposition to evaluate evidence and consider arguments rather than merely going along with one's friends or popular opinion. The acquisition of such a disposition cannot itself be the result of critical inquiry and autonomous reflection because one must already have the disposition needed to engage in critical inquiry and autonomous reflection in order to inquire and reflect. Training that helps immature and not-yet-competent individuals develop such traits is not harmful indoctrination that subordinates critical thinking, but instead part of a social process that develops critical thinkers and autonomous persons.

Similarly, the inner morality of sport, insofar as it forms part of a defensible practice of moral education, does not place athletes in intellectual blinders. Values such as commitment, discipline, respect for the standing of others, and appreciation of excellence are also presuppositions of moral and rational development.

If this position can successfully withstand critical examination, what are its implications for educational policy? In particular, the idea that there is a defensible inner morality of sport as well as of scholarship suggests that moral education of a limited sort is properly the function of our schools and that organized athletics can and should be part of it. Moral education of the kind at issue is limited to promoting those dispositions of mind and of character that can reasonably be regarded as prerequisites of the capacity to engage in autonomous critical inquiry with others. Just which values are to be cultivated will often be controversial, but a strong argument can be made for those core values constituting the heart of what we have called the inner morality of scholarship and sports.

If this approach is defensible, it provides an important reason for athletic programs to be considered a significant part of the curriculum of public education and not just a "frill" to be done away with as soon as school taxes get too high. By reinforcing values taught in the classroom, and bringing together people from diverse backgrounds and perspectives so that they might engage in a common quest for excellence, sports can help to promote and illustrate values that all people who are committed to fostering autonomy and critical thinking, in both public and private life, have reason to support.

SPORTS AND MORAL RESPONSIBILITY

If sports can play an important moral role in society, does it follow that individuals involved in sports have special moral responsibilities to the rest of us? What about the duties of leaders in the world of sport, or of highly visible elite athletes? Let us consider the role of the coach in interscholastic and college athletics.

Coaching and Its Duties

Coaching can take different forms at different levels of sport or different areas of competition. In individual sports such as golf and tennis, the coach can be virtually an independent contractor hired by the athlete to provide technical advice on mechanics, or, like a sports psychologist, to work on improving mental aspects of the game. Thus, famous golf instructors Butch Harmon and, more recently, Hank Haney were hired by Tiger Woods to bring his game to an even higher level, and Haney remained Woods's coach going into the 2010 season. Haney's relation to Woods is different from that of, say, the coach of a high-school team to her players because, for one thing, the contract between Haney and Woods can presumably be dissolved by either party. The high-school coach, in contrast, may have to be a team leader in a way that Haney is not, is responsible for team behavior to some extent, sets practice schedules, and performs many duties in addition to teaching mechanics or form. Although an individual coach also may perform some of these duties at the highest levels of elite individual sports, and the difference therefore is one of degree, there surely is a substantial distinction between coaches of team sports at the high-school and college level, on the one hand, and the golf or tennis professional, on the other.

Coaches of teams may be asked to perform many duties and be evaluated on various factors. Often, in American sports at least, coaches are judged primarily by their wins and losses. At the level of elite intercollegiate sports, coaches in high-profile sports with losing records may not bring in sufficient revenue or create sufficient visibility for the institutions that employ them. At the professional level, winning may relate to profits even more. Coaches also are often expected to promote their program to the general public, to be great recruiters, and at the same time to keep their players in good academic standing and out of trouble.

Many of these functions are legitimate and important, but they can also conflict with each other. Perhaps the college coach can improve the team's competitive record by recruiting students who are marginal academically, or by not enforcing disciplinary codes when star athletes misbehave. At the extreme, as happened at the University of Minnesota (discussed in Chapter 6), the coach might tolerate academic fraud in order to keep players eligible and make sure the team has the best possible chance of winning. In other words, if the main function of the coach is to make sure the team wins games, then important values may have to be ignored and basic ethical principles violated when necessary to achieve that goal.

Perhaps the coach's goal should be to win, but only when the pursuit of victory is limited by appropriate ethical constraints. My suggestion is that the constraints suggested by the basic argument of this book are sufficiently stringent that although coaches should surely strive for competitive success, they should be regarded primarily as educators and evaluated as such as well as on their record of wins and losses.

Indeed, at the level of youth sports, coaches should only minimally be concerned with competitive success. Instead, they should focus primarily on teaching the physical and mental skills central to their sport, on promoting appreciation for the values of the game, and on encouraging friendships, team bonding, and healthy exercise. Surely they perform a more valuable function by helping players develop a lifetime involvement with sport than by winning a youth league championship (although I think it also is reasonable to acknowledge that, as athletes mature and become more skilled, concerns for competitive success may be assigned a higher priority).

In particular, if competition in athletics is best regarded as a mutual quest for excellence through challenge, and the experience of meeting challenges is one in which we learn about ourselves and others, then coaches should, as part of their role, facilitate this experience. This task involves not only teaching the mechanical skills needed to play well but also clarifying the principles behind strategies and setting guidelines about commitments and responsibilities; in this way, athletes will be able to play hard and well in contests while also being successful in class. Most young people play sports to have fun, although serious athletes have fun not by playing loosely or carelessly, but through focused training that enables them to reach their potential in competition. Coaches, therefore, should be evaluated primarily on how well they facilitate this development and on how well they promote understanding and love of the sport. Indeed, our argument in Chapter 6 suggests that in educational institutions, coaches can play an important academic role in integrating academic and athletic values and in ensuring the success of student-athletes in both areas.

Thus, a coach can be successful as a teacher even if he or she does not have a winning record, although it is sadly true that, at many levels of intercollegiate and even interscholastic sports, losing coaches may have trouble keeping their jobs. Sometimes, of course, a continual run of losses or losing seasons may suggest the coach is a bad teacher, but that is not always so.

Even if we do regard the coach primarily as an educator, many ethical issues arise in coaching. Should a coach always play the best players or always aim at winning, even if it means that some players always ride the bench? How is participation to be balanced against excellence? Should a college or high-school coach play a talented freshman over a senior who is less talented but who has been loyal to the program for years? Ethical issues that arise within coaching are extensive and deserve thorough treatment of their own.[10]

For our purposes, however, perhaps the supreme imperative for a coach is to treat the players with concern and respect and not regard them as mere means either for self-promotion or for pursuit of revenue or visibility for an institution. Winning is not unimportant, and there are many reasons why it is not; as argued earlier, for example, the record of wins and losses indicates how well a team has met the challenges of competition. As the level of competition gets higher, greater emphasis appropriately is placed on competitive success.

But athletes are not just means for achieving victory, either; they are persons in their own right. Constraints on the coach that arise from the status of the players limit the pursuit of victory at all levels of sport, although they may apply differently to those at elite levels than to youths and children. Thus, emphasizing participation for all players may be highly desirable in youth sports when players are still in the early stages of developing skills; indeed, young players cannot learn about the nuances of play and how to meet the challenges of the game without competing. At the level of elite sports, however, which athletes freely engage in precisely because of the challenge and the desire for competitive success, a coach normally has good reason to put his or her best players on the field in key situations.

As an aid to developing a broader theory of the rights and responsibilities of coaches and athletes, we might ask what coaches and athletes would expect from one another if they considered the roles impartially, perhaps by employing Rawls's veil of ignorance and asking what principles they would endorse without knowledge of which role they actually would play. Although it is unclear what a full hypothetical social contract between players and coaches would look like, surely there are some fundamentals that neither party could reasonably reject. Thus, it is reasonable for coaches, like other teachers, to expect their athletes to be dedicated, committed to learning, and willing to abide by appropriate team policies. Athletes, for their part, reasonably should be able to expect the coach to be focused on their development, to have knowledge of the game and appropriate teaching skills, and to treat them as persons, not simply as resources to be used in the pursuit of victory. How these guidelines play out in specific contexts will often be debatable, but perhaps such an account can provide an ethical framework that can be brought to bear on specific controversies.

Should Athletes Be Role Models?

In considering the moral responsibilities of athletes, Pete Rose comes immediately to the minds of many observers of sport. Rose, formerly a star Major League Baseball player for the Cincinnati Reds, became known as "Charlie Hustle" because, through hard work and effort, he was able to turn what many regarded as less than extraordinary athletic ability into a distinguished major league career. Rose ended his career having recorded more base hits than anyone else who had ever played the game. His place in the Baseball Hall of Fame seemed assured. To many, Rose was not only a star player but also a symbol of what dedication and commitment to excellence could accomplish.

Following an investigation of charges alleging that Rose, then manager of the Reds, had gambled extensively on baseball games, he was banned from baseball for life in 1989 (although the lifetime ban might now be reconsidered if Rose acknowledged the extent of his involvement in gambling). Not only was Rose accused of being a compulsive gambler, he was convicted of felonies involving tax evasion, presumably committed to support his gambling habit, and served a jail sentence in 1990. In addition, Rose was precluded from election to the Hall of Fame.

Did Pete Rose, as a star athlete and presumably a hero and role model to many youngsters, have a special obligation to behave ethically because of his participation in sports? Do athletes in general have special responsibilities to be good role models for the rest of us, particularly for the children who look up to them as heroes? Or are athletes simply ordinary people with special skills who have the same legal and moral responsibilities as anyone else but have no special obligation to be models for the rest of society? (Note that similar questions could be raised about Tiger Woods, whose dedication to excellence in golf is admirable, but whose status as a moral role model for others was severely undermined by a scandal involving reported marital infidelities that erupted in 2009.)

What does it mean to claim that athletes have special moral obligations to the rest of us to behave ethically? Although it is not always clear what proponents of such a view might be claiming, they might mean that there are reasons over and above those that apply to us all for athletes to behave ethically. A second thing they might mean is that if an athlete behaves unethically, it is somehow more seriously wrong, perhaps because it is more harmful than if someone else who is out of the public eye commits the same unethical act. These might not be the only interpretations of what is meant, but we can work with them in exploring the scope of the moral responsibilities of athletes.

Why should we believe that athletes have special moral responsibilities? Athletes, it might be argued, are just people who have particular skills but in other respects are the same as the rest of us. All of us have obligations not to wrong others. Why should the possession of a special talent, such as athletic skill, carry with it an additional moral obligation to be a moral exemplar for others? Athletes may indeed have special moral obligations within competition to, say, follow the rules and play hard, so as to provide a challenge for opponents, but it is quite another thing to say they have a special responsibility to be ethical generally. Surely, from the premise that certain individuals have unusual athletic talents, it doesn't logically follow that they have special moral obligations outside of competition as well.

It can be argued, however, that athletes occupy a special place in our society. They are often regarded as heroes by children and young people. To many disadvantaged youth, particularly minorities, many star athletes may illustrate that escape from deprivation can be achieved through success in competitive sports. Because athletes are revered by a large portion of the population, they are in fact regarded by many people as models to be emulated. Therefore, they have a special reason to behave morally: The unusually great influence they can have on others arguably generates responsibility and obligation. When they behave immorally, they can do more harm through their influence on others than the ordinary person can. Thus, athletes who are users of addictive drugs, for example, may, however unintentionally, convey the message that it is "cool" to take drugs and so induce their fans to become "copycat" users.

This sort of argument is open to many objections. Instead of expecting athletes to live up to the perhaps unreasonable expectations of many of their fans, perhaps the fans ought to become more realistic. Indeed, the hero worship of athletes can be harmful, especially when it leads youngsters to try to develop athletic rather than academic skills in the grossly unrealistic hope of becoming professional athletes. In any event, why should fans, particularly youngsters, regard athletes, rather than physicians, nurses, teachers, scientists, or their parents, as their heroes? From the perspective of the athletes, why should they have any more responsibilities to be moral exemplars than other entertainers, such as movie or rock stars, who often not only fail to be desirable role models for young people but also are not usually assigned any special moral blame for their derelictions?

These points surely are worth our consideration. But are they decisive? It can be argued that sports not only do but should play a central place in our society because of their concern with excellence and because appreciating sports does not require the special training or background often needed to appreciate excellence in such fields as medicine, science, mathematics, and even the fine arts. Sports, by their very nature, are accessible to large and diverse portions of the population, yet they express and illustrate a concern for excellence. Given the attention paid to sports by the media, and the love that many people, particularly the young, have for sports, it is doubtful that fans will suddenly become "realistic." It is far more likely that they will continue to have special regard for national sports figures as well as local athletes.

What does this have to do with the moral obligations of athletes off the field? Arguably, because of the special connection between competitive sports and the quest for excellence, as well as the broad accessibility of sports, it is not unreasonable for many segments of the population, particularly children and young people, to hold athletes in high regard and seek to emulate them. Top athletes profit from this emulation and are often represented to the public as having exhibited special virtues on the field. For example, Pete Rose was known for his dedication and hustle, Michael Jordan was loved for his enthusiasm for the joy of competition, and Tiger Woods was known for his ability to perform his best under the greatest pressure. Michael Phelps rose to prominence because of his extraordinary success under pressure in Olympic competition. Indeed, our own discussion of an inner morality of sports, and of the function of sports in expressing values, suggests there is an unusually intimate relationship between participation in athletics and ethics.

If so, and if it is therefore not unreasonable for the general public, particularly youngsters, to regard top athletes as heroic figures, and given that many top athletes accept and welcome the benefits of their position resulting from the way they are regarded, then perhaps it is not unreasonable to conclude that they have special reasons for at least avoiding the kind of immoral behavior, such as drug and alcohol abuse, cheating, and lawbreaking, that impressionable young people are likely to emulate. If athletes are regarded as role models in part because of the values expressed through their play, they can do unusual harm if their misbehavior leads their fans either to emulate their misdeeds or to become skeptical of the original values the athletes were thought to stand for.

Perhaps a more important reason for thinking athletes have special moral obligations rests not upon controversial empirical claims about their effect as role models but on the special place values have in sports. If there is an inner morality of sport in which such values as dedication, concern for excellence, and fair play are central, then athletes express such values through their play and benefit from adherence to these norms by other competitors. Without such commitment, we couldn't have the good sports contest and the basic, scarce, and internal benefits it provides. To express such values and benefit from them in a central area of one's life and then undermine them elsewhere seems wrong. Similarly, it is wrong for a professor to claim to value intellectual integrity in scholarship and yet fail to do so outside the classroom by, for example, ignoring evidence in political debate.

Thus, it is not just that sports fans often do look up to and emulate star athletes that underlies the claim that athletes have special reasons to be role models. It is also that the athletes owe much of their fame and fortune to the esteem in which they are held. This esteem arises in significant part not just from their athletic performance but also from the way it expresses an inner morality of sport encompassing such virtues as dedication, commitment, excellence, coolness under pressure, and respect for the game and its challenges. If athletes willingly benefit from their exhibition of such virtues, which are part of their performance as athletes, it is not unreasonable to expect them to respect other often similar virtues off the field as well.[11] This does not mean that athletes must be saints, but it does suggest that they have special reasons to avoid morally immature behavior, to say nothing of criminal actions or the abusive treatment of others; such behavior not only can have harmful effects on young fans but is arguably hypocritical.

Although these suggestions need fuller support than has been presented here and are intended as invitations to reflection rather than as decisive argument, they may have sufficient force to show that the claim that athletes have special moral responsibilities is worth taking seriously. Again, the point is not that athletes should have to meet some unusual moral standard that most people cannot attain, but that they have special reason not to violate minimal standards of good behavior or to discredit values central to the inner morality of sport. Although we could take the opposite tack and argue that athletes should not be our heroes, and should be respected only for their physical skills, the role of athletes in illustrating and expressing important values through their play suggests that sports tend to thrust them into the spotlight in a way that carries some moral obligation.

Perhaps, then, we need to reflect not simply on the fun and beauty of sports but also on the values embedded in the practice of athletic competition. What specific implications this might have for our actual practices, especially within educational institutions, needs further consideration, but at least two possibilities are worth mentioning. First, our discussion suggests that coaches in educational institutions ought to be evaluated more for their teaching than for their record of wins and losses. If appropriate standards of competitive sports have implications for life outside the playing field as well as on it, we need to reward instructors who can teach young athletes to play according to a plausible version of an inner morality of sport rather than fostering an amoral indifference to ethics in the pursuit of victory. For example, coaches in colleges and universities might be accorded faculty status and be judged for retention and promotion by application of criteria that are similar to those used to evaluate the performance of other faculty members. Second, we should expect athletes in our schools not simply to satisfy minimal standards of behavior and academic progress but to be good citizens and committed students as well. Although such specific suggestions may or may not have merit, an emphasis on the inner morality of sport and the lessons it can teach may have a role to play in moral education and, more broadly, in our moral life.

SPORTS, VIOLENCE, AND RESPECT
FOR FELLOW COMPETITORS

Although sports may illustrate or express values such as dedication, commitment, and respect for fair play, we also can find examples of cheating, bad sportsmanship, racism, and violence in sports. Are some sports the collective or institutional equivalent of bad role models for society?

Although it is arguable that indefensible values are not central to sport but can be separated from sport as it should be played, what of the claim that some sports, by their very nature, are ethically suspect? This claim often is expressed about what many would regard as inherently violent sports, such as boxing and perhaps football. How are such claims about so-called violent sports to be assessed? In particular, when is a sport violent? And are violent sports unethical?

Perhaps we should begin by considering what counts as violence. Clearly, a physical assault is violent. But is a hard tackle in football violent? What about a brushback pitch in baseball, where a pitcher throws just inside home plate in order to intimidate the batter and get him to move further away from the plate into a strategically less advantageous position? Or what if a tennis player intentionally hits a hard slam directly at her opponent, who has come up close to play the net?

An important distinction can be made between the use of physical force to achieve a strategic advantage in a sport and the use of force designed to injure or harm an opponent. Although the term "violence" can be applied to both, violence in the former sense generally is ethically unproblematic, as when a golfer uses physical force to hit a 280-yard drive. An observer might say that the golfer "killed" the ball, or speak of the "violence" of the swing, but surely nothing the golfer did was unethical. Accordingly, in our discussion the use of the word "violence" will be reserved for the use of physical force designed to harm others, keeping in mind that sometimes the use of physical force in itself may be ethically questionable, even if there was no intent to harm (for example, the brushback pitch in baseball), and that it sometimes may be appropriate to speak of psychological and well as physical violence.

Applying this distinction, we may well conclude that boxing is a violent sport. Boxers often suffer extensive brain damage, as seems to have been the case with one of the greatest boxers of all time, Mohammed Ali. In addition, hundreds of participants in the sport have been killed or permanently impaired as a result of their boxing injuries. Arguably, the intent of boxers in the ring is to harm their opponents. Even though boxing may have many virtues, including the demonstration of great courage in the face of physical adversity and danger, and although many would argue that boxers consent to the risks of their sport, boxing surely is ethically problematic.[12]

Violence and Contact Sports

Can arguments concerning violence in boxing be carried over to contact sports? For example, if it can be successfully argued that boxing, because it is inherently violent, is morally problematic and perhaps ought to be eliminated or reformed, then shouldn't the same conclusion be drawn about football?

Critics of football maintain that it is a violent sport. Coaches and fans sometimes urge players to "smash," "smear," or "bury" the opposition. The critics see football as a miniaturized version of war. Even players who claim to compete within the rules acknowledge that physical intimidation is part of the game. As former Oakland Raider safety Jack Tatum put it in his perhaps aptly named book, *They Call Me Assassin*, "My idea of a good hit is when the victim wakes up on the sidelines with the train whistles blowing in his head and wondering who he is and what ran him over."[13] Tragically, one of Tatum's hits in a 1978 game against the New England Patriots resulted in the permanent paralysis of Patriots receiver Darryl Stingley.

Tatum claimed that although he hit hard when he tackled, he played within the rules and did not take illegal "cheap shots" at opponents. (The kind of tackle made by Tatum was not against NFL rules at the time, and no penalty was called on the play.) His view was that, as a professional, he was paid to make sure that pass receivers didn't make catches in his territory. A good way to achieve this goal was to make receivers aware that they would get hit hard when running pass patterns. Then, the next time a pass was thrown, the receivers would think more about getting hit and concentrate less on doing their job and catching the ball. As Tatum put it, "Do I let the receiver have the edge and give him the chance to make catches around me because I'm a sensitive guy or do I do what I am paid to do?"[14]

It is understandable why the critics of football would say that it glorifies violence, encourages militaristic attitudes, and amounts to a public celebration of many of our worst values. In effect, these critics claim that football is to our society what bloody gladiatorial contests were to Rome: a distraction for the masses through the presentation of violence as entertainment. Thus, Paul Hoch, author of *Rip Off the Big Game*, a highly ideological critique of American sports that raises many serious issues for consideration, suggested that because violence in football is rule-governed, it "provides powerful ideological support for the officially sanctioned, rule-governed violence in society, in which judges have the final say. In short, the fans are supposed to identify with the distorted framework of law and order, both on the football field and in society, irrespective of what that law and order is supposed to protect."[15]

All of these charges against football can be understood in numerous ways, but two sorts of claims seem especially worth discussing. First, football is held to be a violent sport. Second, football is thought to express or encourage acceptance of officially sanctioned violence while discouraging external criticism or struggle against the official rules themselves. Thus, football, in our society at least, is not ideologically neutral but expresses a conservative bias against social change.

Are these charges justified? In considering them, we need to keep some distinctions in mind. The first concerns whether violence is necessary to football or merely contingently attached to it. The second is the distinction noted earlier between violence and the use of force.

Violence in the sense of force intended to harm an opponent is normally as indefensible in sports as it is elsewhere. Such violence treats the opponent as a mere thing to be used for one's satisfaction or gratification; thus, it violates the morality of respect for persons that is expressed in the ethic of competition as a mutual quest for excellence. But is violence in this strong sense necessarily part of football in the first place?

Football is a contact sport requiring the use of bodily force against opponents; but it does not follow that football is necessarily violent. The use of force is quite distinct from violence, because only the latter covers the intent to harm others. In particular games, or on particular teams, players may indeed act violently toward opponents, but it does not follow that football itself is a violent game, since players who use force need not intend to injure the opposition. (A question we cannot explore here but which is well worth considering is whether there always is a morally significant distinction between intending to do violence and intending only to use force when one knows it is highly probable or even certain that such use of force might result in unintended injury to an opponent.)

How is the line between violence and the use of force to be drawn? When Jack Tatum attempts to intimidate an opponent through hard hits, is he being violent, or is he merely using force efficiently? Tatum could say that because it is not his intent to injure his opponent, he is using force but not ethically indefensible violence. How is this claim to be evaluated?

To begin with, it is clear that many sports often involve the use of physical force applied to opponents to achieve strategic goals. The use of the brushback pitch in baseball, the hard smash directly at the opponent in tennis, and the hard drive to the hoop in basketball can all involve the use of force against opponents. Not infrequently, this use of force carries some risk of injury. Presumably, participation requires that players willingly bear the risk. The key ethical question in fair competition may be whether the use of force takes advantage of an opponent's physical vulnerability. Thus, Major League batters are supposed to have the reflexes to avoid a brushback pitch. The same pitch may be ethically permissible in Major League Baseball but indefensible when thrown against an out-of-shape older businessman who hasn't played ball in years.

If this suggestion has force, it supports what might be called the Vulnerability Principle, or VP. According to the VP, for the use of force against an opponent in an athletic contest to be ethically defensible, the opponent must be in a position and condition such that a strategic response is possible and it is unlikely that injury will ensue. Thus, attempting to block a shot from the front of an opponent in basketball conforms to the VP, but "undercutting" an opponent already in the air from behind does not.

Normal play in football therefore conforms to the VP as long as opponents, using basic skills common among players, can be expected to be able to respond with strategic countermoves. A tackle from the receiver's blind side when the receiver is in a position of·vulnerability is ethically dubious. Indeed, when defensive backs recommended that the rules be redesigned to give more protection to receivers, such protections were added.

Our discussion so far suggests that football can be (although not always is) played without players intending to harm opponents. It is often difficult to draw the line between the defensible and indefensible uses of force in contact sports, although the VP may represent a useful first step in that direction. Perhaps football can be criticized because violence is too prevalent in the sport, or because the use of force creates too much risk for the players, but it does not seem to be true that football by its very nature must be violent.

Sports and Ideology

If football is not necessarily violent in a pejorative sense, the charge that football functions as an ideological defense of officially sanctioned violence is open to serious question. This is because not all instances of football are violent to begin with. However, the thesis that football (and perhaps other sports) is ideologically biased deserves further consideration. Just what does such a charge amount to?

Perhaps the charge means that the attention given to big-time football causes people to tolerate unjust situations and oppose disruptive protest, possibly because sports create identification with the values of those in power, such as the coach or the quarterback, who calls the plays. Alternately, perhaps it means that the values expressed by a sport such as football are inherently objectionable: Football is warlike, or football requires unquestioning acceptance of officially sanctioned violence.

A causal thesis must ultimately be confirmed or disconfirmed by empirical data. Nevertheless, key philosophical points must be kept in mind in interpreting empirical studies. Suppose, for example, that empirical evidence shows that football players and coaches adhere more to traditional values than a control group not associated with football or even interested in the game. Can we conclude that football produces such value commitments? Clearly, the answer is no. As noted in Chapter 2, it is entirely possible that people with certain values tend to become football players and coaches, not that participation in football generates specific values among participants. Even more likely, some third factor, such as socioeconomic background, may tend to promote participation in football and adherence to certain values. Or it may be true that participation in football tends to reinforce values already accepted by those who play. Whatever the relationship truly is, the mere existence of a correlation, if one does exist, does not establish why the correlation holds.

Even leaving this point aside, there is a deeper philosophical point also at issue. If what we are looking for is whether football and other major sports promote such traits as "unquestioning obedience to authority," "acceptance of official violence," "uncritical toleration of injustice," and "unwillingness to challenge the system," we need to be careful that we do not beg the question in favor of certain values over others. What one investigator may see as blind obedience, another may regard as admirable loyalty and discipline. What appears to some as "unwillingness to challenge the system" or "toleration of injustice" may be considered by others as rational allegiance to a defensible set of rules.

Accordingly, although critics of football are quite right to raise the issue of the social significance of sports, they may smuggle in assumptions that have not been adequately defended. For example, they may assume that violence rather than the controlled use of force is a necessary element of football, or that the relationship of players to coaches is more like one of robots to programmers rather than pupils to teachers. Thus, in assessing the effects of sports such as football on participants and spectators alike, we need to be careful to specify just which effects are being looked for rather than jumping to interpret the data so as to confirm our own biases.

What about the idea that, regardless of its effects, football expresses or illustrates conformity, toleration of violence, and blind obedience to authority? Again, although it is probably true that some players, coaches, and teams accept or attempt to promote such values, they do not seem to be necessary constituents of the game. Perhaps many football coaches teach critical thinking about their sport and value good decisionmaking by players rather than mindless conformity to orders.

A good coach, it can be argued, prepares his or her players to think for themselves in the context of the game. Surely it is possible to conceive of the coach as a teacher; but if players are to reach their full potential in the quest for athletic excellence, perhaps it is necessary to conceive of the coach as a teacher. A good coach may insist on discipline and hard work, but it is hard to see why this makes the coach any more of an authoritarian or any more conservative than the philosophy professor who insists that her students work to their best potential.

Thus, our discussion undermines the view that football is necessarily violent as well as the claim that football expresses a bias in favor of conservative political values. Of course, in practice, football and other major sports sometimes may both be violent and express conservative values. But as properly practiced, football and other contact sports should express the values of a mutual quest for athletic excellence, which include respect for opponents, a sense of fair play, and intelligent and critical application of the skills of the game. Even though football, in particular, involves the use of a good deal of physical force, and therefore may be criticized as involving an unacceptable level of risk to the well-being of participants, it need not involve the intention to harm opponents or the support of a particular partisan political ideology.

Having said that, it is worth noting that if one accepts that the idea of a mutual quest for excellence through challenge represents an ethically defensible approach to athletic competition, a case can be made that athletics, properly pursued, support what William Morgan called a "progressive interpretation of sport."[16] That is, the idea of respect for fellow competitors, solidarity with teammates, and a concern for fairness seem to be part of an ethic in which each individual is regarded as important and of concern. Thus, although star players may get special attention, teammates who are injured or who warm the bench are still part of the team and should be given every chance to improve and develop their potential to the fullest. Clearly, there is an affinity between such a progressive idea of sport, as Morgan might call it, and a sensible liberal egalitarian conception of justice that has regard for the rights and well-being of every member of society, including the ill and the disadvantaged, but that still recognizes differences in merit and does not call for identical treatment for everyone.

Accordingly, both the right and the left can make claims that some versions of sport, or some particular sport, express or are best interpreted as supporting their own ideology. My own view is that central values of sport, as interpreted along the lines of broad internalism, as discussed in Chapter 3, constitute what I have called an internal morality of sport. That internal morality need not be unique to sport, and may have much in common with Kantian and perfectionist ethical theories, that is, theories that postulate an ideal of human behavior or human flourishing.

While, as Morgan argued, the most defensible version of an ethic of athletic competition may have more affinity with some versions of liberalism than with some versions of conservatism, we also need to be careful about viewing sports only through the lens of our own ideologies. Thus, the emphasis on merit and achievement in sport may need to be incorporated into some highly egalitarian forms of liberalism, while an emphasis on teamwork and positive obligations to fellow competitors may need to be incorporated into some highly individualistic forms of conservatism. Perhaps a more fully developed account of a defensible inner morality of sports than I have been able to present here would itself have justificatory force independent of political ideologies and even provide grounds for their revision. Maybe sports, when properly conducted, rather than merely reflecting external social and political values, can provide a justification for changing such external values for the better.

A CONCLUDING COMMENT

We have seen that sports raise a host of significant ethical issues. At their best, sports are a stimulating challenge to mind and body; at their worst, they can be a joyless endeavor where losing is equated with being a failure as a person and winning becomes just a means to egoistic self-posturing over others.

But our discussion also suggests that sports, properly conducted, express, illustrate, and perhaps reinforce values of enduring human significance. Through sports, we can learn to overcome adversity and appreciate excellence. We can learn to value activities for their own sake, apart from any intrinsic reward they provide, and learn to appreciate the contributions of others, even when we are on opposing sides. Through sports we can develop and express moral virtues and demonstrate the importance of dedication, integrity, fairness, and courage.

In addition, sports presuppose the importance of standards, including standards of excellent play and standards of appropriate conduct. Whether or not we accept some version of the ethic of the mutual quest for excellence, some moral standard is needed to distinguish sports as they should be conducted from degradations of the sporting ethic. These standards can be arrived at and examined only through the kind of critical reflection that is characteristic of philosophic inquiry.

Moreover, if there are justified standards that really do distinguish excellent from poor play as well as ethical from unethical behavior in sports, they provide reason for questioning the claim of many theorists that all standards are merely subjective and arbitrary preferences simply reflecting our race, gender, socioeconomic status, religion, or cultural upbringing. Although what we learn surely arises from the particular social and historical perspective in which we find ourselves, whether our beliefs are justified is another question. Our discussion about sports suggests that the search for justified standards is not necessarily fruitless. Our particular positions at a given time may always be fallible and subject to criticism, but the claim that there are justified standards of excellence in play and in the ethics of playing morally indicates that the search for justifiable standards need not always be in vain.

We could do worse, then, than to conclude with the remarks of Socrates in Plato's *Republic*. Though he was talking about music and gymnastics, his comments may apply equally to creative activity in general and especially to sports: "There are two arts which I would say some god gave to mankind, music and gymnastics for . . . the love of knowledge in them—not for the soul and body incidentally, but for their harmonious adjustment."[17]

NOTES

CHAPTER 1
INTRODUCTION: THE ETHICS OF SPORT

1. According to one of the most extensive studies done on this topic, the *Miller Lite Report on American Attitudes Towards Sports*, completed in the 1980s, 96.3 percent of the American population frequently played, watched, or read articles about sports or identified with particular teams and players at that time. Moreover, nearly 70 percent followed sports every day and 42 percent participated daily. *Miller Lite Report on American Attitudes Towards Sports* (Milwaukee, Wis.: Miller Brewing Company, 1983). While comparisons over decades are difficult to make, since different studies focus on different aspects of behavior, there is no evidence that interest in sports has declined to any significant extent in recent years. Moreover, if we turn to more recent studies, statistics compiled annually by the National Sporting Goods Association showed that, for 2008, over 75 percent of Americans actually participated in one of the twenty-three sports or related physical activities covered in the report, although disturbingly, children participated less than any other group studied. Moreover, participants may exercise infrequently rather than regularly. See National Sporting Goods Association, "Sports Participation," www.nsga.org/i4a/pages/index.cfm?pageID=3346. Data on attendance for many professional sports also show continued widespread interest by the general population. See, for example, the data on attendance collected by University of Michigan economist Rodney Fort, available at rodneyfort.com/SportsData/BizFrame.htm.

2. In a penalty kick, an offensive player attempts to shoot directly against the other team's goalie in a one-on-one situation. No players other than the kicker and the goalie participate.

3. This incident is described in George Vecsey's column, "Backtalk: When Is It Gamesmanship and When Is It Cheating?" *New York Times*, 8 August 1999, sec. 8, p. 13.

4. Edmund Pincoffs of the University of Texas told me this story some time ago. He was the philosopher in the story and the remark was addressed to him.

5. Allen Bloom, *The Closing of the American Mind* (New York: Simon and Schuster, 1987), 25.

6. My discussion of relativism draws heavily on distinctions made by James Rachels in *The Elements of Moral Philosophy* (New York: McGraw-Hill, 1993), 17–25, particularly the distinctions between various forms of relativism. Errors in their use or in my criticism of crude forms of relativism are entirely my own.

7. There may be a temptation to reply that because science is different from ethics, the example in the text is irrelevant. Disagreement in science doesn't show the impossibility of a rational resolution of a dispute, but disagreement in ethics does. But what entitles the skeptic to assume that science is rational but ethics isn't? The skeptic needs to show just how science and ethics differ in ways that are relevant to supporting skepticism and not simply assume the difference to be self-evident when that very assumption is being challenged. In any event, the logical point still stands. Disagreement on an issue by itself does not establish that we can never tell whether one side has better reasons for its views or is more justified than the other.

8. There are other difficulties with ethical relativism as well. For example, what counts as a culture? Is the sporting community a culture? Is there such an entity as Western culture, or are there only loosely related cultural subgroups within the West? What should we do if we belong to different cultures, each of which makes conflicting moral recommendations? What if our religious culture tells us that abortion is wrong but the secular culture of our peer group says it is permissible? Ethical relativism, which tells us to follow the dictates of our culture, would seem to be useless when the dictates of the cultures to which we belong clash.

Finally, cultures rarely speak with one voice. Thus, the genital mutilation of females as practiced in some African cultures is not only criticized by many Western observers but also by those within the culture itself who oppose the practice. Ethical relativism, by assuming that cultures speak with one voice, obscures the ethical diversity and moral disagreement that exists within them. The important issue concerns not just what a culture asserts but whether the assertion is or can be supported by critical rational inquiry.

9. I discuss the issues raised by this comment, particularly the reluctance by some students to make moral judgments, in "The Paralysis of Absolutophobia," *Chronicle of Higher Education* (27 June 1997): B5–B7.

10. *Nichomachean Ethics*, bk. 1, chap. 2, sec. 25, trans. W. D. Ross, in *The Basic Works of Aristotle*, ed. Richard McKeon (New York: Random House, 1941), 936.

11. See, for example, R. M. Hare, *Freedom and Reason* (New York: Oxford University Press, 1965), and his *Moral Thinking* (Oxford: Clarendon Press, 1981).

12. John Rawls, *A Theory of Justice* (Cambridge: Harvard University Press, 1971).

CHAPTER 2
COMPETITION IN ATHLETICS: IS IT MORALLY DEFENSIBLE?

1. What Lombardi is claimed to have said is "Winning isn't everything, but wanting to win is." Scott Morris, ed., *The Book of Strange Facts and Useless Information* (New York: Dolphin, 1979).

2. The statement by Rice is from *John Bartlett's Familiar Quotations* (Boston: Little, Brown, 1951), 901, and the remark from Evashevski is from *Sports Illustrated* (23 September 1957): 119. For discussion, see James Keating, "Winning in Sports and Athletics," *Thought* 38, no. 149 (1963): 201–210.

3. Judy Cooperstein, as quoted by Gerald Eskanai, "Judy Cooperstein Still Has the Tempo," *New York Times*, 2 July 1981, B12.

4. Quoted by John Loy and Gerald S. Kenyon, *Sport, Culture, and Society* (New York: Macmillan, 1969), 9–10.

5. Utilitarianism is really the name of a family of related positions. For example, utilitarians disagree among themselves over whether we ought to evaluate the consequences of specific actions (act utilitarianism) or of general compliance with rules or social practices (rule utilitarianism). There are different versions of both act and rule utilitarianism. Some philosophers believe that each approach will evaluate the same act differently, as when a specific violation of a promise will have good consequences even when it breaks the rule that promises ought to be kept. Others suggest that a defensible set of rules will have so many exceptions that the very distinction between act and rule utilitarianism blurs or even collapses. For a helpful introductory discussion of utilitarianism, see James Rachels, *The Elements of Moral Philosophy* (New York: McGraw-Hill, 1993), 90–116.

6. Bruce C. Ogilvie and Thomas Tutko, "Sports: If You Want to Build Character, Try Something Else," *Psychology Today* (October 1971): 61–62.

7. James L. Shulman and William C. Bowen, *The Game of Life* (Princeton: Princeton University Press, 2001), esp. chap. 4.

8. Walter E. Schafer, "Some Sources and Consequences of Interscholastic Athletics," in *The Sociology of Sport*, ed. Gerald Kenyon (Chicago: Athletic Institute, 1969), 35.

9. Harry Edwards, *Sociology of Sport* (Homeward, Ill.: Dorsey Press, 1973), 324.

10. The idea of an expressive function of punishment is suggested by Joel Feinberg in "The Expressive Function of Punishment," in his *Doing and Deserving* (Princeton: Princeton University Press, 1970), 95–118. The idea of an expressive function of sport is examined by David Fairchild in his article "Prolegomena to an Expressive Function of Sport," *Journal of the Philosophy of Sport* 14 (1987): 21–33.

11. John Schaar, "Equality of Opportunity and Beyond," in *Nomos IX: Equality*, ed. J. Roland Pennock and John W. Chapman (New York: Atherton Press, 1967), 237.

12. Michael Fielding, "Against Competition," *Proceedings of the Philosophy of Education Society of Great Britain* 10 (1976): 140–141.

13. Richard Harding Davis, "Thorne's Famous Run," in *The Omnibus of Sport*, ed. Grantland Rice and Harford Powel (New York: Harper and Brothers, 1932), quoted by Edward J. Delattre, "Some Reflections on Success and Failure in Competitive Athletics," *Journal of the Philosophy of Sport* 2 (1975): 134–135.

14. Delattre, "Some Reflections," 134.

15. Ibid., 135. Similar themes are developed by Paul Weiss in his *Sport: A Philosophic Inquiry* (Carbondale: Southern Illinois University Press, 1969), one of the pioneering works in twentieth-century philosophic study of sport.

16. A. Bartlett Giamatti, *Take Time for Paradise: Americans and Their Games* (New York: Simon and Schuster, 1989), 35–36.

17. Robert Nozick, *Anarchy, State, and Utopia* (New York: Basic Books, 1974), 240.

18. Can't we just see whether our current performance improves relative to our past performance? Thus, if I shot a 90 in golf last month and an 89 today, haven't I shown improvement? Perhaps so, but whether that improvement is significant or worth noting depends on comparisons with an appropriate reference group. If players of similar athletic ability and training normally improve from 90 to 82 in one month, I may have no justification for regarding my improvement as worth noting, or of significance at all.

19. However, it need not always be so. Winning may breed egotistical behavior or generate excessive self-confidence that may ultimately cause one to lose friends or engage in dangerous risk taking. It can cause a young athlete to neglect academic work and overemphasize athletic success. Whether or not winning is in one's best overall self-interest is an empirical question and depends upon the circumstances at hand.

20. Ronald Dworkin, *Taking Rights Seriously* (Cambridge: Harvard University Press, 1977), 227.

21. Ibid., 272.

22. Ibid.

23. Ibid. For an excellent book-length treatment of desert, see George Sher, *Desert* (Princeton: Princeton University Press, 1987).

24. Based on my memory of a televised postgame interview with University of North Carolina running back Kelvin Bryant in 1981.

25. *New York Times*, 3 February 1999, D4.

26. Nicholas Dixon, "On Winning and Athletic Superiority," *Journal of the Philosophy of Sport* 26 (1999): 10–26.

27. Scott Kretchmar, "In Defense of Winning," in *Sports Ethics*, ed. Jan Boxill (Malden, Mass.: Blackwell, 2002), 130–135.

28. William J. Bennett, "In Defense of Sports," *Commentary* 61, no. 2 (1977): 70.

CHAPTER 3
SPORTSMANSHIP, FAIRNESS, AND COMPETITION IN SPORT

1. Mike Ammann, goalkeeper of the Metro Stars of Major League Soccer, quoted by George Vecsey, "Backtalk: When Is It Gamesmanship and When Is It Cheating?" *New York Times*, 8 August 1999, sec. 8, p. 13.

2. As used here, "sportsmanship" will designate a virtue that can be exemplified equally by all athletes, in particular by males and females of all races, ethnic groups, and socioeconomic backgrounds.

3. James W. Keating, "Sportsmanship as a Moral Category," in *Philosophic Inquiry in Sport*, ed. William J. Morgan and Klaus V. Meier (Champaign, Ill.: Human Kinetics Press, 1995), 144–151.

4. Ibid., 146.

5. Ibid., 147.

6. Ibid.

7. Ibid., 149.

8. This distinction will be criticized later in the chapter. For additional criticism of Keating's position, see Randolph M. Feezell, "Sportsmanship," in *Philosophic Inquiry in Sport*, ed. William J. Morgan and Klaus V. Meier (Champaign, Ill.: Human Kinetics Press, 1995), 152–160.

9. Ludwig Wittgenstein, *Philosophical Investigations* (New York: Macmillan, 1953), 33e (section 66).

10. Bernard Suits, *The Grasshopper: Games, Life, and Utopia* (Toronto: University of Toronto Press, 1978). This book was reissued with an introduction by Thomas Hurka in 2005 by Broadview Press, Buffalo, New York. A series of articles by Suits also has been particularly influential in developing the idea of constitutive rules as central to the idea of games (and most sports). See, especially, "What Is a Game?" *Philosophy of Science* 34 (1967): 148–156, and "The Elements of Sport," in *Philosophic Inquiry in Sport*, ed. William J. Morgan and Klaus V. Meier (Champaign, Ill.: Human Kinetics Press, 1995), 8. For criticism, see Klaus Meier, "Triad Trickery: Playing with Sport and Games," *Journal of the Philosophy of Sport* 15 (1988): 11–30. Volume 35 (2008) of that journal contains a symposium devoted to Suits's work.

11. William J. Morgan, *Leftist Theories of Sport: A Critique and Reconstruction* (Urbana: University of Illinois Press, 1994), esp. chap. 5.

12. This corrects earlier remarks of mine that might have suggested that I thought the internal morality of sport was unique to sport. John Russell offered useful criticism of my earlier confusion in "Broad Internalism and the Moral Foundations of Sport," in William Morgan, ed., *Ethics in Sport* (Champaign, Ill.: Human Kinetics Press, 2007), 51–66.

13. This kind of example, with a squash player who forgets her racquet rather than a golfer whose clubs are lost, was employed by Robert Butcher and Angela Schneider in "Fair Play as Respect for the Game," *Journal of the Philosophy of Sport* 25 (1998): 6, but for an even earlier use of it, see A. S. Lumpkin, S. Stoll, and J. Beller, *Sports Ethics: Applications for Fair Play* (St. Louis, Mo.: Mosby, 1994).

14. See, for example, Warren Fraleigh, "Why the Good Foul Is Not Good Enough," in *Philosophic Inquiry in Sport*, ed. William J. Morgan and Klaus V. Meier (Champaign, Ill.: Human Kinetics Press, 1995), 185–187.

15. For example, see the influential paper by Fred D'Agostino, "The Ethos of Games," in *Philosophic Inquiry in Sport*, ed. William J. Morgan and Klaus V. Meier (Champaign, Ill.: Human Kinetics Press, 1995), 36–49.

16. For Dworkin's criticism of Hart, see "The Model of Rules," in Dworkin's *Taking Rights Seriously* (Cambridge: Harvard University Press, 1977).

17. Much of what follows in this section is taken from and more fully developed in my "Internalism and Internal Values in Sport," *Journal of the Philosophy of Sport* 27 (2000): 1–16.

18. Robert Butcher and Angela Schneider, "Fair Play as Respect for the Game," *Journal of the Philosophy of Sport* 25 (1998): 9.

19. Ibid., 11.

20. Ibid., 18.

21. J. S. Russell, "Are Rules All an Umpire Has to Work With?" *Journal of the Philosophy of Sport* 26 (1999): 27–49.

22. Ibid., 28.

23. Ibid., 14.

24. Ibid., 15.

25. Morgan's *Leftist Theories of Sport* is in part an argument for this conclusion.

26. *New York Times*, 3 February 1999, D4.

27. Bernard Gert, *Morality: Its Nature and Justification* (New York: Oxford University Press, 1998), 191–195.

28. Ibid., 194.

29. Oliver Leaman, "Cheating and Fair Play in Sports," in *Philosophic Inquiry in Sport*, ed. William J. Morgan and Klaus V. Meier (Champaign, Ill.: Human Kinetics Press, 1995), 195.

30. Ibid., 196.

31. Fraleigh, "Why the Good Foul," 269.

32. Kathleen Pearson, "Deception, Sportsmanship, and Ethics," in *Philosophic Inquiry in Sport*, ed. William J. Morgan and Klaus V. Meier (Champaign, Ill.: Human Kinetics Press, 1995), 184.

33. Sigmund Loland and Mike McNamee, "Fair Play and the Ethos of Sports: An Eclectic Philosophical Framework," *Journal of the Philosophy of Sport* 27 (2000): 63.

34. Here, I am indebted to Gert, *Morality*, 191–195, as my emphasis on the rules of sport being evaluated as part of a public system deigned to regulate a common activity follows his theory, although of course, I am responsible for the interpretation of it provided in the text.

35. Pearson, "Deception, Sportsmanship, and Ethics," 184.

36. The reason the penalty is needed is to ensure fairness for other competitors who have not hit their shots into unplayable situations. Without the penalty, there would be no competitive disadvantage for hitting the bad shot that led to the unplayable lie. In a sense, the penalty compensates the other competitors.

37. I owe this point to Warren Fraleigh, who made it to me in conversation.

38. Warren Fraleigh, "Intentional Rules Violations: One More Time," *Journal of the Philosophy of Sport* 30, no. 2 (2003): 166–176.

39. Cesar Torres, "What Counts as Part of a Game? A Look at Skill," *Journal of the Philosophy of Sport* 27 (2000): 81–92.

40. The following discussion draws on my paper "The Ethics of Strategic Fouling: A Reply to Fraleigh," *Journal of the Philosophy of Sport* 32, no. 1 (2005): 87–95.

41. Ken Johnson, "The Forfeit," *Dartmouth Alumni Review* (October 1990): 8–16.

42. Those who would defend Colorado might reply that the Colorado quarterback, if he had known the true situation, would not have intentionally grounded a pass on what he thought was a third-down play, and therefore Colorado might have won if the team had been apprised of the true situation. Because the situation was the same for

both teams, fairness was preserved. But although an argument can be made in defense of Colorado, and although it is clear that Buffaloes and their coaches did not cheat, it also is unclear whether Colorado actually met the test set by the rules and therefore whether the team deserved full credit for the victory.

43. This incident was widely reported. For an online account, see Dan Daly, "Sportsmanship Exists When Money Doesn't," *Washington Times*, 3 June 2008, www.washington times.com/news/2008/jun/03/dany-daly-sportsmanship-exists-when-money-doesn't.

CHAPTER 4
DRUGS, GENES, AND ENHANCING PERFORMANCE IN SPORT

1. See Tom Verducci, "Totally Juiced," *Sports Illustrated* 96, no. 23 (2002): 34–48, and Mark Fainaru-Wada and Lance Williams, *Game of Shadows* (New York: Gotham, 2006). The latter is a report on the BALCO investigation, discussed later in the text, by two reporters for the *San Francisco Chronicle*. A major source of information about steroid use in MLB is the so-called Mitchell Report, more formally *The Report to the Commissioner of Baseball of an Independent Investigation into the Illegal Use of Steroids and Other Performance Enhancing Substances by Players in Major League Baseball*, by former senator George Mitchell (13 December 2003). This report will be referred to as the Mitchell Report hereafter.

2. Mitchell Report, SR-2.

3. See Fainaru-Wada and Williams, *Game of Shadows*, esp. the prologue.

4. Ibid., 296.

5. Testimony before a grand jury is supposed to be confidential, but reports of Anderson's testimony as well as other details were leaked by reporters Fainaru-Wada and Williams, as reported in *Game of Shadows*.

6. For a history of Major League Baseball's reaction to claims of drug use by players, see the Mitchell Report.

7. Mitchell Report, SR-8.

8. John Stuart Mill, *On Liberty* (1849), quoted from the Dolphin edition (Garden City, N.Y.: Doubleday, 1961), 484. Mill's Harm Principle, articulated in the quoted passage, also rules out interference with liberty to prevent acts that merely are offensive to others or to interfere with acts on grounds of their alleged immorality, independent of any harm to others they may produce.

9. Ibid., 576.

10. Mitchell Report, SR 8-9.

11. Carolyn E. Thomas, *Sport in a Philosophic Context* (Philadelphia: Lea and Febiger, 1983), 198.

12. M. Andrew Holowchak, "'Aretism' and Pharmacological Ergogenic Aids in Sport: Taking a Shot at the Use of Steroids," *Journal of the Philosophy of Sport* 27 (2000): 40.

13. For an excellent discussion of different senses of "coercion," and an argument that we should think of coercion normatively as the *illegitimate* interference with the freedom of others, see Alan Wertheimer, *Coercion* (Princeton: Princeton University Press, 1989).

14. Norman Fost, "Let Them Take Steroids," *New York Times*, 9 September 1983, A19. But see also Wertheimer, *Coercion*, chap. 1.

15. Mitchell Report, SR 24-26.

16. Roger Gardner, "On Performance-Enhancing Substances and the Unfair Advantage Argument," in *Philosophic Inquiry in Sport*, ed. William J. Morgan and Klaus V. Meier (Champaign, Ill.: Human Kinetics Press, 1995), 225.

17. See Gardner, "On Performance-Enhancing Substances and the Unfair Advantage Argument," for versions of this sort of argument.

18. Ibid., 229.

19. The idea of a veil of ignorance is presented by John Rawls as part of a complex argument for a conception of social justice in his monumental work *A Theory of Justice* (Cambridge: Harvard University Press, 1971). Part of his argument is that the principles of justice are those we would accept, if we were being rational, from a position of choice in which we were ignorant of our personal characteristics or position in society. This would guarantee that choice was impartial and uninfluenced by such accidents of fate as the wealth of our parents or our genetic endowment.

20. Strictly speaking, athletes behind the veil would be ignorant even of their own values, but would have to take into account the possibility that in the real world they might have such values and vote accordingly.

21. My colleague Richard Werner suggested that a rule-consequentialist argument would lead to the same conclusion through a simpler argument; that is, a rule prohibiting the use of performance enhancers that are harmful to users would have better overall consequences than rules permitting use. However, such an approach would be open to objections of paternalism and, more important, would not explain the intuition of many of us that the use of performance enhancers is unfair. Moreover, the argument presented in the text can be presented without reliance on the "veil of ignorance," which, as Rawls sometimes seems to suggest, can be best viewed as a heuristic aid to impartial thinking. The main point of the argument is simply that if athletes disregard the personal benefits or harms that might accrue to them through steroid use, then the use of steroids to enhance performance makes no rational sense as a general practice. Steroids provide the risk of significant harm to everyone who uses them but at best minimal relative gains in performance.

22. This sort of point has been made by Gardner, "On Performance-Enhancing Substances," 229.

23. Does this argument imply that we also should prohibit athletes from using glasses or contact lenses or from having LASIK surgery? Just when does a technological aid provide an unearned benefit and when should unearned benefits be prohibited? These are difficult questions. One kind of reply, worth exploring further, is that glasses do not modify the challenge of the sport or provide users with competitive advantages over others; they only allow athletes with poor vision to catch up with others. (Does this mean that steroids should be allowed, but only by weaker athletes to make them competitive with naturally stronger ones?)

24. This sort of antipaternalistic argument has been made in a series of articles by Miller Brown. See, especially, W. M. Brown, "Paternalism, Drugs, and the Nature of Sport," *Journal of the Philosophy of Sport* 11 (1984): 14–22.

25. Sigmund Loland, "Record Sports: An Ecological Critique and a Reconstruction," *Journal of the Philosophy of Sport* 28, no. 2 (2001): 127–129.

26. I would like to thank Ronald Weinfeld for making me appreciate the force of this point.

27. Mitchell Report, SR-10 and 11.

28. This point has been developed by Michael Lavin in his paper "Drugs and Sports: Are the Cultural Bans Justified?" *Journal of the Philosophy of Sport* 14 (1987): 34–43. See also in the same issue (74–88) David Fairchild's paper "Sport Abjection: Steroids and the Uglification of the Athlete" for further reasons in favor of prohibition, as well as for some skeptical doubts about whether governing bodies in sport tend to be reasonable or nonarbitrary.

29. For an excellent discussion and summary of issues in this and related areas where legal issues bear on intercollegiate and interscholastic sports, see Matthew J. Mitten, "Rules Limiting Athletic Performance or Prohibiting Athletic Participation: Legal and Ethical Considerations," *Journal of Intercollegiate Sport* 2, no. 1 (2009): 99–113.

30. I first encountered the term "post-human" in David Brin's science-fiction book *Illium* (New York: HarperCollins, 2005).

31. Michael Sandel, *The Case Against Perfection* (Cambridge: Harvard University Press, 2007), 8.

32. Sandel cited the example of an advertisement in the *Harvard Crimson* seeking an egg donor who was athletic; was at least 5 feet, 10 inches, in height; and had combined SAT scores of 1400 as well as other traits regarded as highly desirable by the potential buyer. The ad offered a payment of $50,000. Sandel, *The Case Against Perfection*, 2–3.

33. Nelson Scott, in a review essay on *The Case Against Perfection*, Hamilton College, 2009.

34. Sandel, *The Case Against Perfection*, 87.

35. Ibid., 86.

36. Ibid., 92.

37. Such a conception of respect for persons plays a key role, for example, in the liberal political theory of justice developed by John Rawls in *A Theory of Justice* and his later writings, particularly *Political Liberalism* (New York: Columbia University Press, 1993).

38. Sandel, *The Case Against Perfection*, 36.

39. See Rawls, *A Theory of Justice*, especially p. 104, where he writes that "it seems to be one of the fixed points of our considered judgments that no one deserves his place in the distribution of native endowments any more than one deserves one's initial starting place in society."

40. A similar point can be made about performance-enhancing drugs. In a review of Sandel's book, William J. Morgan recalled a student coming up to him after class

and "exclaiming he didn't see anything wrong in taking such substances to redress the natural inequalities of the genetic lottery." William J. Morgan, review of *The Case Against Perfection, Journal of Intercollegiate Sport* 1, no. 2 (2008): 288.

41. Ibid.

CHAPTER 5
GENDER EQUITY IN SPORT: WHAT DOES JUSTICE REQUIRE?

1. Betty Spears, "Prologue: The Myth," in *Women in Sport: From Myth to Reality*, ed. Carol A. Ogelsby (Philadelphia: Lea and Febiger, 1978), 12.

2. *More Hurdles to Clear: Women and Girls in Competitive Athletics*, Clearinghouse Publication no. 63 (Washington, D.C.: United States Commission on Civil Rights, 1980), 3. For a full account of the development of women's athletics in the United States, see Ellen W. Gerber, Jan Felshin, Pearl Berlin, and Waneen Wyrick, *The American Woman in Sport* (Reading, Mass.: Addison-Wesley, 1974).

3. Althea Gibson, *I Always Wanted to Be Somebody*, Perennial Library Edition (New York: Harper and Row, 1965), 42–43.

4. *More Hurdles to Clear*, 13, 22.

5. Annual Sports Participation Survey of the National Association of High School Federations (1997–1998), available online at www. Balliwick.lib.uiowa.edu/ge. The data from 2006–2007 can be found at www.nfhs.org/custom/participation_figures/default .aspx.

6. "Sport Is Unfair to Women," *Sports Illustrated* (28 May 1973).

7. Richard Wasserstrom, "On Racism and Sexism," in *Today's Moral Problems*, ed. Richard Wasserstrom (New York: Macmillan, 1979), 96–97.

8. Ibid., 10.

9. Eldon E. Snyder and Elmer A. Spreitzer, *Social Aspects of Sport* (Englewood Cliffs, N.J.: Prentice-Hall, 1978), 158.

10. Wasserstrom, "On Racism and Sexism," 104.

11. Pregnancy leaves seem a relevant exception, however, and may show that the assimilationist model should not extend to all areas of economic life or even that it requires severe modification.

12. Perhaps assimilationism can avoid this consequence by distinguishing between the fixed sexual preferences of many people and the social significance or importance attached to such preferences. In this view, the perhaps biological fact of fixed sexual attraction is neither just nor unjust but only given. What is just or unjust is the special significance and preferential status society attaches to such relationships, particularly heterosexual ones. On the other hand, the assimilationist would then acknowledge that literal blindness to the sex of other persons seems neither attainable nor desirable. That is, sexual assimilationism implies more than just nondiscrimination against people with different sexual preferences; it requires virtual blindness to the sex of persons, which seems to be quite another matter entirely.

13. Wasserstrom, "On Racism and Sexism," 97.

14. For such an argument, see Claudio Tamburrini, *The Hand of God: Essays in the Philosophy of Sports* (Gotesborg, Sweden: Acta Universitatis Gothoburgenis, 2000), 104ff.

15. I am indebted here to Randy Carter's much fuller discussion in his unpublished paper, "Are 'Cosmic Justice' Worlds Morally Possible?"

16. For a critique of the identification of sex equality with sex blindness in areas other than sports and athletics, see Bernard Boxill, "Sexual Blindness," *Social Theory and Practice* 6, no. 3 (1980).

17. Betsy Postow, "Women and Masculine Sports," *Journal of the Philosophy of Sport* 7 (1980): 54.

18. Ibid.

19. Jane English, "Sex Equality in Sports," *Philosophy and Public Affairs* 7, no. 3 (1978): 275.

20. James Michener, *Sports in America* (New York: Random House, 1976), 20.

21. For a discussion of the initial opposition to Title IX, see Bradley David Ridpath, Athena Yiamouyiannis, Heather Lawrence, and Kristen Galles, "Changing Sides: The Failure of the Wrestling Community's Challenges to Title IX and New Strategies for Saving NCAA Sports Teams," *Journal of Intercollegiate Sport* 1, no. 2 (2008): 255–283.

22. *Grove City College v. Bell*, 465 U.S. 555 1045 S. Ct 1211 (1984).

23. *Franklin v. Gwinnett County Public Schools*, 112 S. Ct. 1028 (1992).

24. Ronald Dworkin provided an influential explication of fundamental rights in terms of equal concern and respect in his *Taking Rights Seriously* (Cambridge: Harvard University Press, 1987) in the course of a discussion of affirmative action. See especially pp. 227–229.

25. *Final Report of the NCAA Gender Equity Task Force* (Overland Park, Kans.: National Collegiate Athletic Association, 1993).

26. Thus, according to the Annual Sports Participation Survey of the National Association of High School Federations, in 1997–1998 there were roughly 3,763,000 male participants in high-school sports and 2,570,000 female participants. Although the total of female participants had grown since 1993, the disproportion in participation remained basically similar. Reports on participation rates can be found online at www .Balliwick.lib.uiowa.edu/ge.

27. For a critique of the effects of the proportionality requirement on men's sports, see Jessica Gavora, *Tilting the Playing Field: Schools, Sports, Sex and Title IX* (San Francisco: Encounter Books, 2001).

28. See, for example, Carol Gilligan's *In a Different Voice* (Cambridge: Harvard University Press, 1982) and the vast critical literature it has generated. Gilligan argued that women tended to adopt a somewhat different form of moral reasoning than men. This has led to considerable debate in philosophy and psychology over whether there is a difference between an "ethic of care" presumably favored by women and a "justice perspective" presumably favored by men. For a useful account of and contribution to

the debate, see Owen Flanagan and Kathyrn Jackson, "Justice, Care and Gender: The Kohlberg-Gilligan Debate Revisited," *Ethics: An International Journal of Social, Political, and Legal Philosophy* 97, no. 3 (1987): 622–637.

29. James L. Shulman and William G. Bowen, *The Game of Life: College Sports and Educational Values* (Princeton: Princeton University Press, 2001), 245. See also Daniel Fulks, *Revenues and Expenses of Division I and II Intercollegiate Athletic Programs: Financial Trends and Relationships—1997* (Indianapolis: National Collegiate Athletic Association, 1998), for a study and figures provided by the NCAA.

30. What counts as a financial gain or loss can be controversial. For example, should a share of receipts from sale of apparel with a university logo be counted as revenue generated by athletics if sales would have been far less without the visibility of the university's athletic teams? Thus, different accounting decisions might well lead to a different evaluation of the financial gains and losses attributable to intercollegiate athletics. This point is discussed in Chapter 6.

31. See John Rawls, *A Theory of Justice* (Cambridge: Harvard University Press, 1971), 11–22, 60–83.

32. The operative concept here is Rawls's veil of ignorance, a major part of his argument in *A Theory of Justice*. Rawls suggested that just principles are those that would be accepted by rational persons reasoning as if behind a veil of ignorance that obscured from them their personal position in society, their own talents and abilities, and even their values. This would ensure not only that they could not favor their own position but also that arbitrary contingencies, such as initial distributions of natural talents, would not unduly influence the choice of principles of justice. The use of the veil of ignorance has been highly influential and widely criticized—for example, for allegedly requiring that we adopt an impossible "view from nowhere"—and has been deemphasized in Rawls's later work.

I suggest that the concept is a useful tool of moral reasoning if it is used, perhaps in the way Rawls intended, as a device to assist us in reasoning about social arrangements not just from our own surely limited point of view but from the perspectives of others. As such, it does reflect a requirement of moral reasoning: namely, that we subject our own perspective as well as that of others to critical scrutiny and try to understand moral disagreements from a point of view that does not beg the question by implicitly building only our own prejudices and values into the principles we appeal to for adjudication.

CHAPTER 6
SPORTS ON CAMPUS: INTERCOLLEGIATE SPORTS AND THEIR CRITICS

1. Rev. Jon Lo Shiavo, "Trying to Save a University's Priceless Assets," *New York Times*, 1 August 1982, S2.

2. NCAA Infractions Report on the University of Minnesota, 24 October 2000, 2; available online at http://news.mpr.org/features/1999903/11_newsroom_cheating/infractionsreport.shtml.

3. Reports on graduation rates are issued annually by the NCAA and are broken down into various categories. The information in the text is from Steve Wieberg, "Off Court, Top Teams Fall Short," *USA Today*, 18 October 2002, 1c. Data collected by the NCAA on graduation rates, costs of intercollegiate athletics, and other areas of interest are now available at www.ncaa.org by selecting the button "Research" found on the web page.

4. Lo Shiavo, "Trying to Save a University's Priceless Assets," S2.

5. John Stuart Mill is famous for defending freedom of thought and discussion in his *On Liberty* (1859) by arguing that such freedom gives us the opportunity of correcting our ideas when they are false and strengthening them, and therefore appreciating them more fully, when they are true.

6. At some Division I institutions with strong athletic programs, such as Duke, North Carolina, Penn State, and Stanford, athletes graduate at very high rates; at less academically select schools, however, graduation rates can be dismal, and the rigor of courses selected by many athletes is suspect.

7. Quoted in Ira Berkow, "College Factories and Their Output," *New York Times*, 18 January 1983, D25.

8. Based on NCAA statistics reported in "Graduation Rate for Male Basketball Players Falls to Lowest Levels in a Decade," *Chronicle of Higher Education* (21 September 2001). NCAA methodology may tend to underestimate graduation rates, although perhaps not significantly. For example, if an athlete matriculates at Institution A and transfers to and graduates from Institution B, he or she counts as not graduating from A.

9. See, for example, the discussion in James L. Shulman and William G. Bowen, *The Game of Life* (Princeton: Princeton University Press, 2001), esp. pp. xv–xxiv.

10. See Harry Edwards, *Sociology of Sport* (Homeward, Ill.: Dorsey Press), esp. p. 198, for a critique of genetic explanations for the disproportionate participation of African American athletes in many sports.

11. A Louis Harris Poll released in 1990 reported that 55 percent of black high-school athletes expected to play ball in college, and 43 percent said they could make it in professional sports. Only 39 percent of the whites thought they would play in college, and just 16 percent thought they would compete at the professional level. In reality, only about 3 percent of high-school athletes make it in college sports, and only 1 in 10,000 go on to compete at the professional level. This poll was reported in *NCAA News* 27, no. 41 (19 November 1990): 16. On the positive side, the survey also reported that participation in sports may help reduce racial barriers, as 70 percent of the responding athletes said they had become friends with team members from another racial or ethnic group. Moreover, 74 percent of black athletes, a higher percentage than for whites, claimed that participation in sports helped to keep them away from drugs.

12. See, in particular, John Hoberman, *Darwin's Athletes: How Sports Has Damaged Black America and Preserved the Myth of Race* (New York: Houghton Mifflin, 1998).

13. Peter French, *Ethics and College Sports: Ethics, Sports, and the University* (Lanham, Md.: Rowman and Littlefield, 2004), 115.

14. Ibid., 116.

15. For example, NCAA graduation statistics for the 1987–1992 period show 68 percent of female athletes graduating compared to a roughly 58 percent graduation rate for other female students. Male athletes, even in high-profile sports, graduate at very high rates at such Division I scholarship institutions as Duke, Penn State, and Stanford.

16. Myles Brand, "The Role and Value of Intercollegiate Athletics in Universities," *Journal of the Philosophy of Sport* 33 (2007): 10.

17. Ibid., 11.

18. I owe this point to my student Sarah Wissel.

19. I argue more fully for these points in my paper "Does Athletics Undermine Academics? Examining Some Issues," *Journal of Intercollegiate Sport* 1, no. 1 (2008): 40–58.

20. For criticism of the claim of uniqueness for athletics, including cogent objections to some of my own earlier comments, see J. S. Russell, "Broad Internalism and the Moral Foundation of Sport," in *Ethics in Sport*, ed. William J. Morgan (Champaign, Ill.: Human Kinetics Press, 2007), 51–66.

21. For such a view, see Leslie P. Francis, "Title IX: Equality for Women's Sports?" in *Philosophic Inquiry in Sport*, ed. William J. Morgan and Klaus V. Meier (Champaign, Ill.: Human Kinetics Press, 1995), 305–315. Francis defended Title IX as necessary to provide fairness in an ethically suspect practice, intercollegiate athletics, but suggested that replacement of intercollegiate athletics by intramurals would in many contexts be desirable. See, especially, p. 312 of her article.

22. Paul Weiss, *Sport: A Philosophic Inquiry* (Carbondale: Southern Illinois University Press, 1969), 10–13.

23. J. Q. Wilson, "Bowling with Others," *Commentary* 124 (2007): 31.

24. Michael Oriad, "At Oregon State, Basketball Is Pleasing, Not Alarming," *New York Times*, 8 March 1981, S2.

25. Shulman and Bowen, *The Game of Life*. Shulman and Bowen drew upon an extensive database involving cohorts of graduates from the institutions they studied from the years 1951, 1976, and 1989, as well as upon some recent but less complete studies from the 1990s. These institutions included academically respected Division I universities such as Duke and Penn State, the Ivy League schools, selective women's colleges such as Smith, and small, coed, selective liberal arts colleges such as Williams, Swarthmore, Denison, and my own institution, Hamilton. The same database was the basis for another widely discussed book, *The Shape of the River*, in which Bowen and former Harvard president Derek Bok defended affirmative action programs in the colleges and universities they studied. See William G. Bowen and Derek Bok, *The Shape of the River: Long-Term Consequences of Considering Race in College and University Admissions* (Princeton: Princeton University Press, 2000).

26. For a critical discussion of *The Game of Life* that focuses primarily on methodology, see Hal Scott, "What Game Are They Playing?" *Journal of College and University Law* 28, no. 3 (2002): 719–755. Material in the text is drawn from my own review of *The Game of Life* in the *Journal of the Philosophy of Sport* 29, no. 1 (2002): 87–95.

27. The failure to explore this issue is especially surprising. In *The Shape of the River*, a study of the effects of affirmative action based on material from the same database as that discussed in *The Game of Life*, Bowen and Bok did consider such a comparison, although admittedly not in depth. Their tentative conclusion was that students admitted under considerations of affirmative action were not displacing other applicants with vastly superior qualifications but were competing for spots with less qualified candidates (pp. 37–38). Although their discussion of this issue was quite brief, their tentative conclusion certainly was suggestive. For if it also is true to a significant extent that preferred athletes generally are displacing other applicants who are relatively weak academically, then it is far from clear that the effects of the admission of athletes on the academic climate is as great as *The Game of Life* suggests.

28. For example, according to data from *The Game of Life*, in the 1989 cohort at coed liberal arts colleges only 59 percent of the high-profile athletes had fathers with bachelor's degrees, compared to 82 percent of students at large, and at the Division 1A private universities, only 53 percent of the athletes had fathers with bachelor's degrees, compared to 78 percent of the students at large (see Shulman and Bowen, *Game of Life*, 51).

29. Shulman and Bowen found that athletes with faculty mentors outperformed other athletes academically, but are there institutional obstacles to the development of such a relationship (see *Game of Life*, 71–74)? If so, underperformance by athletes might be in significant part a result of experiences of indifference or rejection (as well as other institutional factors that might need to be considered) rather than being due largely to lack of academic commitment on their own part.

30. Albert Camus, "The Wager of Our Generation," in *Resistance, Rebellion, and Death*, trans. Justin O'Brien (New York: Vintage Books, 1960), 242.

CHAPTER 7
THE COMMERCIALIZATION OF SPORT:
MARKETING AND CORRUPTION IN COMPETITIVE ATHLETICS

1. William J. Morgan, *Leftist Theories of Sport: A Critique and Reconstruction* (Chicago: University of Illinois Press, 1994), esp. chap. 3, and William J. Morgan, *Why Sports Morally Matter* (New York: Routledge, 2006).

2. James Michener, *Sports in America* (New York: Random House, 1976), 17.

3. Adrian Walsh and Richard Giulianotti, "This Sporting Mammon: A Normative Critique of the Commodification of Sport," *Journal of the Philosophy of Sport* 27, no. 1 (2002): 62.

4. See Nicholas Dixon, "On Winning and Athletic Superiority," *Journal of the Philosophy of Sport* 26 (1999): 10–26, and Morgan, *Why Sports Morally Matter*, 28.

5. Morgan, *Leftist Theories of Sport*, 147.

6. Morgan, *Why Sports Morally Matter*, x–xiv.

7. Ibid., xiii.

8. Christopher Lasch, "The Degradation of Sport," in *Philosophic Inquiry in Sport*, ed. William J. Morgan and Klaus V. Meier (Champaign, Ill.: Human Kinetics Press, 1988), 407.

9. U.S. Department of Agriculture, U.S. Forest Service, Nationwide Recreation Survey, 1982–1983; and 1994–1995 National Survey on Recreation and the Environment, in Alison S. Wellner, *Americans at Play: Demographics of Outdoor Recreation and Travel* (Ithaca, N.Y.: New Strategist Publications, 1997), 3. Participation rates vary according to various demographic factors, such as age, so caution must be used in evaluating the figures. Wellner provides a helpful discussion.

10. This point also is made by Lasch, "Degradation of Sport," 405–407.

11. Nicholas Dixon supports what he calls "moderate partisanship" in his paper "The Ethics of Supporting Sports Teams," *Journal of Applied Philosophy* 18, no. 2 (2001): 149–158.

12. The distinction between scarce and basic benefits was, to the best of my knowledge, introduced into discussions in the philosophy of sport by Jane English in her article "Sex Equality in Sports," *Philosophy and Public Affairs* 7, no. 3 (Spring 1978): 269–277.

13. Here I am indebted to the work of Alastair MacIntyre on the internal goods of practices, although my conception of internal goods may differ from his. See his *After Virtue* (South Bend, Ind.: University of Notre Dame Press, 1984).

14. See Dixon, "On Winning and Athletic Superiority," and Morgan, *Why Sports Morally Matter*, 28.

15. Stephen Finn, "In Defense of the Playoff System," *Journal of the Philosophy of Sport* 36 (2009): 70.

16. Milton Friedman, *Capitalism and Freedom* (Chicago: University of Chicago Press, 1952), 133.

17. Robert A. Dahl, "A Prelude to Corporate Reform," in *Corporate Social Policy*, ed. Robert L. Heilbroner and Paul London (Reading, Mass.: Addison-Wesley, 1975), 18–19, quoted by Norman E. Bowie, "Changing the Rules," in *Ethical Theory and Business*, ed. Norman E. Bowie and Tom L. Beauchamp, 2d ed. (Englewood Cliffs, N.J.: Prentice-Hall, 1983), 103.

18. Bowie, "Changing the Rules," 103.

19. An excellent account of stakeholder theory as well as an assessment and defense of it is found in Thomas M. Jones, Andrew C. Wicks, and R. Edward Freeman, "Stakeholder Theory: The State of the Art," in *The Blackwell Guide to Business Ethics*, ed. Norman E. Bowie (Malden, Mass.: Blackwell, 2002), 19–37.

20. For an important defense of a libertarian view, see Robert Nozick, *Anarchy, State and Utopia* (New York: Basic Books, 1974), esp. chap. 7.

21. For fuller discussion, see Norman E. Bowie and Robert L. Simon, *The Individual and the Political Order* (Lanham, Md.: Rowman and Littlefield, 2008), esp. chap. 3.

22. See John Rawls, *A Theory of Justice* (Cambridge: Harvard University Press, 1971), and the many discussions of it, as well as Rawls's later work, in the literature. A

discussion of different approaches to justice is found in Bowie and Simon, *The Individual and the Political Order*. An analysis of different approaches to the justice of social and economic institutions, including those of Rawls and the libertarians, can be found in Christopher Heath Wellman, "Justice," in *The Blackwell Guide to Social and Political Philosophy*, ed. Robert L. Simon (Malden, Mass.: Blackwell, 2002), 60–84.

23. For a particularly important treatment of justice as mutual advantage concluding that such an approach is intellectually inferior to one explicating justice in terms of impartial agreement, see Brian Barry, *Theories of Justice* (Los Angeles: University of California Press, 1989).

24. Gunnar Breivik, "Generosity as a Principle in Elite Sport" (paper presented at the annual meeting of the International Association of the Philosophy of Sport, Pennsylvania State University, October 2002).

CHAPTER 8
SPORTS, MORAL EDUCATION, AND SOCIAL RESPONSIBILITY

1. Paul Hoch, *Rip Off the Big Game* (Garden City, N.Y.: Doubleday, 1972), 22.

2. Not all philosophers find such appeal to versions of the so-called Paradox of Relativism convincing or conclusive. According to the paradox, relativists who assert that "there are no truths, only claims which hold within localized cultural, religious, or socioeconomic perspectives" are themselves making a claim, which is either true (thereby contradicting relativism) or itself relative to some particular perspective and therefore need not be accepted by others. But Marxists, for example, might seek to avoid the paradox by claiming that the socioeconomic perspective from which they make their own claims is more developed and comprehensive than earlier, more parochial perspectives, that they have reached the point in history that comes closer to objectivity than ever before. But doesn't this strategy itself involve universal claims about which views are more comprehensive and developed than others that presuppose the possibility by comparing perspectives and making a judgment about them that purports to be objective?

Other thinkers might embrace the claim that their own assertions are themselves relative and context dependent, but claim that they make the best sense of the values inherent in that particular social setting, although critics might respond that such a claim, which purports to be an objective truth, goes well beyond what relativism allows. For an excellent discussion, see Simon Blackburn, *Truth: A Guide* (New York: Oxford University Press, 2005).

3. Many contemporary writers who try to retrieve ideas of worth from the general body of Marx's work need not be reductionists or relativists at all, or accept the cruder deterministic aspects of some Marxist thought. For an example of such retrieval, see Richard Miller, "Marx's Legacy," in *The Blackwell Guide to Social and Political Philosophy*, ed. Robert L. Simon (Malden, Mass.: Blackwell, 2002), 131–153.

4. Drew A. Hyland, *Philosophy of Sport* (New York: Paragon House, 1990), 12.

5. Of course, various versions of utilitarianism or Kantian ethics based on respect for persons also can conflict with prevailing moral beliefs, such as, for example, in a tyranny or repressive theocracy. The internal morality of sport overlaps with elements of many philosophical ethical systems as well as ordinary moral thought. The notion of respect for the opponent, for example, expresses a form of the Kantian injunction never to treat other persons merely as means to one's own goals.

6. As I also pointed out in a note to Chapter 4, this corrects earlier remarks of mine that might have suggested that I thought the internal morality of sport was unique to sport. John Russell offered useful criticism of my earlier confusion in "Broad Internalism and the Moral Foundations of Sport," in *Ethics in Sport*, ed. William Morgan (Champaign, Ill.: Human Kinetics Press, 2007), 51–66.

Perhaps, however, if we give up the uniqueness claim, we run into the problem of triviality. As Mark Andrew Holowchak acutely pointed out in "Review of *Fair Play, The Ethics of Sport*, 2nd ed.," *Journal of the Philosophy of Sport* 31 (2004): 247, "the internal morality of sport is just the inner morality of all properly run social practices." Although I do not have space for a full response here, I would note that because of its visibility, accessibility, and emphasis on fair play, excellence, and challenge, the inner morality of sport, although not unique, pragmatically is, at least potentially, of special social and educational significance.

7. For a discussion of the obligation of educational institutions to be neutral and nonpartisan, see Robert L. Simon, *Neutrality and the Academic Ethic* (Lanham, Md.: Rowman and Littlefield, 1994).

8. Thus, Carol Gilligan, in her book *A Different Voice* (Cambridge: Harvard University Press, 1982), argued that emphasis on impartiality and universality in ethics expresses a moral perspective more associated with males than with females in our society. The implications of a female-oriented approach to ethics is usefully explored by Virginia Held in her "Non-Contractual Society: A Feminist View," *Canadian Journal of Philosophy*, supplementary vol. 13 (1987): 111–137, and more recently in her "Feminism and Political Theory," in *The Blackwell Guide to Social and Political Philosophy*, ed. Robert L. Simon (Malden, Mass.: Blackwell, 2002), 154–176.

9. For a defense of a "core values" approach to moral education along these lines, see William J. Bennett and George Sher, "Moral Education and Indoctrination," *Journal of Philosophy* (1982): 665–677.

10. A very useful discussion of ethical dilemmas that may arise in coaching is found in Jeffrey P. Fry, "Coaching a Kingdom of Ends," *Journal of the Philosophy of Sport* 27 (2000): 51–62.

11. Must athletes *willingly* accept such benefits? What if an athlete does not want to be regarded as exhibiting moral virtues? My own view is that since good sport has an inner morality of its own, athletes who consent to participate and who try to be good competitors are freely committing to the virtues outlined in the text.

12. For further discussion, see Paul Davis, "Ethical Issues in Boxing," *Journal of the Philosophy of Sport* 20–21 (1993–1994): 51.

13. Jack Tatum, with Bill Kushner, *They Call Me Assassin* (New York: Everest House, 1979), 12.

14. Ibid., 176.

15. Hoch, *Rip Off the Big Game*, 22.

16. William J. Morgan, *Why Sports Morally Matter* (New York: Routledge, 2006). See especially the Introduction, Chapter 1, and Chapter 7.

17. Plato, *Republic*, Bk. 3, l. 412.

INDEX